# Dictionary of
# Environmental
# Economics

# Dictionary of Environmental Economics

*Anil Markandya,
Renat Perelet,
Pamela Mason
and Tim Taylor*

# EARTHSCAN

Earthscan Publications Ltd
London and Sterling, VA

First published in the UK and USA in 2001
by Earthscan Publications Ltd

Reprinted 2002

ISBN:    1 85383 529 3

Typesetting by Composition & Design Services (www.cdsca.com)
Printed and bound in the UK by Creative Print and Design Wales, Ebbw Vale
Cover design by Richard Reid

For a full list of publications please contact:

Earthscan Publications Ltd
120 Pentonville Road, London, N1 9JN, UK
Tel:  +44 (0)20 7278 0433
Fax: +44 (0)20 7278 1142
Email: earthinfo@earthscan.co.uk
http://www.earthscan.co.uk

22883 Quicksilver Drive, Sterling, VA 20166-2012, USA

Earthscan is an editorially independent subsidiary of Kogan Page Ltd and
publishes in association with WWF-UK and the International Institute for
Environment and Development

A catalogue record for this book is available from the British Library

Library of Congress Cataloging-in-Publication Data

Dictionary of environmental economics / Anil Markandya ... [et al.].
     p. cm.
   Includes bibliographical references.
   ISBN 1-85383-529-3 (hardcover)
    1. Environmental economics – Dictionaries. I. Markandya, Anil, 1945-

   HC79.E5 D53 2001
   333.7'03–dc21                                                    00-067275

This book is printed on elemental chlorine-free paper

# Contents

# List of Figures and Tables

## Figures

## Tables

# List of Acronyms and Abbreviations

| | |
|---|---|
| AIJ | activities implemented jointly |
| AONB | areas of outstanding natural beauty |
| APE | assimilative potential of the environment |
| APS | ambient permit system |
| BACT | best available control technology |
| BAT | best available techniques *or* technology |
| BATNEEC | best available techniques not entailing excessive cost |
| BAU | business as usual |
| BCA | benefit–cost analysis |
| BEP | best environmental practice |
| BOD | biological oxygen demand |
| BPEO | best practicable environmental option |
| BPM | best practicable means |
| CAA | Clean Air Act |
| CAC | command and control regulations |
| CAP | Common Agricultural Policy |
| CAS | country assistance strategy (World Bank) |
| CATNIP | cheapest available technology not involving prosecution |
| CBA | cost–benefit analysis |
| CD | Cobb Douglas |
| CDM | clean development mechanism |
| CEA | cost-effectiveness analysis |
| CEE | Central and Eastern Europe |
| CFC | chlorofluorocarbon |
| CGE | computable general equilibrium |
| $CH_4$ | methane |
| CHP | combined heat and power |
| cif | cost, insurance and freight, *or* charged in full |
| CITES | Convention on International Trade in Endangered Species of Wild Fauna and Flora |
| CO | carbon monoxide |
| $CO_2$ | carbon dioxide |
| COD | chemical oxygen demand |
| COI | cost of illness |
| CSD | Commission on Sustainable Development (United Nations) |
| CUA | cost–utility analysis |
| CVD | countervailing duties |
| CVM | contingent valuation method |
| DALY | disability-adjusted life year |
| dB | decibels |
| dB(A) | decibels A scale |

## List of Acronyms and Abbreviations

| | |
|---|---|
| DDT | dichlorodiphenyltrichloroethane |
| DNS | debt-for-nature swap |
| DO | dissolved oxygen |
| dr | discount rate |
| DSM | demand side management |
| EA | environmental assessment |
| EAP | environmental action programme |
| EIA | environmental impact assessment |
| EIS | environmental impact statement |
| EKC | environmental Kuznets curve |
| EPA | Environmental Protection Act (UK) |
| EPA | Environmental Protection Agency (US) |
| EPS | emission permit system |
| ERICAM | environmental risk internalization through capital markets |
| ES | environmental statement |
| ETS | effective temperature sum |
| EU | European Union |
| EU | expected utility |
| EuZW | Europäische Zeitschrift für Wirtschaftsrecht |
| EV | expected value |
| FDA | Food and Drug Administration (US) |
| FCCC | Framework Convention on Climate Change |
| FAO | Food and Agriculture Organization |
| GATT | General Agreement on Tariffs and Trade |
| GCM | general circulation models |
| GDI | gender-related development index |
| GDP | gross domestic product |
| GEF | Global Environment Facility |
| GHG | greenhouse gas |
| GMO | genetically modified organism |
| GNP | gross national product |
| GWP | global warming potential |
| HDI | human development index |
| HPI | human poverty index |
| HSI | health status index |
| IEA | International Energy Agency |
| IEA | international environmental agreement |
| IEP | intergenerational equity principle |
| I–O | input–output |
| IPC | integrated pollution control |
| IPM | integrated pest management |
| IPCC | Intergovernmental Panel on Climate Change |
| IPPC | integrated pollution prevention and control |
| IPR | intellectual property rights |
| ISEW | index of sustainable economic welfare |
| IUCN | World Conservation Union (formerly the International Union for Conservation of Nature and Natural Resources) |
| JI | joint implementation |

| | |
|---|---|
| KP | Kyoto Protocol |
| $L_{eq}$ | energy mean sound level (a steady-state continuous sound level with the same energy content as the actual, time-variant, noise level) |
| MAC | maximum allowable concentration |
| MARPOL | International Convention for the Prevention of Pollution from Ships |
| MB | marginal benefit |
| MBI | market-based instrument |
| MC | marginal cost |
| MDC | marginal damage cost |
| MEA | multilateral environmental agreement |
| MEW | measure of economic welfare |
| MNPB | marginal net private benefit |
| MSY | maximum sustainable yield |
| $N_2O$ | nitrous oxide |
| NDP | net domestic product |
| NGO | non-governmental organization |
| $NH_3$ | ammonia |
| NNP | net national product |
| NOAA | US National Oceanic and Atmospheric Administration |
| $NO_x$ | nitrogen oxides |
| NPV | net present value |
| NSPS | new source performance standard |
| $O_3$ | ozone |
| ODA | official development assistance |
| ODS | ozone-depleting substance |
| OECD | Organisation for Economic Co-operation and Development |
| O&M | operations and maintenance |
| OP | option price |
| OVA | objective valuation approach |
| PEA | Pareto-efficient allocation |
| PP | precautionary principle |
| PPP | polluter pays principle *or* purchasing power parity |
| PRA | participatory rural appraisal |
| PSR | pressure, state, response indicators |
| QALY | quality-adjusted life year |
| RA | risk assessment |
| RACT | reasonably available control technology |
| RANDP | resource-adjusted net domestic product |
| RM | risk management |
| SARD | sustainable agriculture and rural development |
| SD | sustainable development |
| SIP | sickness impact profile |
| SMS | safe minimum standards |
| SNA | system of national accounts |
| $SO_2$ | sulphur dioxide |
| SP | stated preference |
| TAC | total allowable catch |
| TCM | travel cost method |

## List of Acronyms and Abbreviations

| | |
|---|---|
| TRIPS | trade-related intellectual property rights |
| TSP | total suspended particulates |
| TSS | total suspended solids |
| UDP | undifferentiated discharge permit |
| UN | United Nations |
| UNCED | United Nations Conference on Environment and Development |
| UNCLOS | United Nations Convention on the Law of the Sea |
| UNDP | United Nations Development Programme |
| UNEP | United Nations Environment Programme |
| UNESCO | United Nations Economic, Social and Cultural Organization |
| UPP | user pays principle |
| VLYL | value of a life year lost |
| VOCs | volatile organic compounds |
| VOLY | value of life year |
| VOSL | value of a statistical life |
| VPF | value of a prevented fatality (formerly VOSL) |
| VPP | victim pays principle |
| WBCSD | World Business Council for Sustainable Development |
| WCED | World Commission on Environment and Development |
| WCS | World Conservation Strategy |
| WRI | World Resources Institute |
| WTA | willingness to accept |
| WTO | World Trade Organization |
| WTP | willingness to pay |
| WTTERC | World Tourism and Travel Environment Research Centre |
| XV | existence value |
| YLYL | years of life years lost |
| ZTCM | zonal travel cost method |

# Preface

Environmental economics as a discipline is expanding rapidly. With this expansion, an increasing vocabulary has been developed to explain various techniques and ideas within the subject area. As a consequence, the need for a dictionary to explain the terms used has arisen. The definitions provided in this dictionary aim to give the reader access to some of the more technical literature that has been produced, as well as a general overview of the main techniques in the subject area of environmental and resource economics.

For most entries, a reference is given. These references denote a source in which the term has been used to date in the literature, and can be accessed by the reader seeking further detail, using the bibliography provided. To aid the reader in his or her study of environmental economics, a list of commonly used abbreviations has been included. Where definitions refer to other entries, these are italicized. Further references to related entries not mentioned explicitly are given where appropriate.

Our hope is that this dictionary will be a useful resource for the reader in accessing the literature relating to environmental economics. Definitions are written so as to be comprehensible to the undergraduate or layman, whilst including the technical detail necessary to elucidate the key concepts.

*A Markandya*
*University of Bath*

# Acknowledgements

A number of people have contributed in various ways to the compilation of this dictionary. In particular, we would like to thank: Adrian Winnett of the University of Bath for his assistance in writing the definition of enclosure; Ibon Galarraga for his definition of eco-labelling; Phil Jones for his definition of the Clarke Tax; Nick Dale, Alistair Hunt and Richard Boyd for assistance in finding literature; Alina Averchenkova and Ruth Hopper for editorial help; and, finally, the production team at Earthscan, particularly Jonathan Sinclair Wilson, Nim Moorthy and Sara Bearman, who have shown great patience throughout the lengthy writing process.

# Aa

**abatement** A decrease in either the level or the intensity of a nuisance, such as pollution or congestion, or the act of decreasing or eliminating a nuisance. Pollution abatement in industry, for example, may occur in response to regulation, consumer demand for cleaner processes, or the diffusion of less pollution-intensive technology. See also *abatement cost; marginal abatement cost; marginal damage; efficient level of pollution.*

**abatement cost** The cost incurred when reducing (in intensity or absolute level) a nuisance such as pollution or congestion. The cost per unit of *abatement* usually increases as the level of the nuisance approaches zero. See also *marginal abatement cost; marginal damage; efficient level of pollution.*

**absolute scarcity** In contrast to relative scarcity of a resource, which implies that demand exceeds supply over a given period of time (and which can apply to any number of resources – *man-made capital, natural capital, renewable* and *non-renewable resources*), absolute scarcity implies that ultimately the supply of the resource is fixed. Thus, absolute scarcity can occur only with *exhaustible resources* such as fossil fuels. See also *scarcity.*

**absorptive capacity** Also known as *assimilative capacity.* The ability of the *environment* to assimilate waste products from the economy. Limits to this capacity may be determined locally, regionally or globally. To the extent that waste emissions exceed the absorptive capacity of the environment, pollutants accumulate and damage results. See also *safe minimum standards (SMS); precautionary principle (PP).*

**acceptability principle** The principle that simple and transparent *economic instruments* are easily internalized by the existing market and institutional system. (Turner, Pearce and Bateman, 1994.)

**acceptable effluent** Acceptable effluent is defined as the *effluent* discharge that results in the *efficient level of pollution*, both in the short and long run. The efficient level of pollution is the load that minimizes the sum of *abatement costs* plus the environmental damage costs.

**accommodating technocentrism** A less extreme position than *cornucopian technocentrism*, accommodating technocentrism maintains that free markets have beneficial effects on the *environment* only if individuals think and act in an environmentally friendly way. Green consumers, investors, citizens and employees are therefore powerful agents for a green economy. From this perspective, although the market has an important role to play, some environmental limits (eg *life support functions*, maintenance and waste assimilation capacity maintenance) must be strictly adhered to (and development activities forgone) if the broader goals of *sustainable development* are to be met. (Turner, Pearce and Bateman, 1994.)

acid deposition

**acid deposition** One of the sources of soil acidification. It involves the atmospheric deposition of sulphur dioxide ($SO_2$), nitrogen oxides ($NO_x$) and ammonia ($NH_3$). Acid wet and dry deposition has effects on water, soil and forests. (Stanners and Bourdeau, 1995.) See also *acid rain*.

**acid rain** Atmospheric stocks of sulphur dioxide ($SO_2$) and nitrous oxide ($N_2O$) accumulate primarily from coal and heavy-oil-fired power generation. As a result, acid rain occurs through two principal processes. In dry deposition, particulate matter is physically deposited, subsequently taking acidic form in conjunction with surface water. The term 'acid rain' is therefore something of a misnomer, as it is not necessarily associated with rain at all. Wet deposition is characterized by acidic substances, particularly sulphuric and nitric acids, being formed in the atmosphere, and subsequently being deposited through rain precipitation or simply movements of moist air. (Perman et al, 1999.) See also *acid deposition*.

**acoustic quality** A measure of noise that takes into account pitch and tone, and compares this against standards. The findings of many studies undertaken in European countries on the effects of noise point out that, to ensure a desirable level of indoor comfort, the outdoor noise level in daytime should not exceed an energy mean sound level ($L_{eq}$) of 65dB(A) (OECD, 1991). The maximum acceptable levels are exceeded in most cities, affecting between 10 and 20 per cent of inhabitants in Western Europe and up to 50 per cent in some cases in Central and Eastern Europe. (Stanners and Bourdeau, 1995.) See also *annoyance costing approach; dB(A) costing approach; noise pollution, valuation of*.

**action programmes** European environmental policy has been developed through the medium of action programmes. These documents establish a proposed action plan for environmental developments over a period of time, usually about five years. They form the basis for policy development in the environmental arena. (Malcolm, 1994.)

**activities implemented jointly** See *joint implementation*.

**acute toxicity** This is present when a short-term exposure to a substance produces a detrimental effect on the exposed organisms. (Tietenberg, 1992a.) See also *chronic toxicity*.

**adaptation** Adaptation refers to changes in ecological, social or economic systems in response to changes in conditions. This term is often applied when discussing *climate change* issues and includes changes in processes, practices and structures in order to moderate damages or to yield benefits from potential opportunities arising from climate change.

There are two reasons why adaptation is important to climate change strategies. The first is that estimating the impacts of climate change requires estimates of the extent to which adaptation will reduce the net damage. The second is that adaptation policy strategies should be developed to minimize the *risks* arising from climate change. Adaptation is needed as a policy strategy since, even with reductions in greenhouse gas emissions, climate change is expected. For example, climate change is expected to lead to a sea-level rise resulting in erosion, flooding and saltwater intrusion in coastal areas. Adaptation here could include the building of sea defences, and will significantly reduce the costs of climate change. It is important that adaptation to climate change be built into coastal zone management. Another type of adaptation is the development of crop *species* that are more tolerant to climatic variations.

Adaptation policy includes three approaches to managing global change:

1   blocking, or preventing, unfavourable impacts of such change on any valuable resources;
2   adjusting or correcting environmental policy to prevent, or make up for, welfare losses resulting from global environmental change; and
3   anticipatory adjustment to strengthen the social systems to lessen losses from uncontrolled environmental change.

In contrast to adaptation policy, a *mitigation* policy consists of measures that reduce, check or delay unwanted effects of global change. (Jepma and Munasinghe, 1998; IPCC, 1996a.)

**adaptive expectation** Expectation of the value of an economic parameter, such as a price, derived by extrapolating the value of the parameter in the recent past. This would imply that to predict the price of a commodity next year an adjustment would have to be made to the previous year's price to account for recent trends. This method will tend to under- or overestimate a variable, because it does not take account of information other than past values that may help to predict future values. In the environmental sphere, predictions of future prices of resources will be systematically wrong if based on such expectations. (Bannock, Baxter and Davis, 1991.) See also *rational expectation; static expectation.*

**adaptive management** 'Sustainable management practices for *ecosystem*s and *species* that are responsive to uncertainties and ecological fluctuations, as well as being reversible and flexible.' (Barbier et al, 1994.)

**adaptive policy** See *adaptation.*

**additionality** In the context of North–South resource flows, the addition of new resources to those flows, as opposed to the repackaging of existing flows, which have now been re-labelled as 'green'. An example would be assistance for global environmental problems which has been provided without reducing official aid for other purposes.

**adjoint method** See *climate change impact assessment – adjoint method.*

**adjusted income** This is a measure of poverty. In contrast to market income, which is the actual amount of money earnt by an individual or household, adjusted income includes cash transfers and in-kind transfers, thus providing a more realistic measure of living standards, particularly for low-income households.

**administrative charges** A type of *economic instrument.* Administrative charges are intended mainly to finance direct regulatory measures, such as the licensing and control activities of environmental authorities. The aim is to lay part of the financial burdens on polluters instead of the general public. In general, administrative charges are acceptable to firms when kept relatively low; otherwise they may compromise relationships between authorities and firms (OECD, 1989a). These *charges* will be environmentally effective if the revenue improves the performance of the environmental authorities. In practice, they rarely operate in this way, since the revenues are not added to the budget of the authorities involved, but to a general budget. In a few cases, administrative charges such as for the registration of harmful products (chemicals or pesticides) are intended as a *disincentive* to their use as well as to raise funds. (OECD, 1989a.)

**aesthetic externalities** Visual *externalities* that include damage to buildings or unsightly developments, in particular near historic monuments or wilderness areas. See also *aesthetic, historical and cultural resources valuation*.

**aesthetic, historical and cultural resources valuation** Negative impacts on sites of particular historical or cultural significance sometimes result from infrastructure construction projects. The loss of scenic resources as the result of a road-building scheme is one example. Such losses are an important consideration when attempting to gain the support of those living in the vicinity of a proposed development area.

It is difficult to quantify the economic value of lost aesthetic, historical or *cultural resources*. One technique that may be applied is the *contingent valuation method* (CVM). However, for aesthetic resources it is common to use the *hedonic pricing* method since, relying as it does on actual consumer behaviour for data, it is thought to produce more reliable results. See also *valuation*.

**affluence** This term is generally used in relation to financial income or wealth. Some environmentalists measure affluence as the per capita material *capital* stock, that is, the physical resources (eg cars, rooms in a house) available for use. The impact, or throughput of *natural resources*, caused by affluence is determined by the material flows required to supply and maintain this material capital stock. (Meadows et al, 1992.) See also *ecological class*.

**afforestation** The establishment of forest cover on land not previously forested. Afforestation may be necessary, for example, to increase the net capacity of the Earth's forests to absorb carbon dioxide ($CO_2$) and other *greenhouse gases*. (Mintzer, 1992.) See also *deforestation*.

**Agenda 21** The global *sustainable development* agenda set out in the Rio Declaration on Environment and Development, which was established at the *Earth Summit* in 1992. Agenda 21 consists of 40 chapters, and at its roots are 27 principles (United Nations, 1993b). There are four broad sections which cover a range of issues: social and economic dimensions; conservation and management of resources for development; strengthening the role of major groups; and implementation. Agenda 21 highlights the importance of national strategies with international cooperation. It includes proposals for the integration of environment and development issues in decision making (Chapter 8) and provisions for international institutional arrangements and legal mechanisms (Chapters 38 and 19). Agenda 21 is an important document which has broad support among nations on all aspects of environment related to social and economic growth. The text of Agenda 21 is online at http://www.un.org/esa/sustdev.

**aggregate abatement information** This refers to information about the average costs of *abatement* across a group of polluters, often in different locations. Regulators can use such data in setting *pollution charges*. *Direct* *regulations* on the other hand often need more accurate and specific information at either the standard-setting or standard-enforcing stage. One debate between pollution charges and direct regulation focuses on the benefits of imposing charges based on such aggregate information, against imposing direct *regulations* on a uniform basis. The advantages of the former are that the consequences of being somewhat inaccurate are not as severe for the polluter or the pollution control agency.

The use of aggregate abatement cost data also has an important institutional consequence. It means that the resources of the opposing sides will be more equal, with environmental pressure groups having a larger influence on the final decision than they would have on *effluent* standard decisions made in a number of smaller legal jurisdictions. Having a centralized decision-making body would facilitate the participation of non-industry engineers and economists in the political process, leading to the implementation of *emissions charges* and other *economic instruments*. (Anderson et al, 1977.) See also *abatement costs*.

**aggregate demand** Total spending on goods and services by all economic agents in the economy.

**aggregate production function** Measures the maximum amount of goods and services that an economy can produce, given its stock of *capital*, human resources, *natural resources* and technology. In conventional economics, it is common for labour and *human-made capital* to be the only *factors of production* considered. However, *environmental economics* emphasizes the productive contribution of land and other natural resources. See also *production function approach*.

**aggregate supply** The total amount of goods and services that producers choose to provide. This may differ from the maximum they can produce given their available *factors of production* for many reasons, one of which is that demand may be insufficient for this level of supply to be profitable.

**aggregation** The aggregation of monetary estimates of environmental damages is an important stage in conducting a *cost–benefit analysis* (CBA) of a proposed project or policy. Problems in aggregating damage estimates may occur when one or more impacts cannot be measured in monetary terms. This is likely to be the case, for example, when certain *ecosystem* damages are considered. The problem may be avoided if individuals are able to establish preferences between monetized damages and non-monetized damages. In this case a weighting system can be derived that will produce proxy monetary values for the original non-monetized damages. Aggregation may also be problematic when conducted over regions with widely differing income levels, such as when aggregating global *climate change* impacts. Alternative weighting systems have been proposed to deal with this problem.

**agricultural potential and climate change** There are two main routes by which *climate change* can impact upon agricultural potential. One is the shift in weather patterns that affect agricultural potential, and the consequent shift of land use and farming types. The other is through changes in yields of crops and livestock. Changes in potential yield in the core areas of the current food production regions will have a larger impact on overall production than shifts in the potential limits for different types of farming at the margin and on the outskirts of present agricultural productivity belts. (Parry, 1990.) See also *agroclimatic indices; climate change, estimating costs of; crop-climate models.*

**agricultural runoff** The transfer of fertilizer or agricultural waste by means of storm water. The washing away of fertilizer is unlikely to benefit the farmer, unlike the washing away of waste. Damages from runoff are an important factor in the contamination of water. (Anderson et al, 1977.) See also *eutrophication.*

**agricultural sustainability** The use of agricultural resources in a way that will at least maintain the living standards of those dependent on agriculture for the indefinite future. It does **not** mean the use of physical practices that can be continued indefinitely. With the few exceptions of countries with still-unexploited reserves of *natural resources*, there is no alternative to further intensification of agriculture, until the world population stabilizes in terms of both numbers and demands. The issue faced by many countries is how and where to intensify agriculture without depleting the resource base and degrading the *environment*.

The United Nations Food and Agriculture Organization (FAO) suggests that sustainability issues require a new policy approach, including:

- The development of a more efficient agricultural production-processing-marketing-consumption system which minimizes waste and pollution whilst maximizing productivity and incomes.
- The reduction of environmental and socio-economic *risks* and increased *resilience* in the use of natural resources in the agricultural process.
- The promotion of diversification in agriculture and related sources of rural income.

*Source*: FAO, 1995.

There are a number of preconditions to be met to ensure agricultural sustainability, some of which are external to the agricultural sector. The implementation of population policies and measures to support agriculture through adequate financing are two examples of prerequisites that have to be met before the agricultural sector can be thought to operate in a sustainable way (op cit). See also *sustainability; sustainable development.*

**agroclimatic indices** This is one of two general techniques for examining the response of agricultural crops to *climate change*: these involve the measurement of crop suitability, whereas the others (*crop-climate models*) provide an estimate of potential productivity. Agroclimatic indices show the growth of a crop in response to climatic variables. A variable often used to represent thermal agroclimate is effective temperature sum (ETS). This usually represents the summation of temperature during the growing period above some base temperature assumed to be critical for crop growth.

An index of precipitation effectiveness and of drought is often used for characterizing moisture aspects of agroclimate. An advantage of these indices is that they do not demand large quantities of detailed data, and can therefore be used for large-area geographical assessments of agroclimatic potential. (Parry, 1990.)

**agroforestry** A form of intercropping in which annual herbaceous crops are interspersed with perennial trees or shrubs. The deeper-rooted trees can often exploit water and nutrients not available to the herbs. The trees may also provide shade and mulch, while the ground cover of herbs reduces weeds and erosion. (FAO, 1995.)

**air pollutant** Any substance in the air that, if sufficiently highly concentrated, could harm humans, other animals, vegetation or materials. See also *air quality criteria; air quality, modelling of; air quality standards; air quality, valuation of.*

**air quality, modelling of** The modelling of the air quality changes which result from pollution emissions involves some complicated processes. Many air quality models have been developed by drawing upon scientific evidence of *dispersion modelling* and changes in the ambient *environment* in response to changes in air quality. See also *air pollutant; air quality criteria; air quality standards; air quality, valuation of.*

**air quality, valuation of** Changes in air quality can be valued using a number of techniques, depending on the impacts being measured. One methodology is suggested in ExternE (1995). The estimation of the damages resulting from a change in air quality may require the *impact pathway approach* technique, whereby the value of a change in quality is estimated on the basis of the health and other impacts. *Dispersion modelling* is used to estimate the dose emitted from a point source to the surrounding area. The dose is then applied to a *dose-response valuation technique* to calculate the impacts, and a monetary value is obtained through the application of such measures as the *value of a statistical life* (VOSL). A recent example of the application of this methodology is included in Markandya and Pavan (1999), in which estimates for health damages resulting from air pollution estimates were obtained for four European countries. See also *air pollutant; air quality criteria; air quality, modelling of; air quality standards; point source pollution.*

**air quality criteria** The levels of pollutant concentration and length of exposure above which adverse health and welfare effects may occur. (Luken, 1990.) See also *air pollutant; air quality, modelling of; air quality standards; air quality, valuation of; health threshold.*

**air quality standards** The level of pollutant concentrations, prescribed by *regulations*, that may not be exceeded during a specified time in a specified area. (Luken, 1990.) See also *air pollutant; air quality criteria; air quality, modelling of; air quality, valuation of.*

**allocation of permits** see *permit allocation.*

**allowance** Allowance in the context of pollution control has essentially the same meaning as *marketable emissions permit*, emissions reduction credit and *tradable emissions permit*, which have all been used in the literature. The term 'allowance' is used to avoid ambiguity and confusion. An allowance is a type of permit which allows the emission of a pollutant or the use of a resource. An allowance allocated under this title is a limited authorization to emit a pollutant, for example sulphur dioxide ($SO_2$), in accordance with the provisions of the title. The giving of such an allowance does not constitute *property right*. That is, the allowance system should not be considered as transferring the public's right to clean air into the right of firms to pollute. (OECD, 1992a.) See also *emissions reduction credit scheme*; *permits*.

**alternative cost approach** An alternative to the *revealed preference* and the *stated preference* (SP) approaches to the *valuation* of environmental impacts. This approach seeks to establish the expenditure which would be required to remove the negative *externality* involved, or to reduce it by a specified amount. This approach has often been used in studies of pollution, and is clearly appropriate where the expenditure is actually incurred and does completely remove the externality. Unfortunately, neither of these conditions is often met in the real world. Turner (1988) gives the example of double-glazing to remove noise nuisance. He argues that where people are actually willing to pay the cost of double-glazing, this may lead to an overstatement of the cost of noise to those individuals. This *willingness to pay* (*WTP*) may result partly from the other benefits of double-glazing such as heat insulation and improved security. On the other hand, the insulation provided against noise by double-glazing does not completely obliterate the problem since it is only effective when the windows are closed and one is inside the building. Finally, the actual payment given for double-glazing may be much less than the maximum amount the person would be willing to pay. For all these reasons, we do not even know the direction of the bias involved in using double-glazing costs as an estimate of the *social cost* of noise.

This *objective valuation approach* is more applicable when environmental standards are established that reflect the society's willingness to pay for an environmental commodity. If it has been decided that set standards of contamination by pollutants must be attained by all water supply sources, the cost of meeting the standard represents society's willingness to pay for that level of environmental quality. It is a similar case if a project involves loss of quality to the natural *environment*, when there is a moratorium on such loss. In these circumstances a shadow project has to be included in the main project, which replaces the lost quality of the natural environment by improving other habitats elsewhere. (Turner, 1988.) See also *shadow project method*.

**alternative development paths** Paths that represent an equitable alternative to the paths typically being experienced by developing countries. The key features are that: developing countries' incomes increase; the income gap between developing and developed countries narrows and ultimately disappears; and that eventually a stationary state is reached across the whole world, in which living standards are maintained rather than increased. Such a development process has many environmental implications. An alternative development path is consistent with *conservation* rather than with a degradation and loss of diverse *natural resources*. One way to achieve this is to use the environmental resources more effectively and efficiently. For example, unique natural resources such as *biodiversity* provide the foundation on which developing countries may stake their claim for a fair share of global output. (Swanson, 1994.) See also *sustainable development*.

**altruism** Altruistic value occurs when an individual is concerned about the wellbeing of others. In the context of *environmental economics*, altruism can imply that the value placed on environmental quality is not based solely on the benefits to the individual. If altruism exists, its value also depends on the opportunity for the enjoyment of increased environmental quality by others. Another area of environmental economics in which altruism is relevant is *sustainable development*, in which individuals may value a sustainable path because of concern for the wellbeing of future generations. (Kahn, 1998.) See also *disinterested altruism; limited altruism; egoism.*

**ambient air** Any confined portion of the atmosphere; open air; surrounding air (Luken, 1990).

**ambient-based standards** Air and *water quality standards* that are based on an ambient quality goal, normally set at a level needed to prevent negative human health and environmental impacts. These standards require explicit agreement on the environmental quality objectives that are to be targeted, and the level of cost that society is willing to bear to achieve those goals. As a result of the fact that ambient standards can be set at differential levels for varying locations, it is possible to use them to protect valuable ecosystems in a way that would not be possible using emission controls. Ambient standards are set for a pollutant by reference to the health effects of different levels of exposure or, more recently, to the capacity of natural ecosystems to absorb environmental pollution, that is, their *absorptive capacity*. See also *air quality standards; direct regulations; regulations; emissions standards; fixed standard approach; quantitative controls.*

**ambient permit system** An ambient *permit* entitles the environmental regulator to vary permitted emissions according to the impacts they have on a receptor, such as a wildlife sanctuary or a drinking water extraction site. The closer a source is to the receptor, the lower the level of polluting emissions allowed by a permit. Sources that are close to the receptor must purchase more permits than those further away to allow a given level of emissions. In this version of the permit system, the polluter pays the same price for each permit, but the level of emissions allowed by each permit varies from location to location. The permit price is determined by the market, yielding an allocation of permits that is cost effective. This method of allocation is called an ambient permit system (APS) to differentiate it from the emission permit system (EPS) applied to achieve an allocation of control responsibility that is cost effective for uniformly mixed pollutants. (Tietenberg, 1992a.) See also *marketable emissions permits; regulations; market-based instruments; economic instruments.*

**amortization** The spreading of the *capital* costs of a project over the lifetime of that project.

**anabolism** The process by which useful matter and energy is converted into living tissue. (Krishnan et al, 1995.)

**ancient monuments, protection of** All countries have laws to protect monuments of national and cultural importance. For example in the UK, under the Ancient Monuments and Archaeological Areas Act 1979 (as amended), the Secretary of State for Cultural Heritage must compile and maintain a list of monuments of national importance. The decision on the scheduling of ancient monuments should be taken in consultation with English Heritage, the organization responsible for the preservation of ancient monuments. Once a monument has been scheduled, then it is an offence to demolish, destroy or damage it without permission. (Malcolm, 1994.) Other programmes for the protection of ancient monuments are administered through international commitments freely entered into by countries. An example is the UNESCO programme for World Heritage Sites (see UNESCO website for more details: http://www.unesco.org/whc/). See also *aesthetic, historical and cultural resources valuation.*

**ancient-growth forests** 'Old forests' or 'ancient forests' have never been logged and as a consequence are in their original, 'natural' state. Old-growth forests are very different from those previously logged forests that have been replanted or those that have been logged and allowed to reforest naturally. There are several reasons for the differences between the *ecosystems* of the old-growth and previously logged forests including the diversity of *species* in ancient forests, the sheer size of the ancient trees and the diversity in tree age of old-growth forests. (Kahn, 1998.)

**ancillary benefits** See *secondary benefit.*

**annoyance costing approach** Technique used in the *valuation* of noise pollution. This technique applies a methodology suggested by Gildert (1993) by valuing noise based on the probability of being highly annoyed. The value of annoyance is deduced from *hedonic pricing* studies and applied to yield an estimate of the damages. (ExternE, 1995.) See also *noise pollution, valuation of.*

**annual incidence** Annual incidence is the lifetime incidence of a health effect adjusted to a yearly equivalent, typically by dividing lifetime incidence by life expectancy. This is used in connection with the estimation of *risks* from environmental pollutants. (Luken, 1990.)

**anthropocentric environmental ethic** A view of the *environment* that is human-centred. More formally it refers to a comprehensive set of principles, obligations and values that are the basis of much of *environmental economics.* Values for the environment derive exclusively from the value that the environment has for individuals, both those alive now and those who have yet to be born. Thus it can address issues of intergenerational equity. The proposal to extend this definition to encompass the existence of moral interests of non-human but potentially conscious beings is known as the *extended rights view.* See also *ethics; environmental ethics; intergenerational equity principle.*

**anticipatory policy** See *adaptation.*

**anticipatory policy response** A type of government policy which anticipates environmental problems and environmental changes before they occur, so that measures to limit the damage associated with the environmental problems are in place before the problems occur. An example would be the building of sea defences in anticipation of a rise in sea levels due to *climate change.* This is distinct from a *reactive policy response.*

**anticyclones** These are continental-sized weather patterns, usually lasting a few days, which can suddenly increase pollution loads on the regional scale, resulting in pollution episodes. (Stanners and Bourdeau, 1995.)

**appropriability** This indicates that a productive input can be possessed and owned by one or more individuals. (Perman et al, 1999.) See also *property rights.*

**appropriate technology** Technology which provides solutions to the problems of local communities that are sustainable, in the sense that the technology can be maintained by the communities themselves and does not introduce dependence on outside support. Appropriate technologies should also be sensitive to the need to reduce pollution by using *renewable energy* sources and *recycling* materials where possible.

An alternative definition of the term is a production method that most efficiently utilizes an economy's *endowment* of factor inputs, such as land, labour or *human-made capital*. For example, labour-intensive technology may be most appropriate for an economy with a surplus of labour and little access to other capital.

**appropriation process** Part of the process of economic *valuation* in which one must measure the economic value of the environmental asset. (Pearce, 1995.)

**appropriative water rights** This is the legal basis for water allocation in the Western US. When there is a shortage, the appropriative doctrine allows those users who acquired rights earliest to draw on the water source before subsequent users. The system is historically based and makes no attempt to measure the user's contribution to aggregate wellbeing. (Hartwick and Olewiler, 1986.)

**aquaculture** The controlled breeding and harvesting of fish or other marine animals and plants. This reduces the problem of overfishing and encourages investment in the resource. The adding of certain nutrients to the water or controlling the temperature of the water can markedly increase the yield in some *species*. Shellfish, catfish, salmon and some other species thrive under the conditions provided by aquaculture, but some fish, such as tuna, will probably never be profitably harvested in this way. Dewalt et al (1996) identify some of the negative impacts of aquaculture, including the effect on mangroves, reduction of fish stocks, and deteriorating water quality. (Tietenberg, 1996.)

**aquifer** An underground layer of water-soaked sand and/or rock; described as either artesian (confined) or water table (unconfined). See also *groundwater*.

**arbitrary standards** Environmental targets are referred to as arbitrary when they are set without reference to *efficiency* criteria. (Common, 1995.) See also *efficient level of pollution*.

**areas of outstanding natural beauty (AONB)** A form of countryside planning control used in the UK. It differs from national parks, which may also be areas of natural beauty, in that while national parks tend to cover large areas, AONBs are normally on a smaller scale. An example of an AONB would be a range of downs that requires special controls for preservation and enhancement. The main purpose of the designation of AONBs is preservation per se, rather than preservation for the purpose of public enjoyment or recreation. (Malcolm, 1994.)

**Arrow's Impossibility Theorem** Kenneth Arrow (1951) defined four minimal conditions which, he argued, all social choices should satisfy. These are:

## asset conversion

1   Consistent (transitivity): This means that if an allocation is preferred to another, and the latter is preferred to a third allocation, then the first allocation will be preferred to the third.
2   Non-dictatorial (democracy): This means that a group's decision must not be controlled by an individual, either in the group or outside.
3   Non-perverse: If the preference of part of the group for a particular allocation increases, then – if that allocation would have been chosen without the change in preference – it should be selected with the change.
4   Independence of irrelevant alternatives: A group rule that involves selecting between two alternative allocations A and B should not depend on any change in the ranking of alternative allocations.

The above criteria are seen by many as being necessary prerequisites for a democratic decision-making rule. Arrow showed, however, that the four criteria cannot be met simultaneously. Violation of consistency or democracy goes hand in hand with the formation of social choice rules. The implications for the environment are that perhaps the democratic processes should delegate some of the decision making to regulators, who are accountable but who select policies by eliciting individual values and comparing them with the costs. (Griffiths and Wall, 1996.)

**asset conversion** Human societies must evaluate the allocation between many different forms of potential assets in building up an optimal portfolio. If the current distribution of assets is different from the optimal portfolio, there will be an incentive to convert some of the assets held to other forms, implying *disinvestment* in some assets (often natural assets or *natural capital*), and investment in others that are human-preferred. The incentive to reduce the level of investment in natural assets in order to invest in the latter is called the 'conversion process'. The natural form of any resource is in competition with other forms of the same assets. For example, a grassy meadow could be converted into a plot for the cultivation of wheat or cattle grazing land, because of the enhanced productivity of this resource. Asset conversion often takes place between natural assets and human-made assets in the course of economic development, for example the construction of a factory on a greenfield site. (Swanson, 1994.) See also *biogeography; debt conversion; debt-for-nature swaps; enclosure; global conversion process; opportunity cost*.

**asset recovery, remanufacturing and recycling** This occurs when parts of end-of-life machines (for example photocopiers or computers) are recovered by the producer for re-use or *recycling*. (OECD, 1998.)

**assignment problem** In *environmental economics* this is the issue of assigning an *externality* to a particular source. It is particularly relevant in the context of regional spillovers, where the relationship between a source and its impacts cannot always be fully described. In these circumstances there are two possible solutions. The first is to make the administered area large enough to internalize all externalities, in order to ensure there are no inter-regional spillovers. The second is to develop a technique to monitor diffusion between regions, which will enforce certain limits to the diffusion between regions. (Siebert, 1987.)

**assimilative capacity** The capability of the *environment* to take wastes and convert them into harmless or ecologically useful products. This is related to the *assimilative potential of the environment*. (Pearce and Turner, 1990.) See also *absorptive capacity*.

**assimilative potential of the environment (APE)** APE is often understood to be the maximum quantity of one or more pollutants that the *environment* can accept without being degraded. It is seen as the basis of environmental standards, such as the maximum permissible atmospheric concentration of harmful substances. It is also a basis for the estimation of *option* and *existence values*, where individuals are asked questions related to their *willingness to pay* (WTP) for the prevention of the violation of the APE. This is related to the concept of *carrying capacity*. See also *absorptive capacity; assimilative capacity*.

**assisted recovery** This refers to the potential for human society to assist in the recovery of an *ecosystem* after it has been degraded. It involves ensuring that any use of the system's services is sustainable. Thus, *non-renewable resources* should not be extracted from the system, any extraction of renewable resources should be sustainable, and only *biodegradable* and non-toxic wastes should be emitted into the system. (Simonis, 1990.) See also *unassisted recovery*.

**assurance argument** This is the argument that people will behave differently if they can be certain that their actions will be followed by similar actions by others. An individual might be willing to make transfers to future generations, but only if he or she is assured that others will do the same. (Pearce et al, 1990.)

**assurance bonding system** This requires that those seeking to use *natural resources* post a bond, equal to the value of the maximum damages that they could inflict on the *environment*, in advance of any activity. Worst-case damage scenarios are to be established by the regulatory authority with the best information available and with the advice of independent scientists. If resource users can demonstrate that damages to the environment are less than the amount of the bond (over a predetermined length of time, specified in the bond), this difference and a portion of earned interest is refunded. Thus, the environmental assurance bonding system ensures that the funds available for protecting the environment are equal to the potential harm facing its resources. (Cornwell and Costanza, 1994.) See also *deposit refund scheme; performance bonds*.

**asymmetrical externalities** These are *externalities* caused by one group, which has the ability to prevent or lessen the externality, and suffered by another group, which cannot act to reduce the consequences of the externality. This concept has been used in the analysis of intergenerational impacts, wherein the present generation which is causing externalities is able to act to reduce them, but future generations cannot act to reduce the impacts of today's actions. (Bromley, 1991.) See also *consumption externalities; production externalities; intergenerational externalities*.

**asymptotic depletion** Asymptotic depletion is a theoretical scenario in which the quantity of a *non-renewable resource* extracted becomes smaller and smaller, but never reaches zero. Hartwick and Olewiler suggest the following example: 'We can think of extracting oil by the bucket, then the cup, and finally by teaspoons and eyedroppers while the price of the resource climbs continuously towards infinity'. This concept is illustrated in Figure 1. See also *choke price*.

# attainment area

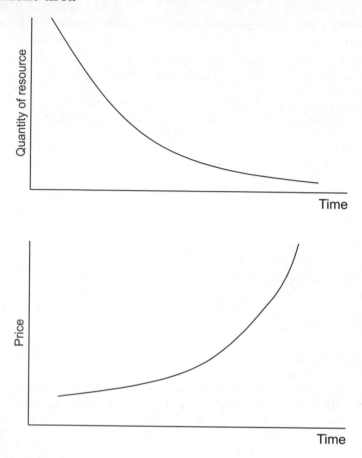

*Source:* Hartwick and Olewiler, 1986.

**Figure 1** *Asymptotic Depletion*

**attainment area** (US) An area in which air quality is as good as or better than national *ambient air* quality standards as defined in the US Clean Air Act (CAA). An area may be an attainment area for one type of pollutant and a *non-attainment area* for others. (Luken, 1990.) See also *air quality standards*.

**attenuation** The process by which a compound is lowered in concentration over time, through absorption, degradation, dilution and/or transformation. (Luken, 1990.)

**attributes of goods and services** A resource can be defined in terms of the services it provides, or its attributes. For example, a park could be defined in terms of its services: boating, fishing, swimming, accessibility (the proximity to an urban centre), and so on. The value of these attributes can be measured using *hedonic pricing* or other *valuation* techniques. (Perman et al, 1996.)

**average cost pricing** A system in which the price is determined by the average cost of production. This system often implies that new higher-cost sources of, for example, *natural resources* are averaged-in with existing lower-cost sources, yielding a price that is substantially lower than the true *marginal cost* (*MC*). Thus the incentive to conserve is diminished, since a reduction in consumption saves less money than it would under *marginal cost pricing*. The expected outcome would be a level of *conservation* that is less than efficient. (Tietenberg, 1992a.) See also *peak load pricing*.

**avertive expenditures** Avertive expenditures are expenditures undertaken to reduce the level of discomfort arising from *externalities*. For example, air and water pollution are known to result in a number of adverse health conditions, ranging from headaches to acute episodes that require hospital care. Expenditures are often made to try to avoid these conditions, an example being the installation of water filters. Avertive costs can be seen as an expression of *willingness to pay* (*WTP*) to avoid the resulting illnesses. (Field, 1997.)

**avoidance costs** see *avertive expenditures*.

# Bb

**background concentration** A term used in pollution *dispersion modelling* to represent the contribution to ambient pollution concentrations from sources not specifically modelled in the analysis. These include both natural and man-made sources. Background concentrations in less polluted areas are used as *baselines* for comparison when valuing environmental degradation for *green accounting*. (Luken, 1990.)

**backstop technology** A technology that is a substitute for one that uses *natural resources*. For example, wind turbines can be thought of as a backstop substitute for the use of coal for electricity generation. Wind power is currently a backstop technology in that it is more expensive than conventionally generated power, but as fossil fuel stocks deplete and prices increase, power generators will switch to the construction of wind turbines. The backstop technology cost is the upper boundary of the price of the natural resource in question since, if the price rose above this level, generators would switch to using the backstop. (Perman et al, 1999.) See also *renewable energy*.

**bads** Water and air pollution and other *externalities* may be considered public 'bads' and their correction a *public good*. The term is used to indicate a negative set of impacts that cause damages to an individual or group of individuals. See also *air pollutant*.

**baghouse filter** A method of pollution *abatement* whereby a large fabric bag, usually made of glass fibres, is used to eliminate intermediate and large (in excess of 20 microns in diameter) particles. (Luken, 1990.)

**banking provisions** See *banking scheme*.

**banking scheme** This term has two applications. The first is an arrangement for pollution *charges* under which enterprises can defer payment of the charges in exchange for making larger reductions in emissions or paying higher *emission charge*s in future. There is a limit on the amount it is permissible to borrow in this way, so that the length of time allowed for paying back the deferred sum of pollution charges is rather short – no more than four years. The banking scheme can be useful when the government is unwilling, in the short run, to bankrupt heavy polluters who are unable to pay their pollution charges. However, the scheme is considered credible only if the authorities take steps to make clear that enterprises which fail to repay their loans will be closed down in future.

In a second definition of this term, credits are stored in return for emissions reductions below permitted levels. Banking encourages firms to invest in new control technologies, and to gain from their investment through the sale or use of the *emissions reduction credit scheme*. A banking system can also reduce costs for firms exchanging credits, be they sellers or buyers. In practice, very few firms have banked *emission credits*. (OECD, 1992a.) See also *emission banking; emissions trading; economic instruments; marketable emissions permits*.

**bans and restrictions** An instrument of policy which either bans a commodity or restricts its use to a defined level. This type of instrument has been used particularly in relation to hazardous materials and to high-volume packaging, including cans. (OECD, 1994b.)

**Barnett-Morse Measure** A method developed to estimate the per-unit *extraction cost* of a resource. Costs are based on actual expenditures on labour, *capital* and other inputs. It can be used to estimate the changing *scarcity* of a resource over time (increasing unit costs reflect increasing scarcity). Barnett and Morse (1963) and Barnett (1979) used this method to conclude that mineral resources became less scarce over the period 1870–1970 due to the discovery of new deposits and the substitution of less scarce resources.

**barriers to entry** Characteristics of particular markets, or measures taken by incumbents in certain markets, which block the access of new participants to the market or part of the market. Barriers to entry thus decrease the likelihood of competition. The existence of patents and licences; concentrated ownership of essential inputs, an example of which could be technology; and very large *economies of scale*, whereby average production costs decrease with increased production, constitute barriers to entry. Such barriers tend to allow incumbent firms to enjoy higher profits. In *environmental economics*, barriers to entry may be created if new entrants have to acquire pollution *permits* from existing polluters, or if regulators make it very difficult for new firms to acquire licences to operate environmentally damaging processes. (Stiglitz, 1993.)

**Basel Convention** Also known as the Convention on the Transboundary Movement of Hazardous Wastes, the Basel Convention came into force in 1992 and stipulated that hazardous wastes could not be moved except between those nations party to the *convention*. The conditions of this convention stipulate the pre-notification and consent of the recipient country. These restrictions were established to encourage the proper management and reduction of hazardous waste at source, and to prevent the transfer of damaging pollution to countries which were not able to control the wastes effectively. (Jha, Markandya and Vossenaar, 1999.) See also *hazardous substances and hazardous waste*.

**baseline** A term often used in *climate change* costing calculations. The baseline is the measure against which policies are compared to evaluate their effectiveness. The 'baseline case' in climate change is, hence, the level of emissions without any *mitigation*. Baseline scenarios display key assumptions on the future use of technology. These include:

1    the efficient baseline case, in which the assumption is that all resources are employed efficiently;
2    the inefficient baseline case, in which the assumption is that some distortions exist and will continue to exist; and
3    the *business as usual emissions scenario*, which assumes that future developments will follow the trend which has been previously observed.

Establishing a baseline scenario is difficult, since the lifetimes of projects for greenhouse gas emissions reductions are long, economic and sectorial policies are constantly changing, and data for the establishment of baseline scenarios are weak or non-existent. See also *mitigation; adaptation; climate change, estimating costs of; business as usual.* (IPCC, 2001.)

**base period** The reference date from which an index number of a time series is calculated. See also *environmental indices; environmental indicators*.

**basic optimist model** A forecast of the future conditions of the world economy that predicts higher per-capita incomes and an intact, human-managed *environment*. See also *optimist model*.

**basic pessimist model** A forecast of the decline and collapse of the world economy in the face of fixed resource constraints and a growing population. This model is typified by *The Limits to Growth* (Meadows et al, 1972), which utilizes *feedback loops* between *environment* and economy, and assumes that natural resource constraints cannot always be overcome by technology.

**beneficiary pays principle** A principle which states that the beneficiaries of a high quality or improved *environment* should compensate resource users for the ongoing costs of maintaining ecological functions, environmental services and attributes that do not bring market benefits and are not required of all people. This principle requires that any additional costs associated with the provision of positive non-market benefits be reimbursed. It differs from the *polluter pays principle (PPP)* in that it assumes that citizens do not hold the *property rights* to a clean environment, and so are responsible for the financial costs of environmental improvement. The PPP, on the other hand, assumes that the property rights to a clean environment lie with citizens, so that a firm must compensate the public for environmental damage. Thus, the beneficiary pays principle and the PPP have different distributional implications. (Young, 1992.) See also *Coase Theorem*.

**benefit–cost analysis (BCA)** A tool of analysis which was originally designed to evaluate the net financial benefits of investment projects, but has lately been extended into the social, environmental and natural resource fields. BCA compares the monetary value of the streams of benefits and costs of a proposed policy, programme or project over defined space and time boundaries. It then ranks alternatives in terms of various measures such as *net present value (NPV)*. Despite the growing use of BCA in the environmental field, critics contend that its methods are flawed, or that the approach (using monetary values for environmental goods and services) is unethical. Although current methods are in principle capable of including almost all benefits and costs, the controversy over the appropriateness of BCA as an evaluation tool continues. Five particular issues arise:

1   how to calculate direct and indirect costs;
2   how to incorporate a societal perspective (BCA has no accepted mechanism to deal with *equity*);
3   how to measure intangible non-market values such as air quality;
4   how to relate the benefits and costs calculated for each future year to a common scale (the use of *discounting*, the standard method for doing this, is much debated); and
5   how to deal with *uncertainty*, both in financial and biological forecasts.

The main criticism is that qualitative factors related to social, environmental or other *external costs* and benefits are very often inadequately dealt with in such analyses and that distributional considerations are marginalized. Nevertheless, BCA is widely used and is an important tool in decision making. When external costs are included in the analysis, it is sometimes referred to as *extended benefit–cost analysis*. (Tolba and El-Khaly, 1992.) See also *judgemental benefit–cost framework; monetization of environmental impacts*.

**benefit function approach** An example of the practice of *benefit transfer*. *Valuation* studies, to measure the economic value of a non-market asset, typically model a relationship between *willingness to pay (WTP)*, the characteristics of the affected population and the *non-marketed good* or service. With the benefit function approach, the entire valuation function model is then transferred to the policy site, and adjusted to conform as closely as possible to the population and physical characteristics at that site. A *zonal travel cost method* model for recreational trips derived at one lake, for example, may be used in conjunction with data on average travel costs, water quality conditions, socioeconomic characteristics, substitute sites and so on at another lake, in order to estimate the recreational benefits of that lake. See also *water quality, evaluation of*.

**benefit principle of taxation** A traditional theory of taxation, which suggests that there should be an allocation of tax burdens to taxpayers in accordance with the benefits they receive from the provision of *public goods*. This is related to the *beneficiary pays principle*.

**benefits-based standards** Standards which limit *effluent* and emissions based on a comparison of potential benefits with potential costs. The development of such standards includes consideration of all the impacts, focusing particularly on the population exposed to the pollution. (Luken, 1990.) See also *direct regulations, regulations*.

**benefit transfer** Benefit transfer is not a *valuation* method per se, but rather refers to the use of existing estimates of non-market values derived in one context or location to estimate values in a different context or location. The site for which the original estimates were obtained is often referred to as the study site, and the site to which the original estimates are now to be applied is known as the policy site. Benefit transfer is, therefore, the practice of adapting available estimates of the economic value of changes in the quality or provision of *non-marketed goods* or services at a study site(s), to evaluate a change in the quality or provision of a 'similar' resource at a policy site(s).

The primary appeal of benefit transfer is that it allows one to obtain estimates of non-market benefits or costs without incurring the expense of new, primary valuation exercises. Most benefit transfer methods utilized to date involve either the *benefit value* or *benefit function approaches*.

**benefit value approach** With the benefit value approach to *benefit transfer*, a single point estimate (typically, the mean or median *willingness to pay (WTP)* per affected unit) is used to represent the results of a primary study, or selection of primary studies, that have been developed in a specific context. The average *consumer surplus* per angling trip, for example, may be taken from a primary *contingent valuation method* study. This unit value is then used to value one

## bequest value

aspect of a change in environmental quality, or the provision of an environmental good or service, at different locations. For example, the average consumer surplus per angling trip at a study site may be used to value the foregone recreational angling benefits resulting from a deterioration in water quality at a policy site. See also *valuation*.

**bequest value** The value that an individual places on having an environmental resource or general environmental quality available for his or her children to experience. It is based on the desire to exchange current value for the increased wellbeing of one's descendants. Bequest values are considered as a *non-use value* of a resource, even though the value derived results from the future use of a resource. Bequest value makes up part of the *total economic value* of an environmental resource. (Kahn, 1998.)

## best available techniques *or* technology (BAT)

'… "Best Available Techniques" signifies the latest stage in the development of activities, processes and their method of operation which indicate the practical suitability of particular techniques as the basis of emissions limit values for preventing or, where that is not practicable, minimising emissions to the *environment* as a whole, without predetermining any specific technology or other techniques…'

(European Commission, 1996, EC Directive 96/61/EC, Article 2.)

In determining whether operational methods constitute BAT, consideration is given to: comparable processes that have been successfully tried; recent scientific and technological advances; the economic feasibility of the methods; and the availability of techniques to carry out the required function. BAT for a particular process will change with time in the light of technological advances and economic and social factors, as well as changes in scientific knowledge and understanding.

BAT reference notes are an important basis of the implementation process. These notes set out the estimated environmental performance and achievable pollution levels of the technologies, processes and subprocesses in an industrial sector and should be taken into account by authorities in determining BAT. Under the IPPC Directive currently being implemented in EU Member States, authorities do not prescribe technologies for particular activities but set conditions and emission values for enterprises to meet. This approach is intended to encourage innovation and provide the optimum solution at the lowest cost to industries.

## best available techniques *or* technology not entailing excessive cost (BATNEEC)
The term BATNEEC was first used in EC Directive 84/360 on the Combating of Air Pollution from Large Industrial Plants and the concept is included in *integrated pollution prevention and control* (IPPC) regulations implemented in the UK Environmental Protection Act (EPA) of 1990.

BATNEEC makes explicit the economic considerations relevant to assessing *best available techniques (BAT)*. 'Not entailing excessive cost' suggests that costs should not be excessive when compared to the benefits of the environmental protection to be achieved. It should be noted that BATNEEC is a forerunner to the concept of BAT subsequently developed in the EU IPPC directive currently being implemented in EU Member States. The IPPC definition of BAT includes economic considerations and is wider in terms of industrial activities covered and environmental impacts than the definition of BATNEEC in the IPPC *regulations*.

**best conventional technology** Effluent *standards* for industrial dischargers that require the application of the best practicable control technology currently available. Links to *BAT* and *BATNEEC* are unclear as the latter have not been used in the same setting as best conventional technology. (Luken, 1990.)

**best environmental practice (BEP)** This is the best environment-friendly company practice that takes into account the following considerations:

- dissemination of information and knowledge among the public and consumers about environmental impacts of products and services, their use and disposal;
- elaboration and application of codes of good environmental practice covering the entire product life cycle; and
- product labelling to inform consumers about possible hazardous effects of the product, its use and disposal.

To determine the combination of measures leading to BEP, consideration is given to:

- danger to the *environment* of the product, its use and disposal;
- the feasibility of using cleaner technologies and substances;
- the scale of product use;
- potential environmental advantages or shortcomings of alternative materials or activities;
- recent advances in science and research and development;
- the time framework needed to change over to the BEP; and
- its socioeconomic effects.

In operational terms the concept is rather loose, and its links with *BAT* and *BATNEEC* have not been fully explored.

**best practicable environmental option (BPEO)** A criterion which requires that an industrial process is undertaken using the least environmentally damaging technique that is financially practicable. It requires information on the available industrial processes and the effects of emissions on the *environment* to identify the *best available techniques not entailing excessive cost (BATNEEC)*. BPEO should account for the environmental impact of the entire life cycle of a product, and should be introduced as early as possible in the design of the industrial process.

BPEO is an important twin concept to BATNEEC within *integrated pollution prevention and control (IPCC)* regulations. According to the UK Environmental Protection Act (EPA) 1990 (Section 7(7)), the determination of BATNEEC must have regard to the BPEO. This means that local conditions of the specific site should be taken into account when determining BATNEEC in order to avoid unacceptable damage to the environment. The concept of BPEO is not included in the IPPC directive currently being implemented in EU Member States.

**best practicable means (BPM)** This criterion implies that pollution control should be undertaken using the best technology that is reasonably practicable, given considerations of cost. As more weight has been given to *benefit–cost analysis* criteria, BPM has been refined into the concepts of *best available*

## bilateral debt swap

*techniques not entailing excessive cost (BATNEEC), best environmental practice (BEP), best practicable environmental option (BPEO)* and most recently, *best available techniques (BAT)*. (Perman et al, 1999.)

**bilateral debt swap** A bilateral debt swap is a form of debt exchange, negotiated between a creditor nation and a debtor nation, that results in a particular public external debt (or part of it) being cancelled in exchange for counterpart funding for a specific purpose. This term has been used in relation to *debt for nature swaps*. (EPIQ/NRM2, 1998.)

**bilateral official (sovereign) debt** Loans owed to specific creditor governments. Official development assistance (ODA) loans are owed to aid agencies. Publicly guaranteed loans are owed to export credit agencies. (EPIQ/NRM2, 1998.)

**biochemical oxygen demand (BOD)** The measure of the oxygen demand placed on a stream by any particular volume of *effluent*. It represents the amount of oxygen, measured in milligrams per litre, required in the oxidation of organic matter by biological action under specific standard test conditions. BOD is widely used to measure the level of organic pollution in wastewater and streams. Sometimes referred to as biological oxygen demand. (Water Quality Association, 1997.)

Emissions from a point source can be translated into *dissolved oxygen (DO)* measures at various locations downstream using modelling. Oxygen sags are one characteristic often seen downstream from an organic effluent source, where the content of DO is lower than at other points. An *ambient permit system (APS)* would aim to raise DO levels at these points, while an *emissions permit* scheme attempts to achieve a particular BOD reduction target. The ambient schemes take the location of the emitter into account, while the emission permit schemes do not. (Tietenberg, 1996.) See also *chemical oxygen demand (COD)*.

**biodegradable** A biodegradable substance is one that is easily decomposed by bacteria. Often cited on product labels, this quality is important for waste management and to reduce water pollution. Many human-made substances are biodegradable, but hard detergents and some pesticides are not, and these may damage *ecosystems*. See also *degradable pollutant; eco-labelling; green consumerism*.

**biodiversity** Biodiversity, or *biological diversity*, can be defined as:

'the variety and variability among living organisms from all sources including, inter alia, terrestrial, marine and other aquatic *ecosystems* and the ecological complexes of which they are part, this includes diversity within *species*, between species and of ecosystems'

(Convention on Biological Diversity, Rio de Janeiro, Brazil, June 3–14, 1992, http://www.biodiv.org/).

The Convention distinguishes between biological diversity and *biological resources*, where biological resources consist of the resources necessary for biodiversity assessments, namely *conservation* areas, scientific collections, genetic resource collections, information and human resources.

The unit of analysis of biodiversity is sometimes thought of as being the number of species in existence. However, three different scales can be applied.

# biodiversity and scientific uncertainty

Genetic diversity is the total genetic information that exists on earth, and accounts for diversity within species. Species diversity refers to the number of species within a system. Species are defined as populations within which breeding can take place; new species develop when populations become isolated and evolve under different conditions. Ecosystem diversity is the variety of habitats, biotic communities and ecological processes in existence.

**biodiversity, economic values of** The *total economic value* of *biodiversity* consists of several components. *Direct-use value* derives from direct use of or contact with *biological resources* or an *ecosystem*, for instance the use of the reserve of a *species* for scientific research or to attract tourism. *Indirect use value* derives from the role of ecosystems in supporting human activity, for example the support given to agriculture by forests that regulate the hydrological cycle. *Option value* is the value placed on preserving an asset that, while not used at present, may be used in the future. An example of option value is the value that people place on preserving ecosystems and landscapes that they may wish to visit in the future. *Bequest value* is the value that people place on preserving natural assets to pass on to future generations, and *existence value* is the value that people place on the knowledge that a particular species or ecosystem exists.

The tools of non-market *valuation* can be used to attach monetary values to biodiversity. These tools include the *contingent valuation method (CVM)*, the *travel cost method (TCM)*, and the *production function approach*. Valuing biodiversity is a way to estimate the extent to which natural ecosystems should be preserved in order to maximize human welfare. Destroying natural ecosystems, such as forests, often brings financial gains. The non-financial value of a forest should be offset against this gain in order to establish whether or not depleting the forest is economically efficient.

**biodiversity losses** Many leading natural scientists are predicting an imminent mass *extinction of species*. Some project losses of 25 to 50 per cent of all life forms over the next 100 years – biodiversity losses. There are various reasons for the loss of *biodiversity*, including overexploitation of *species* and the loss of habitats, also known as the *global conversion process*. (Swanson, 1994.) See also *asset conversion; enclosure*.

**biodiversity and scientific uncertainty** *Biodiversity* is hard to measure, and there remains much scientific uncertainty about, for example, the number of *species* that exist, and the exact nature of the services and functions they perform. For instance, the fact that a certain species plays a crucial role in maintaining an ecosystem is often not apparent until the species is lost. To a certain extent this results from the immense complexity of the interdependence of species and systems. Scientific *uncertainty* means that the formulation of appropriate policy and the assessment and evaluation of its effectiveness is difficult.

One suggestion for policy in this area is to define a *safe minimum standard (SMS)* of environmental quality and ensure that it is met. However, even this is problematic. As MacGarvin (1993) points out, it is difficult to define appropriate SMS for pollution in the Northeast Atlantic and North Sea, as well as to estimate the minimum viable population and optimal depletion of fish stocks.

In the past, population predictions have proved highly inaccurate, and there have been huge differences between model predictions and observations. Pearce (1993) argues that such scientific uncertainty therefore supports the adoption of a precautionary approach to biodiversity *conservation*, at least until better knowledge is gained. This view is endorsed by Hohl and Tisdell (1993) who argue that safe minimum standards for the conservation of species do not exist and that no standard ensures the continued existence of any species. (Pearce, 1993.) See also *precautionary principle*.

**bioeconomic equilibrium** This is a rate of use of *renewable resources* that takes account of biological constraints as well as economic considerations, and that can be maintained for long periods of time. A maximum stock level exists which is determined by the *carrying capacity* of the host *ecosystem*. Above this level, no renewable resource can expand. There may also be a critical minimum stock for some resources, below which the resource cannot continue to exist. There is a range of stock levels between these two extremes that can be maintained indefinitely, involving different levels of harvesting. A bioeconomic equilibrium is one that balances the demand for the resource against the costs of supply. There are a number of possible equilibria, depending on what is assumed about the ownership structure of the resource, and what the underlying discount rates are. For further details see Hartwick and Olewiler, 1986 and Turner, 1988. See also *threshold instruments*.

**bioeconomics** Environmental economists have applied the principle of bioeconomics in terms of estimating human values and applying them in an extended *benefit–cost analysis* framework. Economic modelling is becoming increasingly sophisticated, allowing the development of quantitative estimates of the importance given to human desires and preferences, enabling policy-makers to be better informed in their decision-making process. Pearce (1985) argues that 'economic science has been ahead of the game, developing the foundations of bioeconomics, the integrative analysis of biological and economic systems of man and the natural *environment*'. (Redclift, 1988.)

**bioethical standpoint** This argues either for some kind of equality between anthropocentric value and *intrinsic value* in nature, or for intrinsic value to be given more weight. Intrinsic values are those that are attributed to objects themselves rather than those based on valuations of the objects. According to Turner and Pearce (in Barbier (ed), 1993), environmental economists argue against the bioethical standpoint on three grounds. Firstly, if applied it would have negative impacts on development; thus it has a high *social cost* in terms of the foregone benefits of development. Secondly, social injustice may result from its application in that it may deny development benefits to the less advantaged in society, both at present and in the future. Thirdly, Turner and Pearce argue that this approach is redundant since the '...*sustainability* approach generates many of the benefits alleged to accrue from the concern for intrinsic (non-instrumental) values'. (Barbier (ed), 1993.) See also *ethics; environmental ethics; Kantian ethics; naturalism; extended stewardship ideology; stewardship ethic; anthropocentric environmental ethic*.

**biogeochemical cycles** Naturally occurring cycles that involve biological, geological and chemical processes. One example is the nitrogen cycle. Disruption to these cycles (for example, pollution impacting on the populations of bacteria needed to break down organic matter) affects the productivity of the *ecosystem*. *Adaptation*, such as the use of fertilizers rich in nitrogen, can assist productivity. (Pearce, 1976.)

**biogeography** The study of biology on a geographical basis. An example from Swanson (1994) is the study of islands, which is instructive for looking at the global impact of conversions of habitat. This study has revealed a geometric relationship between habitat conversions and the *extinction of species*, in the sense that the rate of species loss increases geometrically with increased levels of habitat loss. As the technology for conversion becomes more and more efficient, the loss of species will become ever greater. This is what has been occurring on the global level, paralleling the island extinctions from which this relationship was deduced. (Swanson, 1994.) See also *asset conversion; debt conversion; debt-for-nature swaps; enclosure; global conversion process; opportunity cost.*

**biological amplification** Small levels of pollutants can disrupt the *environment* through this mechanism. An example is the food chain, which amplifies the pollution problem because animals higher up the food chain receive doses of pollutants many times higher than the initial exposure. A well-known example of this is the use of dichlorodiphenyltrichloroethane (DDT) as a pesticide. DDT is a persistent pollutant that is absorbed in small doses by insects, but is amplified in birds and other animals including humans higher up the food chain. (Lowe and Lewis, 1980.)

**biological determinist belief** The belief that Darwinian evolution and natural selection apply to socio-economics. Holders of this belief see social organizations as having evolved through the process of natural selection, with firms' survival depending on *adaptation* to change in order to remain profitable and competitive. There is general scepticism among biologists of this use of Darwinian theory. (Pearce and Turner, 1990.)

**biological diversity** See *biodiversity*.

**biological growth** The natural growth process of a renewable resource, such as a *species* of fish or a forest. This process can be described as a mathematical function, with the natural growth at any point in time being determined by the existing level of the resource stock, and the *carrying capacity* of its habitat. (Perman, 1999.) See also *ecological species–area relationship; interactive resources; maximum sustainable yield (MSY); renewable resources.*

**biological oxygen demand (BOD)** See *biochemical oxygen demand.*

**biological resources** These include genetic resources, organisms or parts thereof, populations, or any other biotic component of *ecosystem*s with actual or potential use or value for humanity (Convention on Biological Diversity, Rio de Janeiro, Brazil, June 3–14, 1992, http://www.biodiv.org/)

**biomass appropriation** The use of the net primary product of plant life by the human economy. (Krishnan et al, 1995.)

**biophysical approach to production** This approach sees production as the starting point of economic theory. It takes the basic *factors of production* as being materials, energy, information flows and the biological processes that convert, transmit or apply them, with the primary net input being solar energy. Complementarity of inputs is central to this approach. Its adherents claim that, unlike neoclassical theory, it recognizes the fundamental differences between resource extraction and resource processing. The biophysical approach claims that the movement from a largely *renewable resource* base to a *non-renewable resource* base implies limits to *economic growth*. (Krishnan et al, 1995.) See also *neoclassical economics*.

**biosphere** The region of the Earth, in land, sea or atmosphere, in which life exists. See also *Man and the Biosphere Programme; biosphere homogenization; biosphere reserve.*

**biosphere homogenization** The movement towards humanity's dependence upon a few dozen heavily utilized *species*. (Swanson, 1994.)

**biosphere reserve** Site considered by IUCN or UNESCO to be of international importance for *conservation*, study and *sustainable development*. By 1999 there were 357 such sites around the world. For further details on biosphere reserve, including current sites, see the UNESCO website at http://www.unesco.org/mab/wnbr.htm. See also *Man and the Biosphere Programme; biosphere homogenization; biosphere.*

**biotechnology** The application of biological science techniques to industrial processes. This includes the *genetic modification* of food and the *recycling* of wastes.

**black list** One of three classifications of pollutants under the *Oslo Convention* for the Prevention of Marine Pollution by Dumping from Ships and Aircraft. Those on this list are the most detrimental and their dumping is prohibited except in cases of emergency, or where they appear only as trace elements. Leeson (1995) lists the black list substances as being:

- organohalogen compounds and compounds which may form such substances in the marine *environment*, excluding those which are non-toxic, or which are rapidly converted in the sea into substances which are biologically harmless;
- organosilicon compounds and compounds which may form such substances in the marine environment, excluding those which are non-toxic, or which are rapidly converted in the sea into substances which are biologically harmless;
- carcinogenic compounds under the conditions of disposal;
- mercury and mercury compounds;
- cadmium and cadmium compounds;
- persistent plastics and other persistent synthetic materials which may remain in suspension in the sea, and which may seriously interfere with fishing or navigation, reduce amenities, or interfere with other legitimate uses of the sea.

(Leeson, 1995.) See also *grey list; white list.*

**black markets** These are illegal markets that arise when *regulation* creates 'rents' – that is, profit that can be gained simply by evading the regulations. The most common reason for the development of black markets is the avoidance of tax. In the environmental sphere, a number of controls could create black markets. One example is *hazardous substances and hazardous waste* for which a black market could be created if there were strict controls on its acceptance in regular landfills. The holder of the waste would pay a fee in excess of normal waste fees to a black market operator, who would dispose of the waste illegally. The extent of black markets depends on the size of the resulting rents and the probability and consequences of being caught. See also *fly tipping*.

**'black spot' policy** Governmental *regulation* policy aimed at the concentration of pollution-intensive activities in certain areas. A spatial separation approach in planning policy is used to try to bring about a specialization of national territory. Such a policy focuses what Siebert (1987) calls the 'public bad' in designated areas. This policy may also lead to the placement of black spots close to borders, shifting the *externality* from the polluting country to its neighbour, as has been seen in Sweden, where heavily polluting industries have been located close to the border with Norway. (Siebert, 1987.)

**BOD** See *biochemical oxygen demand*.

**BOD5** The amount of *dissolved oxygen (DO)* consumed in five days by the biological processes that break down organic matter. (Luken, 1990.) See also *biochemical oxygen demand*.

**border price** The price of a commodity in international prices, measured as the landed price, including cost, insurance and freight (cif) for imports; or without taxes and *subsidies*, delivered to the point of export, in the case of exports. Border prices are used in *benefit–cost analysis (BCA)* as representing the *opportunity cost* of the commodity.

**bottom-up modelling:** Bottom-up models are based on detailed analysis of technical potential, and hence are disaggregated compared to the aggregate *top-down modelling* technique. The relative merits of these two modelling techniques are presented in IPCC (1996b). In essence, bottom-up models are better at simulating detailed substitution potentials, and top-down aggregate models are used to estimate the expected impacts on the wider economy. Two approaches for bottom-up modelling are spreadsheet modelling and optimization modelling. The former uses simultaneous equations in describing the potential for the adoption of a given technology in an economy, while the latter simulates investment decisions endogenously. See also *climate change, estimating costs of*.

**Brownian Motion** Arbitrary or uncontrolled movement of particles or physical objects. The reference to this in environmental economic arises because of the uncertainties inherent in such things as prices. Hence, the profitability of natural resource use can be estimated using equations based on this concept. Hanley et al (1997) use this concept in estimating the returns from fishing.

**brown issues** Issues that refer to the pollution of land, air and water from household and industrial activities. Distinguished from green issues, which refer to environmental problems in the fields of natural resource *conservation*, *biodiversity* and so on.

**Brundtland Commission** The World Commission on Environment and Development (WCED) (1984–87), the chairman of which was Dr Gro Harlem Brundtland, former Prime Minister and Environment Minister of Norway.

## bubble policy

The commission was selected in cooperation with and approved by the United Nations Secretary General, and its report *Our Common Future* (World Commission on Environment and Development, 1987) elaborated on the concept of *sustainable development (SD)*. The Commission is known for its broad use of public hearings in various regions of the world to discuss its findings and probe public opinion about them.

**bubble policy** A feature of an *emissions trading* system which can be used to ensure that, over a certain area, average exposure to a certain pollutant is reduced. A bubble is best thought of as an imaginary glass dome covering several different sources of pollution, either several points within one plant, or several different plants. The aim is to prevent total emissions from this area rising above the level called for in the standard-setting procedure. Excessive emissions from one point within the area can be redressed through the purchase of emissions reductions credits from another area within the bubble. The bubble policy reduces or controls the average level of environmental exposure to one pollutant, in contrast to traditional *command and control policies* which set a uniform maximum level of pollution for each emitter. A time dimension may also be included, determining the period in which compliance has to take place. (OECD, 1992a.) See also *permits; regulations*.

**bubble trades** This refers to the trades that take place under a *bubble policy*, by means of which a firm can increase emissions at one source without incurring additional regulatory burdens by purchasing emissions reduction credits from another source within the bubble area. (OECD, 1992a.)

**budget constraint or budget line** This represents the combinations of goods and services that an individual can afford. An example of a budget constraint is shown in Figure 2. Two goods are represented, an environmental good and all other goods. The consumer can spend all income on the environmental good (point A), all of income on other goods (point B), or any combination between these two points. Line AB is the budget constraint for the individual. The slope of this line represents the relative prices of the two goods. The budget curve represents the range of different consumption possibilities for an individual or society. Economic analysis is used to determine which of these possibilities should be chosen.

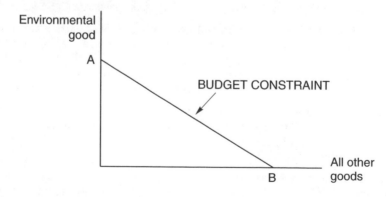

**Figure 2** *Budget Constraint*

**buffer zones** These are zones between areas of intensive land use, such as logging or farming, and areas of strict *conservation*. They can help to reduce encroachment onto conservation areas if they offer employment opportunities that are more attractive than encroachment. (Panayotou, 1993.)

**bundle of entitlements (or rights)** This refers to the rights and responsibilities of an owner over the use of a resource. There are generally several entitlements, including privileges (such as construction, exclusive use, or subsurface resource mining) and limitations (such as prohibited activities or obligation to sell to the government in some circumstances.) See also *property rights*.

**business as usual (BAU) emission scenario** This measures emissions of a pollutant on the assumption that no specific measures are taken to reduce them. (IPCC, 1996b and 2001.) See also *baseline*.

# Cc

**capacity building** Term often used in the *sustainable development (SD)* literature to denote the development of the ability of individuals, groups, organizations and institutions in a society to find and implement solutions to environmental issues as part of a wider effort to achieve the goal of sustainable development. This term encompasses more than simply formal training, and includes collaboration and partnership with overseas experts in improving the functions of civil society and local bureaucracies. (OECD, 1995.)

**cap-cum-trading** The combination of *cap setting* and *emissions trading*.

**capital** Any asset that provides economic or social services over a period of time. The main types of capital used in *environmental economics* are *human-made capital, human capital, natural capital* and *social capital*. Human-made capital consists of assets, such as buildings, equipment, plants and machinery, and tools. Human capital is made up of the investment in education and training embodied in the workforce. Natural capital is made up of the stock of environmental assets such as soil and forests, wildlife and water, biological *species*, landscape, and wetlands. Social capital consists of the network of institutions and social relationships in society, which are the basis of the proper functioning of legal and economic systems. Capital is a particularly important concept in the analysis of sustainability and sustainable development, since an economy's capacity to ensure wellbeing for its citizens can be reduced over time if the aggregate capital stock is not maintained, or if there is insufficient investment in a certain type of capital. See also *weak sustainability; strong sustainability*.

**capital asset pricing** The value of a resource stock can be expressed as the *net present value (NPV)* of the stream of service flows it is expected to yield over the lifetime of the resource. Such a method for arriving at the price of a resource is referred to as the *capital* assets pricing method. Calculating NPV involves using the technique of *discounting*. (Perman et al, 1999.)

**capital–resource elasticity** A measurement of the degree of substitutability between *human- or human-made capital* and *natural resources* in production. For example, suppose that the *elasticity of substitution* is infinite (perfect elasticity) between tractors and hectares of arable land in agriculture. This implies a fixed rate of substitution between tractor months and land. Then a farmer with access to 12 months of tractor services and 100 hectares of land should be able to produce as much agricultural output as one with access to 24 tractor months and 50 hectares. Clearly perfect substitutability is not possible, but there is a great deal of debate about the extent to which *natural capital* and *human-made capital* are substitutable. See also *weak sustainability; strong sustainability*.

**capital wealth** The physical and monetary value of the stock of all *capital*.

**cap management** The monitoring, *enforcement*, inspection and other administrative presence required to ensure that the enforcement of ceilings on total allowable emissions of a pollutant (caps) will be strict. (OECD, 1989a.) See also *cap setting*.

**cap setting** Establishment of a cap or ceiling on the total allowable emissions, based on the best available scientific information, local needs, societal preferences, *willingness to pay (WTP)*, and so on. Caps should correspond to current and forecast emissions levels, estimated from air quality monitoring and assessment capabilities. Overall, caps need to be aimed at meeting regional requirements. (UNEP, 1993.) See also *cap management; cap-cum-trading*.

**capture theory** This theory proposes that an industry can turn environmental *regulation* to its advantage through exerting pressure and influence over the regulating agency, because it is the sole supplier of regulation-related data to the agency, or because it is a key partner in various forms of collusion or cooperation. See also *regulatory capture*.

**carbon budget approach** An approach to framing an optimal *climate change* policy. An alternative to *benefit–cost analysis (CBA)* for global warming, this method ignores damage considerations and imposes an upper atmospheric concentration or warming limit, determined on the basis of ethical, political or precautionary considerations. Under the carbon budget approach, the costs of the constraint applied are reflected in the shadow value of emissions, and the shadow value will bear no relationship to the global warming damages occurring. The advantage of this technique is that no modelling of global warming damages is needed, although the question remains as to how stringent the carbon constraint should be. Fankhauser (1995) reports that the *shadow prices* from carbon budget models are often far greater than actual *social cost* estimates, at least in later time periods. (Fankhauser, 1995.)

**carbon cycle** This is the process by which carbon moves among its main repositories: the atmosphere, animals and plants, and oceans. The carbon cycle operates as a balanced system in which emitted carbon is absorbed by *carbon sinks*, notably oceans and forests. This is an example of a *biogeochemical cycle*.

**carbon dioxide ($CO_2$)** Formed from the burning of all fossil fuels and wood, organic decomposition, human and animal exhalation and the reaction of acids with carbonates such as limestone. $CO_2$ has no smell and is non-toxic, but it can asphyxiate. This gas is the most significant contributor to *climate change*.

**carbon monoxide (CO)** A colourless, odourless, poisonous gas produced by incomplete fossil fuel combustion. (Luken, 1990.)

**carbon offset deals** A trading mechanism between countries which lowers the global costs of reducing *greenhouse gas (GHG)* emissions. An offset deal might involve a commitment of forest users to a forestry management plan which maximizes *carbon sequestration* in exchange for an annual payment which represents a carbon credit for the financier. The use of such a mechanism is discussed under *Kyoto Protocol*. (OECD, 1996.)

**carbon sequestration** The biochemical process through which carbon in the atmosphere is absorbed by biomass such as trees, soils and crops. (IPCC, 1996a.) See also *carbon cycle; biogeochemical cycles*.

**carbon sinks** Chemical processes which absorb *carbon dioxide (CO$_2$)*. Forests constitute carbon sinks since as they grow, they absorb and store carbon dioxide. (IPCC, 1996a.)

**carbon tax** A tax imposed by an international agency, a country or a local political administrative unit on the *greenhouse gas* emissions in a particular area. The tax may be defined in terms of dollars per metric ton of carbon or dollars per ton of *carbon dioxide (CO$_2$)*, although the former is more common. The chemical relationship is that one ton of carbon equals 3.5 tons of CO$_2$. A carbon tax is an *economic instrument*, aimed at the *mitigation* of *climate change*.

**carrying capacity** The maximum level of a biological population that an *ecosystem* can sustain. Once a population, such as a fish stock or a forest, grows to the level of the carrying capacity of its *environment*, its growth will then be sufficient only to replace losses due, for example, to mortality. The net growth in the stock is zero. Carrying capacity can also be used to refer to the capacity of the environment to support humans, including its capacity to assimilate the wastes of production and consumption. See also *assimilative capacity, absorptive capacity*.

**carrying (holding) cost** The cost of reducing pollution (and so improving the quality of the *environment* and adding to the value of the *environmental resource* stock) by one unit for one period. (Perman et al, 1999.)

**cash cropping** The growing of crops for sale, including for export. Environmental problems arise from this form of cropping in that soils are often degraded by overexploitation. Senegal, for instance, borrowed heavily to install refining capacity for a million tonnes of groundnut and as a result of this intensive cultivation the soil quality has declined. (George, 1991.)

**catabolism** Process that converts living tissue into degraded matter and energy. (Krishnan et al, 1995.)

**catalytic converter** A device which converts *carbon monoxide (CO)* and hydrocarbon pollutants into *carbon dioxide (CO$_2$)* and water. This typically consists of a finely divided platinum-iridium catalyst in which emissions are combined with excess air. This is an example of the *mitigation* of environmental damage.

**catchment basin** Geographical area from which rainfall and other waters drain into major rivers.

**catch per unit effort** The amount of harvest from fisheries (for example, mass or number of fish) resulting from a unit of fishing effort (for example, man-hours or boat-days). In estimating the depletion of fish stocks when the latter cannot be measured, it is important to account for changes in fishing effort, and not to look just at the landed catch. This is because the need for a greater effort to harvest a given catch is an indication that stocks are being depleted; this would not be revealed by figures on landed catch alone.

**categorical pre-treatment standard** An *effluent* restriction based on the use of technology by an industrial facility which discharges into a municipal sewer system. This is similar in stringency to *best available technology (BAT)* for direct dischargers. (Luken, 1990.)

**cause** A number of statutes, in defining offences in the environmental field, provide that the wrong occurs when the perpetrator 'causes or permits' or alternatively 'knowingly causes or knowingly permits' the prohibited act. In the UK the meaning of 'cause' was given judicial consideration in the Rivers (Prevention of Pollution) Act 1951, which created the offence of 'causing poisonous, noxious or polluting matter to enter a stream'. Leeson (1995) cites the case of Alphacell v. Woodward (1972), in which Viscount Dilhorne summarized his view saying 'What then is meant by the word "caused" in this subsection? If a man intending to secure a particular result, does an act which brings that about, he causes that result. If he deliberately and intentionally does certain acts of which the natural consequence is that certain results ensue, may he not also be said to have caused those results even though they may not be intended by him? I think he can, just as he can be said to cause the result if he is negligent, without intending that result.'

**cell fusion** This involves uniting the cells of *species* that would not normally mate to create new types of plants different from parent cells. See also *biodiversity; genetic modification*.

**certification** In the environmental context this word is used to refer to *regulations* which require approval at key points in the conduct of certain programmes and activities. One example from Swanson (1994) is certification of users and managers of natural habitats. They would be required to ensure that wildlife stocks are maintained and that diverse natural habitats are conserved for low-intensity uses. Suppliers would be certified on the basis of their demonstrated management of the natural habitat and wildlife resources for which they are responsible.

**chain store paradox** An illustration in *game theory* of the problem wherein, if a country has to negotiate with two or more countries on transboundary pollution issues, or deal with the same country on several issues, then too fast an acceptance of the *victim* or *beneficiary pays principle* in the negotiations on one of these issues may give the country a reputation as a 'weak' negotiator. (Helm, 1991.)

**change in productivity approach** An *objective valuation approach (OVA)* to valuing environmental damages. This approach involves inferring the value of an environmental damage, such as an increase in pollution, by calculating the value of production lost due to the damage. This approach can be applied, for instance, where increased air pollution results in loss of agricultural productivity. See also *valuation*.

**charges** Charges, in an environmental context, impose an explicit price for an environmental service or resource. Effectively applied, charges change a polluter's behaviour by providing price signals that more fully reflect the cost of using environmental resources and services. Charges produce revenues to fund *environmental management* and provide companies with the correct incentives to significantly reduce pollution. Charges are seen as penalties for bad behaviour. Although in theory they are efficient mechanisms for pollution reduction, in practice they often have little incentive effect (see *economic instruments*) and often their main purpose is to raise revenues, for example for financing collective wastewater treatment plants.

# cheapest available technology not involving prosecution

In Eastern Europe, charges are determined on the basis of the targets of the *environmental fund*s concerned. Theoretically, for a charge to be economically efficient, its level per unit of pollution should be set at the level of emissions at which *marginal abatement costs* and *marginal damage* costs are equalized. Such a charge is, however, difficult to determine in practice. Moreover, it will only coincidentally equal the level of a charge whose purpose is to raise revenues. For example, the level of water effluent charges is far below the desired level from an *efficiency* point of view in many countries that have such charges. Low charge levels imply the necessity of *direct regulations* in order to achieve the objectives of environmental policy. Three types of charges most often used are *emission* or *effluent charges, product charges* and *user charges*. (OECD, 1989a.)

**cheapest available technology not involving prosecution (CATNIP)** There is some evidence that a polluter will apply a technology which is as superficial and inexpensive as is possible without facing prosecution from the regulatory authority. It was this context that generated the acronym CATNIP. (Leeson, 1995.) See also *best available technology (BAT); best available technology not entailing excessive cost (BATNEEC); best practicable environmental option (BPEO).*

**chemical oxygen demand (COD)** A measure of the oxygen-consuming capacity of inorganic and organic matter present in water or wastewater. It is expressed as the amount of oxygen consumed by a chemical oxidant in a specified test. This measure does not differentiate between stable and unstable organic matter and thus does not necessarily correlate with *biochemical oxygen demand (BOD).*

**chlorofluorocarbons (CFCs), legislation against** CFCs are one of the main causes of the depletion of the *ozone* layer, and various international and regional agreements have been put in place to limit their use. One example is the Vienna *Convention* for the Ozone Layer, negotiated in 1985, and the subsequent protocol to the convention, the 1987 Montreal Protocol on substances that deplete the ozone layer. The Montreal Protocol required industrialized countries to phase out the use of CFCs by 1996. It also set out provisions for the transfer of new technology from industrialized to developing countries, and placed limits on trade in ozone-depleting substances (ODSs). (Malcolm, 1994.)

**choke price** This is defined as the price at which demand for a good, for example a fossil fuel, drops to zero. That is, it is the highest price at which there will be any positive demand for a good. The choke price is used in estimating total *willingness to pay (WTP)*. If a choke price exists, then the resource will not experience *asymptotic depletion*. (Hartwick and Olewiler, 1986.)

**chronic toxicity** Chronic toxicity is said to be present when a negative effect arises from continuous or frequent exposure to a *hazardous substance*. Tests for chronic toxicity usually involve subjecting animal populations to sustained low-level doses of the substance over an extended period. (Tietenberg, 1996.) See also *acute toxicity*.

**cif (cost, insurance and freight, or charged in full)** The full price of a good that is shipped to a buyer includes the costs of transportation to the destination port specified in the contract, and the insurance against loss or damage to the goods during transportation. See also *border price*.

**circular economy** The *environment* and the economy can be characterized as a circular relationship, whereby everything is an input into everything else. Such a relationship is shown in Figure 3. The extraction of raw materials leads to production, but also produces waste. Consumption follows production, and also leads to more waste. The end result of consumption is waste material. Waste material is either dumped into the environment, thus using the environment as a sink, or is recycled into a raw material, and goes back into the cycle. For further details see Pearce and Turner (1990).

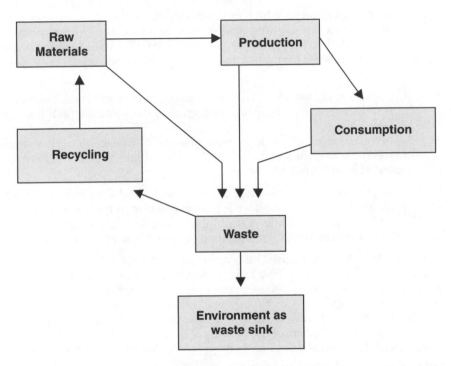

**Figure 3** *The Circular Economy*

**CITES** The *Convention* on International Trade in Endangered Species of Wild Fauna and Flora (CITES) regulates commercial trade in endangered and other *species*. When a species reaches a certain level of *vulnerability*, the parties to the Convention list it in one of three appendices. This determines the extent to which trade in the species is permitted. Appendix I species are those 'threatened with extinction and are or may be affected by trade'. Trade in Appendix I species is prohibited for 'primarily commercial purposes'. Appendix II contains species that 'although not necessarily now threatened with extinction, may become so unless trade in specimens of such species is subject to strict regulation in order to avoid utilisation incompatible with their survival'. Trade in Appendix II species is prohibited if authorities in the country of export determine that the export will be detrimental to the survival of the species. Appendix III lists species that a country has identified as 'subject to regulation within its jurisdiction for the purpose of preventing or restricting exploitation, and as needing the cooperation of other parties in the control of trade. Unlike species in Appendices I and II, the listing of species in Appendix III does not require a vote of the conference of parties. Trade in these species requires the presentation of appropriate export documents at the time of importation'. (Jha, Markandya and Vossenaar, 1999.) See also *regulation*.

**Clarke Tax** The Clarke Tax is used to induce individuals to reveal the true level of their demand for public goods. The essence of the tax is to convert a 'large' number situation (in which individuals believe they have no influence on outcomes) into a 'small' number situation (in which individuals are held to account according to the action that they take). If individuals have to choose between two options (for example, two levels of public good output), the Clarke Tax procedure is:

- Ask voters how much they would be prepared to offer for each option.
- Sum the totals for each option and choose the option which has the highest total.
- Levy a Clarke Tax on each individual equal to the absolute difference between the two total sums when the individual's preferences are not included in the summations.

In this way, the tax that any individual pays will equal the extent to which their participation changes welfare for everyone else in the community. As such, each individual is made accountable for actions taken and it can be shown that there is no better strategy than to honestly reveal preferences.

**Clark Model of Extinction** The economics of the *extinction of species* was initially modelled by Clark (1973). He showed that where a resource is subject to *open access*, it will be exploited to the point at which the price it fetches is equal to the average cost of extracting one unit of the resource. This can result in extinction if growth rates are low, and if the price is high relative to the costs of extraction. For a criticism of the model see Swanson, 1994. The extinction of a species under open access is an example of the *tragedy of the commons*.

**classical economics** Classical economists were interested in standards of living and the process of *economic growth*. *Natural resources* were seen as determinants of national wealth and growth; moreover, differences in resource *endowments* were perceived as influencing income differentials between economies. Since land was fixed in supply, and was a necessary input in production, classical economists ranged from being actually pessimistic about the future of mankind (the Malthusian viewpoint) to taking the less stringent view that economic progress was necessarily limited in the long run. (Perman et al, 1999.) See also *neoclassical economics*.

**Clawson-Knetsch Method** See *travel cost method (TCM)*.

**clean development mechanism (CDM)** The CDM was established as one of the flexibility mechanisms of the *Kyoto Protocol* which facilitate the reduction of global carbon emissions. Under this proposed mechanism, *emission credits* could be gained by Annex I countries (that is, developed countries) in exchange for investments in emission reduction projects that promote *sustainable* *development (SD)* in developing countries. The Kyoto Protocol, at time of writing, is yet to be ratified and the structure of the CDM is still under negotiation. Major difficulties in the establishment of the CDM include: the establishment of the appropriate *baseline* and hence the net emission reduction brought about; the monitoring of emissions; and the establishment of eligibility for participation in CDM. For a good review of work to date on the CDM see Chapter 6 in IPCC (2001).

**clean production** A comprehensive way to minimize the ecological damage caused by the design and consumption of products. Clean production offers a way to limit the unsustainable use of materials and energy. It is based upon the circular concepts of the product life cycle and utilizes the *precautionary principle* to approach material selection and system and product design. It also aims to protect biological and social diversity. For further reading see *Rachel's Environment and Health Weekly* (1999).

**climate change** Climate change has become one of the most important areas of research in the field of the *environment*. The impact of human emissions of *greenhouse gases* on, for example, the climate has been the subject of much research, particularly by the IPCC (1996a, 1996b, 2001). This concept is commonly known as global warming or the *greenhouse effect*, although in recent years 'climate change' has replaced these terms, owing to the diverse nature of the impacts. Greenhouse gases trap heat and lead to changes in the global average temperature. However, in a given country the temperature may be either increased or decreased depending on location, leading to shifts in weather patterns. The impacts of climate change include: potential sea-level rise; changes in weather patterns, including *El Niño*; increased incidence of severe weather conditions; *desertification*; and impacts on human health (see *climate change and human health*). Potential policy responses include *mitigation* and *adaptation* policies to reduce the impacts of climate change, either through reductions in emissions or through changes in behaviour or government spending patterns in response to the problems caused by climate change.

Modelling climate change is difficult, involving as it does the use of complex *general circulation models*, among other tools. The *valuation* of the damages arising from climate change is also complex: see *climate change, estimating costs of* for further details.

In response to the problems posed by climate change, an *international environmental agreement*, the *Kyoto Protocol*, has been established under the *Framework Convention on Climate Change (FCCC)*. This agreement paves the way for *mitigation* and *adaptation* policies, including the use of *emissions trading*, the *clean development mechanism (CDM)* and *joint implementation*. The Kyoto Protocol, which has yet to be ratified, also establishes greenhouse gas emissions targets for countries and regions.

Climate change is expected to occur over a long period of time, leading to issues of intergenerational equity in the formulation of policy. It is thus an important issue for *sustainability* and *sustainable development (SD)*. The distribution of impacts is also under debate, with poorer countries being less able to adapt to the effects of climate change. See IPCC (1996a, 1996b and 2001) for an indepth analysis of climate change. See also *agricultural potential and climate change; climate impact assessment; intergenerational equity principle.*

**climate change, estimating costs of** The costs of *climate change* fall into three categories: the costs imposed on society by the impacts of climate change; the costs of reducing the gases that cause climate change (*mitigation* costs); and the costs of adapting to the change in the climate (*adaptation* costs). *Climate change impact assessment* has proved to be extremely difficult; the physical impacts are highly uncertain and human responses are also not easy to predict. Consequently, the range of damage estimates is very large. One particularly controversial variable is the value attached to the increased *risk* of death from the greater incidence of diseases such as malaria. If one bases this value on the *willingness to pay (WTP)*, the figures for poor countries are much lower than those for rich countries. Allowing this disparity to become the basis of policy is considered by many to be unacceptable.

In the case of mitigation costs, the issues are less problematic, although there remain difficulties there as well. Broadly *bottom-up modelling*, which looks at the use of energy at the plant and household level, comes up with very low costs of reduced emissions, whereas macroeconomic models, which look at energy use in the context of a broad macroeconomic framework, generate much higher cost estimates. A relatively under-researched area is that of the costs of implementing changes in practice and in introducing new polices. Typically these are underestimated, resulting in too optimistic a cost prediction from the bottom-up models.

The costs of *adaptation* are also relatively little researched. Again, any cost assessment is bedevilled with *uncertainty* about the impacts. The range of options and the timing of the actions need to be considered in a comprehensive benefit–cost framework, as well as in a decision-making framework that gives due importance to the uncertainty. Further details of all these issues are to be found in Markandya (1998b), ExternE (1999), IPCC (2001), and Toth (1998). See also *agricultural potential and climate change; carbon budget approach*.

**climate change and human health** *Climate change* is likely to have broad and mainly negative impacts on human health. The health impacts will probably result from both direct and indirect causes, with the indirect impacts, in the longer term, likely to predominate. Indirect impacts include disease caused by the increase in the range and season of organisms such as mosquitoes. Direct health effects include increases in mortality and illness as a result of increases in the intensity and duration of heatwaves. A rise in the mean temperature in colder areas would be expected to result in fewer cases of death as a result of cold weather. It is anticipated that extreme weather conditions will arise more frequently, resulting in higher incidence of death, injury, psychological disorders, and exposure to contaminated water supplies. Possible *adaptations* to reduce the severity of these health impacts include disaster preparation, vaccinations and appropriate health care. (IPCC, 1996a.)

**climate change impact assessment** The emission of *greenhouse gases (GHGs)* into the atmosphere, and the consequent change in climate, is likely to have a significant impact on the planet in a number of areas including human health, the *ecosystem* and industrial production. Attempts have been made to value these impacts using complex models of climate–economy interactions.

The *valuation* of climate change impacts is greatly influenced by the discount rate used in the analysis. This is due to the fact that climate change impacts are spread over a long time horizon.

# climate change impact assessment

There are many models which attempt to estimate the damages caused by climate change. The results yielded by the FUND model (Tol, 1999) are presented in Table 1. The table shows the distribution of damages by sector and by geographical region. A negative sign represents a net benefit, as is the case for agriculture under a 10 per cent discount rate. As can be seen, the major category for impacts is expected to be sea-level rise. As mentioned above, the discount rate applied significantly affects the level of damages anticipated.

There is a great deal of *uncertainty* regarding these impacts. On a global scale, average temperatures are expected to increase by 1 to 4.5°C. The level of the sea has increased by 10–25cm since 1900 (Jepma and Munasinghe, 1998). The sea level is expected in many scenarios to increase by 13–99cm in the next century (Wigley, 1999).

Valuing the impacts of climate change requires numerous, difficult, and essentially normative judgements. These include judgements on how to treat *equity* considerations, that is whether to take a single *value of a statistical life (VOSL)* figure and apply it across the world or whether to adjust this to reflect per capita income through *benefit transfer*.

Many advances have been made in recent years in the estimation of climate change impacts. With more sophisticated modelling and a greater understanding of the climate–economy linkages, including the inclusion of *adaptation*, climate impact assessment is likely to continue to advance. (IPCC, 2001.) See also *Climate change impact assessment – adjoint method.*

**Table 1** *The FUND Model*

| Net present value of total damage 1990–2100 as a function of discount rate[a] | | | | | |
|---|---|---|---|---|---|
| | 0% | 1% | 3% | 5% | 10% |
| **Percentage by sector** | | | | | |
| Sea-level rise[b] | 57.8 | 61.1 | 68.6 | 75.1 | 82.1 |
| Agriculture | 2.7 | 2.4 | 1.5 | 0.7 | −0.6 |
| Extreme weather[c] | 33.5 | 30.1 | 22.7 | 16.3 | 9.5 |
| Species | 0.9 | 0.8 | 0.6 | 0.4 | 0.2 |
| Malaria | 5.2 | 5.6 | 6.7 | 7.6 | 8.7 |
| **Percentage by region** | | | | | |
| OECD (America) | 0.3 | 0.3 | 0.3 | 0.3 | 0.3 |
| OECD (Europe) | 0.5 | 0.5 | 0.5 | 0.4 | 0.4 |
| OECD (Pacific) | 0.1 | 0.1 | 0.1 | 0.1 | 0.1 |
| Central and Eastern Europe and former USSR | −0.1 | −0.2 | −0.2 | −0.2 | −0.2 |
| Middle East | 6.9 | 6.9 | 6.6 | 6.2 | 5.5 |
| Latin America | 12.3 | 12.7 | 13.6 | 14.5 | 15.8 |
| South and Southeast Asia | 42.0 | 42.5 | 44.2 | 46.4 | 50.3 |
| Central planned Asia | 6.4 | 5.6 | 3.7 | 2.1 | 0.3 |
| Africa | 31.7 | 31.7 | 31.3 | 30.2 | 27.5 |
| **Total (billions of 1990 US dollars)** | 519,500 | 248,800 | 74,400 | 31,800 | 10,100 |

a    Damages calculated under a commonly used climate change scenario.
b    Coastal protection, dryland loss, wetland loss and migration.
c    Hurricanes, extra-tropical wind storms, river floods, hot spells, cold spells.

*Source:* Eyre et al, 1998.

**climate change impact assessment – adjoint method** This method for assessing the damages of *climate change* estimates the sensitivity of different media to climate change and the threshold levels of climate change effects. The advantage of this approach is that it can help distinguish between changes of climate that are significant and those that are not. (Parry, 1990.)

**closed system** A system which exchanges neither energy nor matter with its *environment*. The Earth is a system which is closed with respect to materials. The matter on Earth is fixed in quantity so that material inputs to production originate from the Earth, and the residuals from the productive process remain on the Earth. However, with respect to energy, the Earth is an *open system*; it receives energy from the sun and loses energy to the surrounding system. (Perman et al, 1999.) See also *Second Law of Thermodynamics*.

**club good** This is a good that is neither purely private nor purely public. Use of the good is excludable, in that only a limited number of consumers may be able to use it, but is non-rival among this limited number, in that one user's use does not reduce the availability of the good to the other users. However, there is likely to be an optimal number of users. Examples of club goods would include cinemas, parks, and recreational facilities. See also *public goods; clubs, theory of*.

**Club of Rome** Set up by an international group of economists, scientists, technologists, politicians and others in 1968, this organization's purpose is the study of the interactions between humans and the *environment*. These interactions include the economic, scientific, biological and social components of the human situation. The Club was established with the goal of eventually being able to predict the results of government policies and to formulate alternative policies where deemed necessary on environmental and survival grounds. The *Limits to Growth* and *Beyond the Limits* studies by Meadows et al (1972, 1992) were supported by the Club of Rome. See also *systems analysis*.

**clubs, theory of** Buchanan (1965) introduced the theory of clubs to explain the conditions required for *efficiency* in the provision of goods that are non-rival in consumption but excludable. Parks and recreational facilities are examples of goods that may be considered *club goods*, so long as no congestion externalities are present. See Cullis and Jones (1998) for a full explanation of the theory of clubs, including the derivation of the optimum size of a club.

**Coase Theorem** This shows the theoretical conditions under which bargaining between two parties will lead to a Pareto efficient level of pollution so long as one of the parties (it does not matter which) holds the property rights to the environmental good in question. The theorem is of some importance in policies to regulate *externalities*. If the polluter and the pollutee can bargain to an efficient solution, then there is no role for a regulator, and indeed a regulator can make things worse. The consensus is that the Coase solution works when property rights are well defined and when the parties are few in number. There are problems with the solution, however, when transaction costs are significant, and when information about the impacts is limited. Nevertheless, Coase-type negotiations do take place and policy-makers need to be aware of them in designing and enforcing *regulations*. See also *Pareto efficiency*.

**Cobb Douglas (CD) production function** The production function, that is the relationship between output (Q) and the inputs of *capital* (K) and *natural resources* (R) may be represented in many ways. One is the Cobb Douglas, whereby output is a product of a constant (A) multiplied by the product of K and R raised to coefficients $\alpha$ and $\beta$, which are constants determined by technology. If the sum of the coefficients a and b is less than, equal to, or greater than 1, then the production function is said to display diminishing, constant and equal returns to scale, respectively. The Cobb Douglas production function for a technology utilizing capital and resources may be represented as follows:

$$Q = AK^{\alpha}R^{\beta}$$

The Cobb Douglas production function is often used in *neoclassical economics* and was, for instance, the production function used in the development of the *Hartwick rule*. It has been criticized by ecological economists because it embodies the assumption that there is a large degree of substitutability between natural and *human-made resources*. See also *elasticity of substitution; weak sustainability*.

**cobweb model** The fluctuations in supplies of food and swings in the prices of food can be explained through the cobweb model, as illustrated in Figure 4. Suppose, due to a weather-induced shortage, $Q_0$ is supplied, driving the price up to $P_0$. For the next growing season, farmers have to plant well in advance of harvest time. Their decisions about how much to plant depend on the price they expect to receive. Suppose that they use this year's price as their guess of what next year's price will be. They will plan to supply $Q_1$. At price $P_0$, the

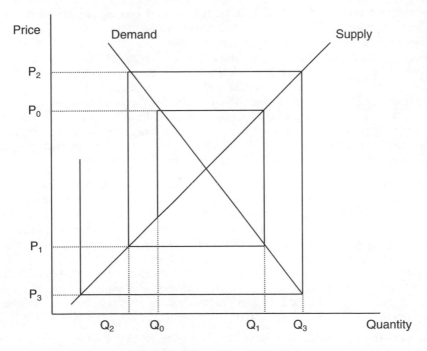

**Figure 4** *The Cobweb Model*

41

market cannot absorb that much of the commodity so the price falls to $P_1$. If farmers use that price to plan the following year's crop, they will produce $Q_3$. This will cause the price to rise to $P_3$, and so on. The model demonstrates how price fluctuations can arise in markets in which there are considerable lags between production decisions and goods being available for purchase.

**cognitive dissonance** A psychological phenomenon which has been used in *environmental economics* to explain why individuals appear to view small losses differently to small gains. Given an initial position, they may value a given additional benefit at $X. However, a loss of the same magnitude is seen differently, perhaps due to the fact that they may see it as an infringement of what they consider to be theirs by right. Hence the loss is given a greater value than $X. This phenomenon affects the applicability of the *willingness to pay (WTP)* and *willingness to accept (WTA)* measures. (Pearce and Turner, 1990.) See also *loss aversion*.

**collective wellbeing** In any theory of *ethics* it is well recognized that individual rights, choices and opportunities cannot be unlimited. One person's freedom can constrain or violate the freedom of many others. Some people have used this to argue against the excessive individualism of the free market, and for socially responsible forms of development. They contend that individual and collective wellbeing are intertwined, and human development requires strong social cohesion and equitable distribution of the benefits of progress to avoid tension between the two. The power of collective action is an essential driving force in the pursuit of human development. (http://www.undp.org, 'What is Human Development?')

**command and control (CAC) policies and excess abatement cost** Command and control (CAC) *regulations* have been criticized as generating higher *abatement costs* than necessary to achieve a given level of emissions. This problem is highlighted in Markandya (1998b) which shows the clear cost advantages of *market-based instruments (MBIs)* over CAC policies. Most CAC mechanisms impose *emissions standards* or force the use of a certain technology. This is less efficient (that is, the total cost of achieving a given reduction in environmental damage is greater) than the use of *market-based instruments* and other *economic instruments*, as illustrated by the *least-cost theorem*. See also *ambient-based standards; emissions standards; fixed standard approach; direct regulations; regulations; quantitative controls; standard setting*.

**commodity bubble** A type of *bubble policy* within a *marketable emissions permit* scheme, in which the scheme is extended to include more than one type of pollutant. Under such a policy, emissions of one pollutant can be traded for reduced emissions of another, which often allows further flexibility in complying with *regulations*. For example a commodity bubble could include $CO_2$ as well as methane ($CH_4$), both of which are greenhouse gases (GHG). The trade would have to recognize the different impact in terms of radiative forcing by specifying that 1 ton of $CO_2$ was worth 25 tons of $CH_4$, the latter value being determined by the relative impacts each has on climate (this is debated, but 25 is one number that has been suggested). (OECD, 1992b.)

**commodity specification bias** This is a form of bias that may arise in the application of the *contingent valuation method (CVM)*. It arises if the environmental good being described in the questionnaire is badly explained, leading to a distortion in the *willingness to pay (WTP)* measures obtained. (Folmer and van Ierland, 1989.)

**The Common Agricultural Policy (CAP) and the environment** The Common Agricultural Policy (CAP) of the EU attempted to raise productivity to ensure self-sufficiency, fair incomes for farmers and stable consumer prices. In its initial formulation there was little concern for the environment. These policies placed significant pressure on land resources and encouraged intensive agricultural practices, leading to environmental degradation. Recent reforms of the CAP, in line with EU Agenda 2000, have included the encouragement of less intensive agriculture and the use of organic techniques, though the environment is still not a major part of the policy. (UNEP, 2000) (See http://europa.eu.int/scadplus/leg/en/lvb/l60002.htm)

**common burden principle** This principle supports the case for the state to offer compensation from public funds in situations where the polluter cannot pay (perhaps on grounds of bankruptcy), or where it would be inequitable to ask the polluter to pay. (O'Riordan and Cameron, 1994.)

**common property** The control and use of any asset, but typically land, by a group of individuals who constitute more than one family. (Tietenberg, 1996.) See also *property rights*.

**common property resource** A resource which is not controlled by a single agent or source. The management of *common property* is highly complex, and a common property resource is not necessarily an *open access* resource, which can be exploited on a first come, first served basis. (Tietenberg, 1996.) See also *property rights*.

**commons** A historical term for common land. A key reference in *environmental economics* is Hardin's *Tragedy of the Commons* (1992). See also *common property, common property resource; property rights; tragedy of the commons*.

**communalist ecocentrisim** This supports the idea of a green economy. Supporters of this position argue that the absolute level of economic activity should neither increase nor decline. This translates into a call for zero *economic growth* and zero population growth in order to establish the *steady-state economy*. (Turner, Pearce and Bateman, 1994.)

**community ecology** This is an extension of the study of population *ecology* in which the focus is the competition among two or more *species*. (Barbier, 1989.)

**compensated demand curves** The compensated demand curve is constructed in such a way that compensation is made which eliminates the income effect of a price change. Movements along a demand curve thus represent the pure substitution effect of a price change. When we draw a two-dimensional compensated demand curve in price-quantity space, all points on the demand function represent points of constant *utility*. (Perman, 1999.)

**compensating surplus** In *environmental economics*, compensating surplus is used to measure the value to an individual of a change in the availability of a pure *public good*, such as clean air. Suppose that an individual's *environment* deteriorates, for example because of increased air pollution. The compensating surplus is the amount of money the individual would require to maintain the

## compensating variation

level of *utility* which existed before the environmental change. In other words, this is the amount of money that is required to compensate for the environmental change. Note that the compensating surplus is defined with respect to the original level of utility. The distinction between compensating surplus and *compensating variation* is that the calculation of compensating surplus assumes that the individual cannot vary her consumption of the good. That is, it is a pure public good. This measure is thus appropriate for valuing changes in *air quality standards* and similar environmental factors. (Markandya et al, 2002.) See also *equivalent surplus; equivalent variation*.

**compensating variation** In *environmental economics*, compensating variation is used to measure the value to an individual of the availability of a good which is not a pure *public good*, such as a change in the quality of a national park. Suppose that the quality of a national park increases due to a programme of environmental *conservation*. For an individual who uses the park, and whose *utility* would increase as a result of this change, the compensating variation is the amount of money that would have to be taken from the individual for him to be at the same level of utility as he was before the environmental change. That is, it is the amount of money that is required to compensate for the environmental change. Note that the compensating variation is defined with respect to the original level of utility. The distinction between compensating variation and *compensating surplus* is that the calculation of compensating variation assumes that the individual can vary his consumption of the good in question. See also *equivalent surplus; equivalent variation*.

**competitiveness and environmental regulation** One major argument for the international harmonization of environmental standards is that variable standards will encourage both the loss of competitiveness in the regulating country and the migration of industry to countries with the lowest standards. Evidence for this, however, is limited. There are several studies which look at the same issues, but mainly in developed countries (see Dean, 1992 for a survey). In general their findings are that the competitiveness effects are small. A recent study of developing countries generally supports that conclusion, but there are a few cases where the effects on specific industries have been noticeable (Jha, Markandya and Vossenaar, 1999).

In contrast to the negative impacts of environmental regulation there are also some positive effects to consider. There will be some growth of a domestic pollution *abatement* industry. Even if much of the technology is imported, various studies have shown that adaptation to local conditions is almost always necessary. This will generate some economic activity. Then there is the view that stricter *regulations* will benefit the more innovative and enterprising firms. This may be because they are able to find ways of meeting the standards at lower cost, or because they can respond more quickly and more effectively.

**compliance data system** The compliance data system is an EPA-managed database management system which reports on the degree of compliance of *stationary sources* with their *emissions permits*. (Luken, 1990.)

**compliance schedule** A schedule of environmental targets which a company or country has to meet in accordance with a specified timetable. The targets may be set by the government or by private certifying organizations. This would be part of a system of environmental *regulation*.

**compliance with standard reporting** This is a system wherein firms account to society for their success or failure in meeting environmental standards established either by law or by professional or trade associations. (Perman et al, 1999.)

**computable general equilibrium (CGE) models** CGE models divide the economy into a number of markets and model supply and demand in each of these markets. The degree of disaggregation varies depending on the questions that the model is intended to answer, but it consists of, at a minimum, two to three goods markets and two factor markets. The key internally determined parameters are the prices. Whether or not markets clear depends on the assumptions made, but the standard (though not universal) assumption is for market clearance. In general, CGE models cannot be solved algebraically, but thanks to the explosion in computing power and the development of solution algorithms they can be solved computationally. These developments have stimulated a rapid growth in applied CGE modelling, particularly on issues related to taxation, trade, structural adjustment and the *environment*. (See Reed, 1997; Markandya et al, 2002.)

**concessional loan** A type of loan offered to a country to assist, among other things, environmentally sound development. These loans are usually offered at very low rates of interest. In September 1997, for example, Japan gave a loan on very preferential terms to strengthen Egyptian efforts to combat *global warming*. The projects considered eligible for such loans include energy saving technologies, new and *renewable energy* sources, forest *conservation*, and measures against air pollution (http://www.infojapan.org/embjapan/egypt/oda/s-loan.html).

**conditionality** The use of restrictions in loans, usually those offered by multilateral organizations and developed countries. Such restrictions might require changes in taxation and expenditure policies by the government, or changes in the way the *environment* is protected, such as requirements to guard against the overexploitation of *natural resources* and the *extinction of species*. Critics on one side claim that environmental conditionality has reduced the development or productive value of such loans; on the other they criticize the donors for not being strict enough about protection of the environment and in some cases actually exacerbating environmental damage.

**conditionally renewable resources** Resources which can be regenerated biologically after harvest or removal. These serve three types of functions:

1    They can be harvested and consumed by man.
2    They provide a host of environmental services which are essential for the maintenance of environmental integrity, including the assimilation of waste.
3    They provide a wide array of amenity, historical and cultural values.

Often one natural resource provides all three functions simultaneously, an example being a native forest. (Young, 1992.) See also *renewable resources; non-renewable resources; maximum sustainable yield*.

**conservation** Conservation, according to the World Conservation Strategy (WCS), is 'the management of human use of the *biosphere* so that it may yield the greatest sustainable benefit to the present generation while maintaining its potential to meet the needs and aspirations of future generations.' (IUCN, 1980.) See also *Agenda 21; biodiversity; biosphere reserve; conservation easements; debt-for-nature swaps (DNS); development rights approach to resource conservation; eco-vests; global conversion process; sustainable development (SD).*

**conservation easements** These limit the activities which can be permitted in the process of using a resource. An example is the permission of traditional uses of a forest by the indigenous population, although clear cutting is banned. (Tietenberg, 1996.) See also *conservation.*

**conservation investor** The *conservation* investor acts as an intermediary to negotiate a debt swap between a creditor and debtor in order to support a defined conservation objective in a *debt-for-nature swap*. Conservation investors raise funds from donors, which are then invested in the debt-for-nature swap. Conservation investors have included non-governmental organizations (NGOs), research institutes and universities. (EPIQ/NRM2, 1998.)

**conservation trust fund** *Conservation* trust *funds* (in countries whose systems are based on UK or US models) or foundations (in civil law countries) are funds which legally set aside assets whose use is restricted to the specific environmental purposes set out in a legal trust instrument, for example funds for the protection of *biodiversity*. (EPIQ/NRM2 1998.)

**conserver society** A society in which labour and *capital* are substituted for energy use. The transition from such a society may be aided by a tax on energy, which may benefit from a *double dividend*. (Krishnan et al, 1995.)

**constant capital rule** Requirement sometimes put forward as a rule for *sustainable development (SD)*. If there are no specific reasons for highlighting one form of *capital*, the requirement for SD then becomes one of leaving to future generations an aggregate capital stock whose value is no smaller than the one which exists now (Hartwick, 1978; Solow, 1986). This constant capital rule is often called *weak sustainability*. Weak sustainability implies that the form in which we pass the capital stock on to future generations is unimportant, so long as its value is maintained. (Hartwick and Olewiler, 1998.) See also *constant economic value; genuine saving index.*

**constant economic value** A principle which states that one can allow for a declining physical stock with a rising real price over time, so that the economic value remains constant. Another interpretation of this principle states that the price of the *capital* stock should remain constant over time. (Pearce et al, 1989.) See also *weak sustainability; constant capital rule; genuine saving index.*

**constant elasticity demand curve** Demand curve on which the elasticity is the same at every price.

**consumer surplus** A monetary measure of the net benefit to an individual of consuming a good. That is, the excess of the *willingness to pay (WTP)* for a given quantity of the good over the sum which is actually paid out. A socially efficient allocation of resources would be one which maximizes the total benefit across all goods and *factors of production*. One component of total benefit is consumer surplus, another is *producer surplus* and the third is net external benefit. See also *externalities.*

**consumption discount rate** This is used to compare future and present consumption benefits. It is determined by the relationship between society's rate of *time preference* for current over future consumption, and the growth rate in the economy. Typically, consumption discount rates range from 1–4 per cent. The alternative is a rate based on the *opportunity cost* of *capital*, which can be higher. See also *discounting; utility discount rate; Ramsey rule; time preference*.

**consumption externalities** Consumption externalities arise when the consumption of a good by one person affects the welfare of another person, and that effect is not fully taken into account by the first person in making her decision to consume the good. An example of a consumption *externality* would be the playing of excessively loud music. See also *externalities*.

**consumptive use value** A *direct-use value* which is related to the consumption of an environmental resource. It is distinguished from *use values* derived from the pleasure of seeing someone else benefit from a good (altruistic use value or *bequest value*). See also *total economic value*.

**content standard** A standard which sets a minimum quality for a product, or dictates the amount of a certain substance in a product, or the recycled content of packaging.

**contestable concept** According to Common (1995), this is a concept which can be interpreted in a variety of ways, but which, at the same time, is widely agreed as representing a desirable state, an example being *sustainability*. The value of sustainability as a concept is in the expression of it as a goal and not in the debate on the particulars relating to it. Common argues 'Contestable concepts as policy objectives are central features of the democratic political process. Consider for examples: liberty, *justice*, democracy, freedom and equality. Definitive definitions of these concepts do not exist, yet it is rarely suggested that these are not useful concepts, or that they cannot, or should not, inform policy.'

**contingent ranking** A technique related to the *contingent valuation method (CVM)*. Contingent ranking studies offer a choice from a list of alternatives. Respondents are asked to rank two or more of the options in order of preference. The important attributes or characteristics of each item on the menu are identified, and the extent of one or more of the characteristics is varied for each option on the list. For example, if a researcher were to attempt to value different endangered *species* he might consider it important to consider taxonomic distinctiveness and some measure of a particular variation, such as size in the case of charismatic megafauna (an elephant or tiger, for example). Economic *valuation* can enter by introducing the preservation cost for each option. Respondents compare the additional monetary cost to the additional pay-off, and rank the preferred option highest according to the benefit derived. Through this technique, it is possible to estimate the value of a marginal improvement in different characteristics of a good; in the case of endangered species these could include the chance of survival, population size, and so on. (Brown, 1997.)

**contingent valuation method (CVM)** A technique used in the *valuation* of environmental goods, to estimate either the *willingness to pay (WTP)* for an improvement in the quantity or quality of some environmental good, or the

# contingent valuation method (CVM)

*willingness to accept (WTA)* compensation for a deterioration in environmental provision. This is done by either employing an experimental approach, based upon simulation or game analysis, or, more commonly, by using data derived from questionnaire or survey techniques.

This method uses survey questions to elicit people's preferences for *public goods* by asking them how much they would be willing to pay for specified improvements or to avoid specified deterioration or losses. Thus it is a *stated preference (SP)* valuation method, as opposed to a *revealed preference* method. Alternatively, respondents to CV surveys might be asked what level of compensation they would require for a loss, or for the failure to receive an improvement in environmental quality.

Consider the following example, in which the analyst elicits the value of the loggerhead sea turtle. The study asks respondents hypothetical questions about their monetary valuation of a situation, such as 'suppose that a $10 contribution would be needed to support and fund the loggerhead seaturtle programme. Would you be willing to contribute $10 each year to the "Loggerhead sea turtle preservation fund?"' Prior to this question, background information about the natural resource setting and circumstances must be provided. Care must be taken to explain the quantity, quality and duration of change in the *natural resources*. A payment instrument has to be chosen; in the example above, the respondents were asked if they would contribute a specific amount of money to a hypothetical *fund*. In another famous study (the Exxon Valdez oil spill case), respondents were asked if they would vote for a tax increase. In other surveys, the payment vehicle is an increase in product price, as when harvest restrictions to preserve wild salmonid *species* in the Pacific Northwest result in an increase in retail salmon prices.

The background information and payment vehicle are not independent elements. The challenge is for the researcher to develop a plausible scenario and an acceptable payment vehicle. Unless there is a careful design, respondents will refuse to respond or respond inappropriately if, for example they are against taxation and the vehicle is a tax change (see *payment vehicle bias*); if they are told but do not believe a cost incident will be passed on to the respondent; or if they think a special purpose public fund for a limited duration will be used for purposes other than funding the environmental improvement in question, will be extended longer than was stated or will be spent wastefully – liberties that respondents may have observed public authorities taking in similar situations in the past.

There is a growing debate about how people should be asked to pay – the appropriate method of elicitation. Is the respondent asked to state the maximum amount she is willing to pay (the open-ended method)? Or, as in the study of turtles, is she asked if she would pay $X for the environmental change (or no change) in question (the dichotomous choice method)? The amount, X, is systematically varied across the sample population to discover the distribution of responses or values.

CVM has been severely criticized for its subjective bias in value setting (see *hypothetical bias*). However, the standing of this technique has been greatly improved now that it has been legally authorized for use in natural resource assessment in the US, and the estimated damages are perceived by some companies to be large. A recent review of the method has come up with 'good practice' guidelines (see *National Oceanic and Atmospheric Administration*). More than one thousand studies using CVM have been conducted throughout the world and the number is growing rapidly. See also *embedding phenomenon; commodity specification bias; strategic bias; information bias.*

**convention** An *international environmental agreement* which, when ratified or acceded to by a country, has the binding force of international law. The national laws of a country must be brought into conformity with its provisions. See also *ozone; biodiversity.*

**conventional pollutants** Pollutants which are statutorily listed and which are well understood by scientists. These may include organic waste, sediment, acid, bacteria and viruses, nutrients, oil and grease, or heat. (Luken, 1990.)

**Convention on Biological Diversity** One of the two international environmental *conventions* signed at the 1992 UN *Earth Summit* in Rio de Janeiro, the other being the *Framework Convention on Climate Change (FCCC)*. It calls for the *conservation* and sustainable use of *biodiversity*, and for the benefits of its use to be shared equitably.

**Convention on Climate Change** See *Framework Convention on Climate Change (FCCC).*

**convexity of benefits and damage function** In identifying the *efficient level of pollution* as being the level at which the *marginal abatement cost (MAC)* is equal to the *marginal damage* cost (MDC), it is assumed that both the damage cost and *abatement* cost curves are convex. This means that as the pollution level rises, the marginal abatement cost falls, and the marginal damage cost rises. If this condition is not satisfied then setting marginal abatement costs equal to marginal damage costs may not identify the *efficient level of pollution.* There are various reasons why damage cost function may not be convex, including the possibility that, beyond a certain pollution level, the additional damage is zero since, for instance, an *ecosystem* has already been destroyed. (Perman et al, 1999.)

**cooperative solutions** Solutions to situations in which a failure to coordinate could result in two or more players (individuals, firms or countries) being worse off than they would otherwise be. An example is the agreement of an *international environmental agreement*, whereby total wellbeing is increased as each country observes higher environmental standards. See also *prisoners' dilemma; non-cooperation; game theory.*

**cornucopian technocentrism** Supporters of this position believe that the mechanisms of the free market are the best way to maximize human wellbeing. In particular, constraints should not be placed on the exploitation of *natural resources*, since technological progress can be relied upon to provide substitutes for resources as they become scarce. Part of this view is the belief that the value of natural resources and assets, including animal and plant *species*, derives purely from their use to humans. That is, they have only *instrumental value* and not *intrinsic value.* (Turner et al, 1994.) See also *accomodating technocentrism.*

**costate variables** see *shadow price.*

**cost–benefit analysis (CBA)** see *benefit–cost analysis.*

## cost–effectiveness analysis (CEA)

**cost–effectiveness analysis (CEA)** A tool which is concerned with minimizing the cost of achieving a specified environmental or economic objective. For example, in the *acid deposition* field, the objective might be to meet a target loading of sulphur at minimum cost over a large region, taking into account that control costs vary from industry to industry and that the costs of control increase with increasing severity of control. Another example would be the minimizing of the costs of reducing *greenhouse gases (GHG)* by a given amount. A number of options may be available and the objective would be to minimize the costs per ton of GHG. Cost–effectiveness analysis ignores the benefit side of *benefit–cost analysis* but concentrates on the cost side.

**cost-effectiveness principle** The principle that *economic instruments* should have low bureaucratic and low compliance costs. Thus the practical difficulties of designing the instruments, monitoring and control should be minimized. (Turner et al, 1994.) See also *regulation*.

**cost-of-illness approach (COI)** An *objective valuation approach (OVA)* to placing an economic value on environmental damage. The financial costs of illness caused by, for example, air pollution can be calculated by adding the costs of treating an illness to the costs of lost work-time. The full cost of the illness would then require a measure of the value that the individual places on the suffering that it causes, but this must be measured using a technique such as the *contingent valuation method (CVM)*, which is not an objective valuation approach. See also *valuation*.

**cost recovery** Cost recovery occurs when the costs of a project are recovered from revenues generated by the project. There may be full cost recovery, whereby 100 per cent of the operations and maintenance (O&M) costs and *capital* costs of a project are recovered, or recovery of variable costs. Many projects fail because, although the *benefit–cost analysis* is correct in identifying large net benefits, insufficient account is taken of the recovery of the costs, without which implementation cannot be successful.

**cost–utility analysis (CUA)** Cost–*utility* analysis is a type of economic appraisal which focuses on the quality of health resulting from health programmes and treatments. There are many similarities between cost–utility analysis and *cost–effectiveness analysis (CEA)*, and some authors see CUA as a particular case of CEA (Weinstein and Stason, 1977). CUA requires final output effectiveness data, such as lives saved, and the final outcome may be expressed as a cost per *quality-adjusted life year* (QALY) gained. (Drummond et al, 1987.)

**costs of environmental damage** The economic and *social costs* of environmental damage are usually divided into three broad categories: health costs (health consequences of environmental damage – sickness, premature death, and so on); productivity costs (reduced productivity of *natural resources* and *human-made capital*, disruption of environmental services such as the natural cleansing of water or the yield from fisheries, spending more time on cleaning and maintaining houses and other buildings); and the loss of environmental quality, or amenity costs (a loss of *biodiversity*, a clear view, a pristine lake, a mature forest, and clean and quiet neighbourhoods, and so on). The economic values of these costs can be estimated using *valuation* methods such as the *contingent valuation method (CVM)*.

**countervailing duty** This usually refers to import duties imposed by an importing country on goods from an exporting country which are subsidized, and thus have an unfair advantage in trade. With reference to the *environment*, CVDs have been proposed to correct the implicit subsidy of lax environmental regulation in the exporting country. The reasoning is that, whether or not another country chooses to protect its environment from production *externalities*, producers who are more environmentally responsible should not be held at a competitive disadvantage.

**coupons** Coupons are used to ration commodities, so that a buyer must have a coupon in addition to paying the price of the good. In the environmental field they are also a form of *permit*. One novel application would be to use them in the *regulation* of trade in endangered *species*. Once a given number of coupons are printed, a regulatory system would work by refusing to admit the regulated good without a coupon. When coupons are distributed to the designated suppliers, the task of controlling access to the species becomes one of controlling access to the coupons instead, which is usually less costly than direct controls. (Swanson, 1994.)

**cowboy economics** A term coined by Boulding (1966) to describe the apparent assumptions behind current production and consumption decisions. Cowboy economics assumes that there are no effective environmental or resource constraints, so that inputs to production are easily found, and the wastes of production and consumption can easily be absorbed. The term is inspired by early North American settlers, whose *environment* seemed unlimited relative to the demands that they placed on it. This analogy was intended to illustrate the fact that the world's economies cannot continue to live indefinitely by this assumption. The fact that the natural environment and its capacity to provide services is finite means that the global economy is more similar in nature to a spaceship, which must recycle its wastes. (Perman et al, 1999.) See also *spaceman economy*.

**cradle-to-grave analysis** See *life cycle approach or analysis*.

**criticality criterion** Discussed by Turner (1988), the critical nature of a material or *natural resource* is assessed in terms of how essential it is to the military and industrial wellbeing of a country. Criticality depends on such factors as the opportunities for substitution, effective material utilization and/or *recycling*; and the degree of domestic economic damage likely to result from either a failure of supply or an increase in price.

**critical load** Critical load analysis means estimating quantitatively the exposure to one or more pollutants below which significant harmful effects on specific sensitive elements of the *environment* do not occur, according to present knowledge. An example of the use of critical loads is the estimation of acid depostions and their effects on the forest health.

**critical zone resources** The critical zone sets the limits above which the effects of depletion on the flow of renewable resources are irreversible. Critical zone resources can be defined in terms of a sustainable flow of renewable products or services. If the critical zone for a particular use has been exceeded, lower use is encouraged. (Dixon et al, 1989.) See also *irreversibility*.

**crop–climate models** Parry (1990) identifies two broad classes of models: empirical statistical models and simulation models. Empirical–statistical models build upon regression analysis of the relationship between climatic data and crop yields. This is not necessarily founded upon the understanding of the causal relationships between *climate change* and the extent of crop yield, and hence it is seen by some as a black box approach, meaning that the process by which the model generates its outputs is not made clear. In some cases, however, empirical–statistical models are derived from detailed analysis of crop physiology, and so can be effective in *climate change impact assessment*.

Simulation models analyse crop growth through a set of mathematical equations which examine the linkages between plant, soil and climate processes. Parry argues that, when based on a close understanding of plant-growth processes, these models are the most accurate means of estimating plant responses to change. The most effective means of analysis would probably use a combination of models, with relatively simple agro-climatic indices being used to characterize the varying sensitivity of large areas to climate change, thus identifying appropriate sample points for more detailed study with the use of crop–climate models. (Parry, 1990.) See also *agricultural potential and climate change*.

**cross compliance** This occurs when compliance in one area is required for access to another. An example of this is in the US where the right to participate in certain commodity-price-support programmes is contingent upon practising soil *conservation*. (Bromley, 1991.)

**cross-media approach** An integrated approach to addressing environmental problems which takes into account interrelationships between various elements (components) of the *environment*, such as air, water and soil. (See also *medium-by-medium approach*). It is important to avoid improving quality standards in one environmental medium at the expense of other media. A cross-media approach recognizes the integrated nature of the environment, seeks to reduce the overall pollution at source by improving *energy efficiency* (avoiding the generation of waste as a whole as well as in any one media, and its transferral to other media), and introduces clean technologies. In the UK it has been the basis of the *integrated pollution prevention and control* policy.

**crowding diseconomies** Crowding diseconomies occur where the benefit from using a resource is reduced because others are also using the resource. These are important in *open access* situations as there is a tendency under open access for there to be more users and more exploitation of a resource than would be considered economically efficient. Perman et al (1999) give the example of the fisheries. Each fishing boat's catch reduces the chance of catch for other boats, thereby imposing a cost on the other users of the resource. Thus, the costs of catching a certain quantity become greater and as a consequence an *external cost* or *externality* is imposed on the others in the industry. (Perman et al , 1999.)

**crustal abundance (of a mineral)** In contrast to reserves of a mineral, which are known amounts which could be extracted profitably from the Earth given current prices, abundance refers to the amount of a mineral existing in the 'average rock', which may be present in minute concentrations and currently uneconomical to extract. It is generally recognized that, extraction and environmental cost aside, the potential availability of minerals considered 'scarce' in reserves terms is many times larger in terms of crustal abundance; thus consumption of the minerals may continue for much longer than currently forecast. See also *extraction costs*.

**cultural resources** These include history, language, religious customs and traditional communal practices. Losses of these resources are hard to quantify in physical terms, let alone in monetary terms. Cultural resources are thought of as one of the components of *social capital*. See also *aesthetic, historical and cultural resources valuation; ancient monuments, protection of*.

**current expenditure** The sum of a firm's expenditure on the purchase of inputs, the salaries and wages of its employees and the taxes it pays, less any *subsidies* it receives. Current expenditure does not include the *depreciation* of fixed assets.

**customary law** Historically, this has been the major source of international law. It has developed from patterns of use, which have crystallized into law. A customary law may eventually be accepted by a national or international court as the formal expression of law.

According to Malcolm (1994) customary law is not a significant source of environmental law. There are, however, some general principles, such as the obligation on one state not to injuriously affect another state, which could be applied to environmental law.

**CVM** See *contingent valuation method*.

# Dd

**damage assessment** The damage caused by pollution can take many different forms. It may impact on human health, on crops or materials or on the natural environment more generally. The assessment of damages in monetary terms is becoming increasingly important, especially in the US where the government can seek compensation for damages to the *environment* arising from spills and releases of hazardous waste. Damage assessment may be made through the *impact pathway approach* or through other methods such as the *contingent valuation method, hedonic pricing* and the *travel cost method*. The impact on health, crops and materials can be measured and a value attributed to the damage. See also *costs of environmental damage*.

**dB(A) costing approach** A *valuation* technique used in the estimation of the damages attributable to an increment in the noise level arising from an activity. The noise increment is valued on the basis of the noise *depreciation* sensitivity index, an index which uses *hedonic pricing* to estimate the impact on house prices of different noise levels. This technique was recommended by ExternE (1995) for the estimation of damages arising from noise pollution. See also *noise pollution, valuation of; acoustic quality; dB scale*.

**dB scale** A measurement of noise levels, also known as the decibel (dB) scale. It is based on a logarithmic scale of base 10, which means that the noise level at 60dB is 10 times louder than it is at 50dB. Weighting scales are used to discriminate between the impacts of high and low frequency sounds and those in the middle of the scale, which have the greatest impact due to the relative sensitivity of the human ear in this range. The most commonly used variant using these weights is the *dB(A)* or A-scale. Other variants of this scale exist, including $L_{Aeq}$ which is equivalent to the mean sound energy level. Many European nations have *regulations* on noise based on these scales. (ExternE, 1999.) See also *dB(A) costing approach*.

**dB(A) scale** See *dB scale*.

**deadweight loss** An *efficiency* loss which results from an allocation of resources other than that which maximizes welfare; which is, the sum of *consumer surplus* and *producer surplus*. Deadweight losses are often associated with *market failures* such as monopolies and distortional taxation. In *environmental economics* they arise, for example, when taxes are used to collect revenue to finance pollution control.

**debt buy-back** Repurchase by a debtor of all or a portion of its debt, usually at a discount from face value. The World Bank and bilateral donors finance commercial debt buy-backs for low-income countries. Some aid agencies finance buy-backs of publicly guaranteed export credits or private debt owed by debtor governments for conversion into local currency funds for *conservation* and/or development. (EPIQ/NRM2, 1998.)

**debt conversion** The exchange of one form of claim on a debtor country for another form of claim, such as *debt-for-nature swaps*. A secondary market for developing country debt emerged in 1992 as a consequence of the accelerating international debt crisis triggered by Mexico's announcement that it could no longer service its debts. Private banks predominate in this trade. There are different debt conversion categories such as debt-for-bonds, debt buy-back, debt-for-debt swap, debt-for-equity swap, and debt-for-nature swaps. See also *asset conversion; global conversion process*. (Larrain and Velasco, 1990.)

**debt-for-development swap** The cancellation of a debt in exchange for funding or investment in another asset to support development objectives (such as education, health, poverty reduction) in the debtor country. (EPIQ/ NRM2, 1998.)

**debt-for-nature swaps (DNS)** The basic principle behind the debt-for-nature swaps mechanism was first outlined in Lovejoy (1984). The basic transaction is the purchase of developing countries' debt at a discounted value in the secondary debt market, and cancelling the debt in return for environment-related action on the part of the debtor nation. Such secondary debt is sold by existing holders at a discount, reflecting the market's judgement on the probability of repayment. In a debt-for-nature exchange, the holder then offers to give up the debt holding in exchange for an undertaking by the debtor country government or an acting *conservation* organization to protect a given area or to undertake another environmentally positive activity, such as training conservationists.

**decision theory** Branch of *game theory* which is used in the analysis of decision making. This involves the calculation of the various pay-offs of policy decisions. Four decision rules which have been established under this are the maximin rule, the maximax rule, the minimax regret rule and the assignment of subjective probabilities. For a review of the application of decision theory under *uncertainty* see Perman et al (1999).

**declining block pricing** A technique of pricing, commonly used in charging for water, whereby the costs of water increase at a decreasing rate as the amount consumed rises. This means that consumers pay a higher *marginal cost (MC)* for lower levels of water consumption, meaning that low-income households, whose consumption is low, pay relatively more than high-income households. The incentives to conserve water that this system provides, while greater than those under a flat-charge system, are relatively weak. A system of increasing block pricing provides low-income households with cheaper water, electricity and so on, at the expense of higher-income households. (Tietenberg, 1996; Markandya and Pemberton, 1990.) See also *average cost pricing; marginal cost pricing; peak load pricing*.

**decreasing returns to scale** This describes a production technology for which an equal percentage increase in all inputs (ie, with relative shares of input factors unchanged) yields less than an equivalent percentage increase in output. One implication is that long-run average costs rise. See also *diseconomies of scale*.

**deep ecology** The deep *ecology* movement was founded by Arene Naess. It argues that humans are part of a larger *ecological system*, and that the realization of this interconnectedness is vital for maintaining the health and integrity of *ecosystem*s. (Krishnan et al, 1995.)

**defensive expenditure method** A method of evaluating an environmental attribute. It is based on the assumption that individuals and communities spend money on mitigating or eliminating damages caused by adverse environmental impacts. The installation of double-glazed windows to reduce traffic noise is one example. Others are extra filtration for polluted water, air conditioning to avoid polluted air, and so on. These expenses can be considered to be minimum estimates of the benefits of reducing environmental damage, since it is assumed that the benefits derived from avoiding damages are at least as great as the costs incurred in avoiding them. The advantage of this technique is that it is easier to know the expenses incurred than to estimate the environmental damage. (Markandya et al, 2002.) See also *valuation*.

**defensive expenditures** Expenditures to mitigate the impacts of environmental damage. An example is the installation of double-glazing to reduce noise from traffic. One problem with defensive expenditures is identifying how much of the expenditure is for protection against the *environment*, and how much is for other improvements or enhancement in the quality of life generally. Double-glazing, for example, reduces heat losses and thereby provides a benefit distinct from the noise-reduction benefit. A second problem is that the expenditure only provides partial protection against the environmental damage, and it is difficult to estimate how much is mitigated and may cause other nuisances. Again, double-glazing provides a clear example; only some of the noise is blocked. Furthermore, on hot days one may have to chose between too much heat (or increased expenditure on air conditioning), or more noise. See also *abatement; abatement costs; mitigation*.

**deferred pain strategy** This is a method of setting *charges* so as to minimize immediate damages from a high charge. Legislators introduce a charge which increases gradually over time, providing an incentive for firms without efficient *abatement* techniques to begin research and investment. (Anderson et al, 1977.)

**deforestation** The loss of forest cover. The destruction of forestry resources can cause *soil erosion* and damage to watershed areas, including the silting up of water courses and flooding. These effects have long-term, negative and possibly irreversible implications for agricultural productivity and for *economic growth* and welfare.

The FAO's definition of deforestation is a change of land use with depletion of tree crown cover to less than 10 per cent. (FAO, 1995.) See also *afforestation*.

**degradable pollutant** This type of pollutant is broken down into its component parts, usually by bacteria, when released into the *environment*. (Tietenberg, 1996.) See also *biodegradable*.

**Delphi technique** Method whereby, through an iterative process, experts are asked to place a value on a particular good. This technique has been applied in many cases including the derivation of preservation values for endangered *species*. The qualifications of the experts involved will affect the results obtained through the use of this method, as will the method used to extract the valuations. (Dixon et al, 1986.) See also *valuation*.

**demand-side management** Any activity designed to alter a customer's timing or use of a resource or good. In electricity supply, such actions are designed to reduce consumers' demand during peak periods, and to increase *efficiency* in energy use. It is argued in *bottom-up modelling* of *mitigation* that demand-side management is a very cost-effective way of reducing energy use. For example, energy-efficient light bulbs are a demand-side management option in which the direct costs are lower than the value of the energy saved under a wide set of assumptions. One question that is frequently posed is why such options are not implemented in all events, if their benefits are so clear. This raises the issue of implementation costs. (IPCC, 1996a, 1996b.)

**demographic transition** The process by which a country moves from high fertility and high mortality to low fertility and low mortality. Four stages have been identified in demographic transition:

1   High birth rates and high death rates. In certain cases, the high death rate reflects attempts to stabilize the population size, including infanticide, infant neglect and senilicide.
2   Declining death rates as a result of improved nutrition and developments in public health following improvements in incomes. In this stage there are also reduced pressures on families and communities to control population growth. The second stage, therefore, has rapidly rising population levels.
3   Social and economic forces lead to reduced birth rates. Factors include increased educational and employment opportunities for women.
4   Birth and death rates converge leading to a stable population level.

Source: Perman et al, 1999.

**demonstration process** Part of the process of economic *valuation* wherein one must demonstrate that an environmental asset has economic value. (Pearce, 1995.)

**depensation** A term used to describe models of *renewable resource* growth. If the growth rate is an increasing function of the stock or population, the function is said to show depensation over the relevant range of values of the population. (Hanley et al, 1997.)

**depletion premium** This is a part of the price of a natural resource under competitive conditions. The full price consists of the *marginal extraction cost* and the depletion premium. The latter reflects the *scarcity* of the resource, and the rent that it can earn by virtue of its scarcity. It is also known as the royalty, the *resource rent* or the *marginal user cost*. See also *asymptotic depletion; critical zone resources; depletion quotas*.

**depletion quotas** Depletion quotas set a restriction on the amount of a resource which can be used or extracted. It is suggested that they offer an important advantage over taxes as a means of reducing the use of a resource because of their direct control of the throughput of the resource. Money could be raised through the auctioning of depletion quotas by the government, unless non-market criteria such as *grandfathering* are used in the allocation of the *permits*. (Lang and Hines, 1993.) See also *asymptotic depletion; critical zone resources; depletion premium; permit allocation*.

**deposit refund schemes** Deposit refund schemes require a deposit to be paid upon the purchase of potentially polluting products. This deposit is refunded if the product or its residues are returned for disposal and *recycling*, thereby avoiding pollution. This is a type of *economic instrument* which is designed to encourage recycling, and/or to cover the costs of environmentally sound waste disposal. These systems provide incentives to prevent pollution, and reward good behaviour. Deposit refund systems are often applied to widely used products such as beverage containers, and have sometimes been applied to car hulks. They can be considered a valuable tool for *environmental management*, although in general they are not powerful enough for major environmental problems, because of their voluntary character and the low value of the deposits. Their use on bottles, cans and so on has proved very effective in reducing the amount of such material disposed of into the general waste stream.

Deposit refund systems are being extended beyond bottles and cans to include disposable batteries, lubricating oils, electronic equipment, white goods (refrigerators, stoves, washing machines) and automobiles. They encourage companies and consumers to take a *life cycle approach* to product management. Designed appropriately, they can provide an accurate reflection of environmental costs. They also offer new ways for companies to provide services to their clients, such as leasing products instead of selling them, and they can also encourage repeat business. (OECD, 1989b, 1998.) See also *assurance bonding system; performance bonds*.

**depreciation** The reduction in the value of *capital* equipment as a result of its use or of the passage of time since its construction. At the macroeconomic level it refers to the sum of depreciation across all types of *human-made capital*, which is deducted from *gross domestic product (GDP)* to yield the *net domestic product (NDP)*. The term may also refer to a fall in the value of a nation's currency.

**desertification** This is a sustained reduction in the biological productivity of the land. The end result is desert, or skeletal soil that is irrecoverable. Desertification takes two forms: desert spread, and induced desertification in more humid areas. Hence it does not necessarily imply the encroachment of the desert into otherwise green areas. (FAO, 1995.) See also *climate change*.

**development rights approach to resource conservation** An approach to resource *conservation* which takes the view that a developing country has a right to develop its *natural resources* in its own self-interest. If the international community wishes to ensure the conservation of such resources it must be willing to provide a stream of payments to compensate for the foregone development. (Swanson, 1994.) See also *biodiversity; global conversion process*.

**differentiated taxation** A form of *economic instrument* whereby taxation is applied to different goods at different levels, depending on the level of environmental damage attributable to each good, or the waste created by its consumption. This has been used to some effect, particularly on fuel; sizeable reductions in the use of leaded petrol have resulted, in part, from the proportionately greater taxes imposed on it than those imposed on unleaded.

**dilution ratio** The relationship between the volume of water in a stream and the volume of incoming water. The ratio affects the ability of the stream to assimilate waste. When a pollution charge is set in terms of concentrations in wastewaster, polluters may be able to get round it by diluting the waste. To avoid this, the charge would have to be calculated on concentrations and volume. (Luken, 1990.) See also *absorptive capacity; assimilative capacity*.

**diminishing returns to a factor** In contrast to *decreasing returns to scale*, the law of diminishing returns refers to changes in one factor input (holding other factor inputs constant). It states that each unit increase of the factor will yield a smaller increase in output than the previous unit. For example, diminishing returns to labour will occur if the number of cashiers is increased while the number of cash registers remains the same. Also known as the law of diminishing returns.

**dioxins** Dioxins are a family of synthetic compounds known chemically as dibenzo-p-dioxins. These have been shown to be some of the more toxic human-made compounds. They are extremely persistent, which means that the stock of dioxins in the environment is approximately equal to the sum of all historical emissions. (USEPA, 1998.)

**direct regulations** Direct *regulations*, or *command and control (CAC) policies*, aim to reduce environmental degradation by specifying, for example, the amount of a polluting substance that a firm may emit, or the production technology that the firm should use. Polluters are legally obliged to comply and various penalties, such as fines, imprisonment or the closure of offending sites, are used to enforce compliance. Direct regulations are particularly important for toxic or dangerous materials and health-related pollutants where no margin of error can be tolerated. They are more effective in controlling limited pollution problems, when individual sources have similar pollution characteristics, impacts are understood and technological options are known.

Direct regulations are often limited by weak implementation and *enforcement*, and piecemeal and *reactive policy responses* addressing only particular problems. They are generally designed to control end-of-pipe pollution emissions. They are less effective in controlling numerous non-point pollution sources comprised of individual households, small enterprises and farms. The use of concepts such as *best available techniques (BAT)* give companies little incentive to go beyond regulatory norms and can lock firms into traditional technologies. Direct regulations tend to impose uniform standards on all polluters while each polluter faces different options and thus different costs to reach *abatement* requirements. Hence, they are less cost effective than measures that use *economic instruments*, as illustrated by the *least-cost theorem*. Administering and complying with environmental regulations is very costly. (OECD, 1994b.) See also *environmental shirking; ambient-based standards; command and control (CAC) policies; emissions standards; fixed standard approach; regulation, quantitative controls; standard setting*.

**direct-use value** Value which is derived from direct use of the *environment*, now and in the future. This includes *consumptive use value*, altruistic value and *bequest value*. See also *total economic value*.

direct valuation

**direct valuation** This is a class of methods for placing an economic value on an environmental asset such as a lake or a forest, or environmental improvements such as improved air or *water quality standards*. These methods measure the money value of such goods directly, either by creating hypothetical markets in which individuals are asked to state their value of the good (the *contingent valuation method, CVM*), or by looking at the markets for goods which are related to the environmental good (the *travel cost method (TCM)* and *hedonic pricing*). See also *valuation; revealed preference; stated preference (SP)*.

**disability-adjusted life year (DALY)** The disability-adjusted life year (DALY) combines a measure of healthy life years lost because of premature mortality with those lost as a result of disability. This allows mortality and morbidity estimates to be compared across countries. (World Bank, 1993.) See also *quality-adjusted life year (QALY)*.

**discounting** Discounting is the practice of placing progressively lower numerical values on future benefits and costs the further into the future they occur. The practice of discounting arises because individuals attach less weight to a benefit or cost in the future than they do to a benefit or cost now. Impatience, or *time preference*, is one reason why the present is given more weight than the future. A second reason is that, since *capital* is productive, a dollar's worth of resources now will generate more than a one dollar's worth of goods and services in the future. Hence, the markets value a dollar now more highly than a dollar in the future. This argument for discounting is referred to as the marginal productivity of capital argument.

If a form of damage, valued at $X today, but which will occur in T years time is to be discounted at a rate of r percent, the value of X is reduced to $X/(1+r)^T$. Clearly the higher r is and the greater T is, the lower the value of the discounted damages will be.

Excluding questions of *risk*, the three main contenders for the choice of the social discount rate are: the individual rate of time preference, based on the rate of individual trade-off between present and future benefits and costs; the *opportunity cost* of *capital*, based on the marginal productivity of capital; and the social rate of time preference, based on ethical considerations about the rate at which present and future costs should be traded off.

The individual rate of time preference would be equal to the opportunity cost of capital if there were efficient markets and no taxes. In practice, the range of individual time preference rates is large and does not coincide with the rates for the opportunity cost of capital. Broadly speaking the individual rate of time preference could be around 6–20 per cent (possibly higher in developing countries and depending on whether the individual is borrowing or lending), whereas the (risk-free) opportunity cost of capital rate would be around 7 per cent.

The social rate of time preference, on the other hand, is different to both of the above. Broadly speaking the rate at which economists and philosophers would regard it ethically justifiable to discount future damages would be in the region of 1–3 per cent.

More recent thinking on discounting has looked at rates which vary with the time period considered. From surveys of individual trade-offs over time, Cropper et al (1994) estimate a nominal rate of around 16.8 per cent, based on a sophisticated questionnaire approach to valuing present versus future *risks*. Most importantly, however, this paper points to a declining rate of discount – that is, to a rate which is not constant over time but which gets smaller as the time horizon lengthens. So, whereas the 16.8 per cent rate applies to a 5-year time horizon, a rate of only 3.4 per cent applies to a 100-year horizon. In a survey of 1700 professional economists, Weitzman (1998) finds that economists believe that lower rates should be applied to problems with long time horizons, such as those being discussed here; and that they distinguish between the immediate and the far-distant future. The discount rate implied by the analysis falls progressively, from 4 per cent to 0 per cent, as the perspective shifts from the immediate (up to 5 years hence) to the far-distant future (beyond 300 years). The author suggests that the appropriate discount rate for long-lived projects is less than 2 per cent, based upon this analysis. See also *net present value (NPV)*.

**discrete time:** Time measured in intervals (for example a year), rather than as a continuous variable. (Hanley et al, 1997.)

**diseconomies of scale** An increase in long-run average costs as the scale of production rises. Diseconomies of scale which are internal to a firm include optimum technology production levels beyond which costs rise, and bureaucracy which increases with a firm's size. Diseconomies which are external to firms include pollution and traffic congestion. Diseconomies of scale are synonymous with *decreasing returns to scale*. (Bannock et al, 1991.)

**disincentives** In the environmental context, this is any mechanism which internalizes the costs of the use of and/or damage to environmental resources, and in so doing provides *economic incentives* to reduce the use of or damage to the *environment*. Disincentives include: user fees, *non-compliance fees*, fines for damages, *liability rules* and *performance bonds*.

**disinvestment** Disinvestment occurs when any *capital* asset depreciates without compensating investment being made. Thus, if a firm's stock of machinery is allowed to depreciate over time, without investment in alternative assets being made, then the value of the firm's assets declines, and it can be said to be disinvesting. Disinvestment in one form of capital can involve its conversion into another form. For instance, a biological asset such as a forest may be converted into a human-made asset such as a log cabin. In this case society has disinvested in the forest but invested in a log cabin, so that the value of net investment may be positive. See also *asset conversion; constant capital rule; constant economic value; weak sustainability; genuine saving index*.

**disinterested altruism** When one generation uses resources so as to leave the next generation with the maximum scope for choosing what they want, the first generation is said to have exercised disinterested altruism. (Turner, Pearce and Bateman, 1994.) See also *altruism; limited altruism*.

**disjointed incrementalism** In most highly industrialized nations, production and consumption involve specialized activities performed by millions of decision makers. Each of these specialists makes little or no attempt to consider all of the potential spillover effects of their behaviour on others. Rather, each individual acts in a self-interested way (in the private sector) or according to a mixture of his own interest and that which he perceives as the public interest (in the public sector). Within the private sector, this is called free enterprise.

## dispersion modelling

Within the public sector 'it is called muddling through by most people, but disjointed *incrementalism* by decision theorists. It is disjointed because millions of individuals act separately without explicit coordination; it is incremental because each acts mainly to solve immediate problems rather than to carry out some long-range comprehensive plan'. (Bain, 1973.)

**dispersion modelling** Models which estimate concentrations of pollutants at receptors downwind (or downstream) of a pollution source. These draw upon mathematical equations which relate pollution concentrations to the level of emissions, stack height and meteorological factors like wind speed and temperature. See ExternE (1995) for a good summary of some of the main dispersion models. See also *air quality, modelling of; air quality, valuation of.*

**dissolved oxygen** The oxygen level available in water. This is important for the survival of fish and other aquatic life, and to prevent odours. Traditionally, the level of dissolved oxygen has been seen as the single most important indicator of the ability of a river or lake to support life. See also *biochemical oxygen demand (BOD), water quality standards.*

**dose–response evaluations and functions** These form part of the process of *health risk assessment.* They define the relationship between the pollution, or dose, to which an agent is exposed and the probability of a specific adverse effect, whether environmental or human damage – the response. Estimates are based on statistical studies of exposure, to which monetary values can then be attributed. Used in the *green accounting* methodology to estimate the responses of crops, building materials and health to increases in the level of pollution. See also *air quality, valuation of; epidemiology; valuation.*

**dose–response valuation technique** A conventional market approach to the *valuation* of environmental resources which uses market prices for the environmental service which is affected when output is measurable. The dose–response valuation technique takes the *dose–response* function and values the damages. Methods of valuation could be based on market prices (if they exist), corrected market prices (when the market prices are distorted), or on techniques such as the *contingent valuation method (CVM), hedonic pricing,* and the *travel cost method (TCM).* Dose–response valuation has been used to value the effect of air pollution on health, physical *depreciation* of material assets such as metal and buildings, aquatic *ecosystems*, vegetation and *soil erosion.* (ExternE, 1995, 1999; Markandya and Pavan, 1999.) See also *air quality, valuation of; epidemiology.*

**double burden argument** The argument that imposing a pollution charge on industry takes away money which the industry would otherwise have spent on pollution reduction. (Anderson et al, 1977.)

**double dividend** The benefits arising from the application of *environmental taxation* are sometimes considered to have a double dividend. This is said to be the case when there are two pay-offs: an improvement in environmental quality; and extra benefits obtained by using the revenues from environmental taxes to reduce pre-existing distortions in the economy, such as taxes on socially desirable items like labour. See also *pollution taxes.*

　　One case which has been studied in some depth is the use of a pollution charge to generate revenue which then allows a government to reduce employment taxes. This can result in an increase in employment while allowing pollution to drop, without affecting the budget. (O'Riordan, 1997.) See *double dividend, strong form; double dividend, weak form; environmental double dividends*.

**double dividend, strong form** The strong form of the *double dividend* looks at a revenue-neutral swap of *environmental taxation* for a representative normal tax (for example employment) which may also be called a distortional tax. The claim is that this result involves a saving in the gross costs of taxation, ie it improves the *efficiency* of raising taxes. Economists have shown that this is rarely the case. (Goulder, 1995.) See also *double dividend; double dividend, weak form; environmental double dividends*.

**double dividend, weak form** the weak *double dividend* is simply concerned with what is done with the revenue from *environmental taxes*. It states that it is better to use this revenue to reduce the rates of distortional taxes than to provide lump sum payments to citizens. This has been shown to hold in most cases. See also *double dividend; double dividend, strong form; environmental double dividends*.

**dynamic efficiency** An allocation of resources across a given period of time is dynamically efficient if it maximizes the *net present value (NPV)* of benefits from the resources over that time period. (Tietenberg, 1996.) See also *efficiency, static efficiency*.

**dynamic games** From the *game theory* literature. A situation wherein a game is played repeatedly, and players change their position based on their perception of the other's likely moves. (For an example of a dynamic game see Hanley et al, 1997.)

# Ee

**earmarked environmental funds** Funds that are allocated specifically to environmental programmes, as opposed to *environmental investments* which come from the general budget. Earmarked funds come in many forms. *Industrial pollution funds* finance environmental investments in the most polluting industries, such as metallurgy, chemicals, pulp and paper, and non-mineral metal products (UN ECE, 1994). Off-budget environmental funds receive tied revenues, such as road funds financed by gasoline taxes, and have a very mixed record around the world. One criticism is that they tend to distort government spending decisions and, if they become widespread, they can narrow the scope for fiscal policy to an unacceptable extent.

**earmarking** Earmarking, also known as hypothecation, is the assignment of revenues from a particular tax to a certain expenditure or type of expenditure, or to a specific government department or agency. It follows from the commitment to earmark tax revenues, on which the budget of the recipient department or specific project is dependent, rather than being decided by review and with reference to alternative possible uses for funds. The latter process is more usual in the setting of public expenditure budgets. Earmarking thus involves a degree of pre-commitment on the part of the government in the use of the tax. Earmarking tax revenues may enhance the overall political acceptability of a tax change, though it also leads to potential inefficiencies in the allocation of public funds to different activities. Barde (1999) suggests that earmarking revenues to certain expenditures may lead to rigidities and over-investment in the sectors involved. Earmarking may lead to a precedent in the allocation of public funds to certain activities, which may not result in social *efficiency*. (O'Riordan, 1997.) See also *environmental taxation*.

**earthquakes** Earthquakes are a natural environmental phenomenon, but one which scientists believe can be influenced by human activity. They are caused by stresses beneath the Earth's surface which can be either volcanic or the result of movements in the tectonic plates which make up the Earth's crust. These stresses result in sudden movements or shaking of the Earth's surface. There are thousands of earthquakes each year, the majority of them extremely mild or located beneath oceans. Serious oceanic earthquakes can cause tidal waves. Serious earthquakes in built-up areas, of which there are around 5 per year, kill an average of around 15,000 people as well as destroying material and environmental assets.

The scientific study of earthquakes is known as seismology. A major objective of seismologists is to forecast and detect earthquakes in an attempt to minimize the number of lives and the amount of resources which they claim. However, it is extremely difficult to accurately predict earthquakes. The fact that a major earthquake is possible in any area of the world is used as an argument against the further building of nuclear reactors, particularly where the likelihood of a major disaster is significant.

Some scientists believe that humans can affect the likelihood of earthquakes with large civil engineering projects such as the creation of huge new dammed lakes. The fear is that the enormous pressure which the body of water exerts on subterranean rock formations could cause earthquakes. From an environmental viewpoint this presents a case for setting policy for *adaptation* in such a way as to take account of the *risks*. It is also an area where the *precautionary principle* could be relevant.

**Earth Summit** The United Nations Conference on Environment and Development (UNCED) held in June 1992 in Rio de Janeiro, Brazil. This summit adopted, with the participation of more than 170 national state delegations, 4 major documents – the Rio Declaration, consisting of 27 principles complementing the 26 principles adopted by the UN (Stockholm) Conference on Human *Environment* (June 1992); Agenda 21, a plan of action for *sustainable development (SD)*; 2 global environmental *conventions*, namely the *Framework Convention on Climate Change (FCCC)* and the Convention on *Biodiversity* – and 1 statement on forest degradation.

**easements** In the environmental context, these are contractual arrangements between private landowners and public or non-governmental organizations (NGOs), which involve specified *conservation* practices on land. Agreements are often initially voluntary and accompanied by some financial compensation for required management practices. Subsequently, the arrangement is a contractual one. (OECD, 1996.)

**Easterlin Paradox** Easterlin (1974) published a review of surveys of human happiness, gathered through responses to questionnaires, conducted in 19 countries in various stages of development. The object of each survey was to estimate an index of happiness, in order to know the extent to which people with a higher income were systematically happier than those with a lower income. Likewise, the comparison of results for different countries was intended to compare measured happiness between countries at different levels of income. For one country, the US, a time series of observations between 1946 and 1970 was analysed, with the aim of measuring changes in happiness over time, along with economic development and increased income.

The term 'Easterlin Paradox' derives from the fact that these studies came to a counter-intuitive conclusion. While within each country, people with higher incomes systematically stated that they were happier than did those with lower incomes, this result was not reproduced in the cross-country studies. That is, people in low-income countries were not proportionally less happy than those in high-income studies. Likewise, for the time-series study in the US, happiness was not observed to rise proportionally with income. This result has been used by some to argue that the aim of indefinite *economic growth* is not necessarily desirable.

**eco-balance in taxes** See *environmental taxation*.

**eco-compass** A measure which aims to assess potential product innovations against 6 scales: service extension, *recycling*/reuse, mass (material) intensity, energy intensity, potential *risk* to health, and *environment* and resource *conservation*. An existing product is arbitrarily assigned a score of 2 on each scale. Product innovations are scored relative to the existing product, resulting in a graphic display of their strengths and weaknesses. An ideal product would score 5 on all 6 objectives. The eco-compass can be used to identify more eco-efficient alternatives to existing products and to show the relative benefits of different alternatives. (OECD, 1998.)

**eco-development** Eco-development is defined as development which induces desirable change for a human social group. Thus, it is held to be not only better for the social group but also to promote economic, social and ecological equilibrium. Under such development, there is a concern for self-reliance and an attempt to optimize the balance between human needs, locally available resources and culturally desirable lifestyles. (Riddell, 1981.) See also *sustainable development (SD)*.

**eco-efficiency** This term describes patterns of production which exploit the positive correlation between *economic efficiency* and ecological *efficiency*. That is, the achievement of eco-efficiency involves continuing to produce goods and services which satisfy customer needs at competitive prices, while reducing over time the environmental resources used in, and the environmental damage caused by, their production. A measure of eco-efficiency would be the ratio of the value of goods and services produced to the environmental inputs used and damage associated with their production. Specific means by which eco-efficiency can be improved include reducing the materials and energy used to produce goods and services, limiting waste emissions from the production process, maximizing the potential for *recycling*, and maximizing the sustainable use of renewable resources.

Government policy to improve eco-efficiency includes taxing natural inputs and the emissions of toxic wastes. This, by internalizing the *external costs* of production, reduces the gap between private and social aims and values, in that the creation of such *economic incentives* would make saving energy and materials more profitable. The World Business Council for Sustainable Development (WBCSD) adopted eco-efficiency as a business concept in 1992, in its report to the Rio *Earth Summit*. The concept of eco-efficiency is related to the *ecological footprints* associated with production and consumption, and to the attempt to limit ecological impacts and resource use to a level within the Earth's estimated *carrying capacity*. (OECD, 1998.) See also *energy efficiency; technical efficiency*.

**eco-feminism:** A movement which argues that the ideology which causes men to dominate and misuse nature is identical to that responsible for the domination of women by men. Eco-feminists argue that androcentrism (male-centred thought) is the cause of environmental problems, and therefore that the solution lies in overthrowing androcentrism. (Krishnan et al, 1995.)

**eco-labelling** Eco-labels, green labels or environmental labels are easily identifiable seals on product packaging. They inform consumers about the effects that the production, consumption and waste of products and services have on the *environment*. They have two objectives. The first is to provide consumers with information about the environmental effects of their consumption with a view to encouraging more environmentally friendly consumption patterns. The second is to encourage governments, firms and other agents to raise environmental standards in general.

The most common eco-labels are Type I labels, which certify a product's environmental standards relative to other products. They are third party voluntary programmes and are usually government supported, aiming to certify products and processes on multiple criteria covering the product's entire life cycle (eg the 'Blue Angel', Germany). Type II labels are one-sided informative environmental claims made by manufacturers or distributors. They refer to a specific attribute of a product, such as 'chlorofluorocarbon-free'.

Eco-labels are granted by a public or private body on the basis of criteria which establish a product to be less destructive of the environment than similar competitive products. These criteria reflect a holistic, overall judgement of the product's environmental quality. As such, eco-labelling excludes negative labels, which warn of particular dangers, and specific matters such as the use of recycled materials. Germany issued the first environmental label in 1978. National programmes for such labels are usually based on a government assessment of the aspects of a product design, within a product category, which could potentially effect a significant reduction in environmental damage. Once the product category has been selected, the types and degrees of environmental damage caused by the products in the category are examined. The product scope is defined, and criteria are established with expert working groups. Manufacturers voluntarily submit products for consideration, agree to contractual agreements, and pay to use the label for a period of years. Initial criteria may be expanded if the industry as a whole improves its environmental performance. Labelling programmes are difficult to administer due to a need to assess comprehensively the life cycle of the product, provide financing, and establish product categories and criteria. However, their use continues to spread. (Zarrilli et al, 1997.) See also *fair trade*.

**ecological carrying capacity** The maximum use to which a natural habitat can be put without degrading it. This is determined by environmental factors, for example the maximum number of animals the land can hold without being subject to density-dependent mortality and environmental degradation. (Barbier, 1993.) See also *carrying capacity; economic carrying capacity; absorptive capacity; assimilative capacity*.

**ecological class** This concept has been developed by radical environmental economists who argue against free market forces. They contend that free trade economics has meant the pursuit of wealth and consumption for the world's richest inhabitants only, to the detriment of the rest of the world's population and of the *environment*. Alan Durning of the US-based Worldwatch Institute argues that this has led to the emergence of a new ecological global class system. The richest ecological class is thus in effect a 'consuming class' as it consumes a disproportionate share (64 per cent) of the globe's resources and enjoys 64 per cent of the world's income. (Lang and Hines, 1993.) See also *affluence*.

**ecological consumerism** Consumerism which is sensitive to the environmental impacts of its consumption. Besides considering a product's quality and price, the ecological consumer considers its impact on health and the *environment*, not only at home but across the world. For example, the ecological consumer will prefer to consume food which has been produced close to home in order to minimize the pollution and other costs associated with transportation. (Lang and Hines, 1993.) See also *green consumerism; environmental product declaration; eco-labelling*.

**ecological deficit** Measured as the amount by which a country's *ecological footprint* exceeds the locally available ecological capacity.

**ecological dumping** See *environmental dumping.*

**ecological economics** This is a transdisciplinary approach to economics which emphasizes the relationships between economic and *ecological systems*. Humans are considered to be a major component of the overall economic–ecological *ecosystem*, rather than being the dominant and central component. Human society is thought of as co-evolving with the natural world. Ecological economics accounts not only for the financial constraints on consumption, as in conventional economics, but also for the natural constraints implied by the limited ability of the *environment* to provide *natural resources*, and to absorb the wastes of production and consumption. These constraints, which do not necessarily bind in the present but may reduce the capacity of the economic–ecological system to provide for human wellbeing in the future, are particularly relevant to *sustainability* and *sustainable development (SD)*. Sustainable management of the economic and ecological system is one of the major focuses of ecological economics, and the time frame of the analysis is typically longer than that considered in conventional economic analysis.

Ecological economics brings three concepts from the natural sciences into economic analysis. The first is throughput (from basic inputs of *natural resources*, including water and soil, to the use of the natural environment as a waste sink). The second is the concept of *carrying capacity* (whose variability and unpredictability call for caution, or the *precautionary principle*. The third is *entropy*. Ecological economists see the *Second Law of Thermodynamics* as having relevance for economics, and in particular the economics of sustainability. They note that in terms of entropy, the cost of economic activity is always greater than the benefit. (Costanza, 1997.) See also *environmental economics*.

**ecological footprints** Each person, city or country has a certain ecological impact due to the products and services of nature which are used to produce the goods and services which they consume, and due to the waste products of that consumption. The term 'ecological footprint' is a figurative term used to describe the amount of land needed to provide the *ecological services* corresponding to the consumption of each social unit, from the individual to the country.

The calculation of an ecological footprint requires knowledge of the *natural resources* used to produce the goods and services consumed, and the amount of land needed to produce these resources. It also requires knowledge of the wastes generated, and the biologically productive area necessary to assimilate these wastes. Of course, in reality the footprint is not a single piece of land; rather, the actual ecological footprint of any person or country is likely to be spread across the globe.

A comparison of a country's ecological footprint with its available biological capacity provides a measure of its *ecological deficit*. (O'Riordan, 1997.) See also *ecological remainder.*

**ecological funds** Most countries in Central and Eastern Europe have established ecological funds to receive and disburse revenues from *pollution charges*. The advantage of these funds is that they tend to reduce opposition to pollution charges, since the firms which pay the *charges* see that the revenues raised are used to finance environmental expenditures. There are two main disadvantages of these funds. The first is that *earmarking* taxes tends to raise questions as to whether the benefits of the expenditure for which the taxes are earmarked are as great as those of alternative projects. The second is that funds set up to finance specific classes of investment tend to become bureaucratic. This has led to suggestions that ecological funds should be established with a limited mandate, and their activities reviewed regularly. See also *earmarked environmental funds.*

**ecological irreversibility** This occurs where environmental functions, or unique ecosystems, are destroyed or irreparably damaged. (Pearce and Warford, 1993.) See also *irreversibility.*

**ecological remainder** Also known as remaining ecological capacity. Countries with *ecological footprints* smaller than their locally available ecological capacity are endowed with an ecological remainder – the difference between capacity and footprint. In many cases, this remainder is occupied, through production for export, by the footprints of other countries. See also *ecological deficit.*

**ecological services** Ecological functions which are currently perceived to support and protect the human activities of production and consumption or affect overall wellbeing in some way.

**ecological sensitivity** Ecological sensitivity refers to the ecological degradation sustained by an *ecosystem* as a result of a given level of stress, such as pollution or depletion. An example would be the degradation caused by *acid rain*, which is less in some areas than in others due to different geological conditions. It could also be argued that the damage caused by certain pollutants depends on the use which people make of an area of land. For instance, pollutants which cause reduced visibility result in more damage to the value of national parks than they do in other areas where visibility is less important. (Tietenberg, 1996.)

**ecological species–area relationship** This refers to the positive relationship between the area of land which an *ecosystem* occupies and the numbers and types of *species* which can exist on it. Thus, it is a relationship between an area of land and a measure of *biodiversity*, and reflects the fact that habitat loss – as land is converted from natural ecosystems to alternative uses – is a major factor in *biodiversity loss*. The species–area relationship is complex and depends on many environmental, climatic and other factors. (Barbier, 1993.)

**ecological stability** The ability of an *ecological system* to maintain a relatively constant level, or equilibrium, of *biodiversity*, biomass and productivity, in response to normal fluctuations and cycles in the surrounding *environment*. (Pearce et al, 1989.) See *sustainable shock, resilience, vulnerability.*

**ecological sustainability** See *environmental sustainability; sustainability.*

**ecological systems** 'A dynamic complex of plant, animal and micro-organism communities and their non-living *environment* interacting as a functional unit.' (*Convention on Biological Diversity*, Rio de Janiero, Brazil, June 3–14 1992). Ecological systems, or *ecosystems*, can also be defined as systems in which *species* live and evolve. The process of natural selection means that any species which proves to be ill-suited to the ecological system is eliminated while better-suited species survive. An ecological system is in equilibrium when the different species achieve balance in which no species is growing or declining over time. (Tietenberg, 1994.) See also *biodiversity*.

**ecology** The study of natural systems. The scope of this study can range widely. At the most detailed extreme, ecologists may study the life cycles of individual plants and animals, including for example the effect on these life cycles of changes in their habitat. At the opposite extreme they study the entire planet, which is itself an *ecosystem*, and the effect on its processes of changes such as the loss of tropical rain forests and other types of habitat.

The research of ecologists, and in particular their discoveries regarding the effects on ecosystems of pollution and resource depletion, has been an important factor in the development of the green, or environmental, movement. However, it is important to recognize that ecology is a scientific subject and does not imply a particular philosophical or political stance. (Pope et al, 1991.)

**econometric modelling** The use of statistical techniques to represent quantitative relationships between economic variables in the form of an equation or set of equations. Econometric modelling using regression analysis is a common technique used in *environmental economics*. Econometric techniques are used, for example, in the application of the *hedonic pricing* method (see Markandya et al, 2002) and in estimating the effect of socio-economic variables on the *willingness to pay (WTP)* for environmental goods obtained by the *contingent valuation method (CVM)*. For a good introduction to econometric modelling see Gujarati (1992).

**economic benefit or cost** See *social cost*.

**economic carrying capacity** This is determined by economic factors, for example the stocking rate of animals which offers maximum economic returns to producers, given their economic objectives and the definition of 'productivity'. It may differ from *ecological carrying capacity* in that some degradation may be acceptable if economic returns are to be maximized.

**economic depletion** Depletion of a mineral resource to the point where *extraction costs* equal market price. At the point of economic depletion, there may be a remaining stock, but it is not profitable to extract because the costs of extraction exceed the market price of the resource. This contrasts with the notion of *physical depletion*, which means that the stock of the resource is exhausted. See also *non-renewable resources*.

**economic efficiency** A situation in which the costs of a project, programme or policy are minimized. Much economic analysis is constructed around the concept of economic *efficiency*. Economic efficiency requires that production increase until *marginal costs (MCs)* equal *marginal benefits (MBs)* (productive efficiency). In the allocation of inputs, it requires that there is no alternative allocation which would reduce the total costs of producing a given output. In terms of the allocation of outputs it requires that no alternative allocations exist which would make at least one person better off without making someone worse off. This is called allocative efficiency, and is also known as *Pareto efficiency*. Proper economic efficiency does require that all costs referred to above are *social costs*, in other words that there should not be *external* production costs which are suffered by society but which are not accounted for by the producer. Efficiency is usually thought of as being distinct from the concept of optimality. See also *efficient level of pollution, efficient level of durability, technical efficiency.*

**economic failure** The inability of existing markets to capture the 'true' value of *natural resources* and other assets. Three sources of failure can be identified: *market failure, government failure* and *institutional failure.*

**economic growth** The increase in real output, and output per capita, over time. One of the major concerns of *environmental economics* and *ecological economics* is that the depletion of stocks of *natural resources* and accumulation in the natural *environment* of pollutants may mean that economic growth is not sustainable. For a review of various models that have been suggested to explain economic growth see Romer (1996). See also *Easterlin Paradox, sustainability.*

**economic incentives** In the environmental context these are measures which encourage households and enterprises to reduce pollution and waste, by providing them with economic gains if they adopt less polluting measures, or by imposing economic penalties if they do not. Examples are *pollution charges,* and various *economic instruments.* See also *disincentives.*

**economic instruments** There are a large number of regulatory measures which qualify as economic instruments. Broadly speaking a distinction can be drawn between instruments which act directly on pollution, and fiscal and financial instruments which provide an indirect *economic incentive* through their effect on prices paid for the inputs or received for the outputs of a production process. Table 2 overleaf shows a taxonomy of instruments which may be used for pollution control. The choice as to the most appropriate instruments for pollution control depends on a number of factors including:

- *Cost effectiveness.* The relative costs of different instruments is an important issue in policy making. *Market-based instruments (MBIs),* those which work through market forces, have been shown to be less costly than *command and control (CAC) policies.*
- Dynamic incentives certainly exist under economic instruments. Indeed, since the firm has to pay a price for every unit of pollution it produces (or alternatively must buy a *permit* for every unit of pollution it produces), the firm always has the incentive to reduce its emissions so as to reduce its total tax payments (or sell permits it no longer needs). Such incentives are much reduced under (CAC) since under this policy, the firm can pollute up to the standard free of charge. Once it complies with the standard, it has little incentive to do any better.
- Implementation issues. A number of issues concerning the implementation of different instruments, such as administration cost, monitoring or *capacity,* can arise in the use of economic instruments.
- Flexibility. Certain instruments, such as tradable permits, may be preferred to pollution *charges* because of the flexibility provided by such instruments, in that there is no need for further intervention if permits are sold, whereas charges must change to reflect different conditions in order for the desired emissions level to be attained.

## economic rent

While pollution charges and tradable permits appear considerably superior, CAC has overwhelmingly been the preferred method of intervention. Many reasons may explain this phenomenon. Economic instruments have often been perceived as a licence to pollute as opposed to a genuine instrument by which social optimality may be restored. The impact of economic instruments on the competitiveness of enterprises has also been much debated.

**Table 2** *Economic Instruments*

| Direct economic instruments | |
| --- | --- |
| Charge systems | Pollution charges |
| | User charges |
| | Access fees |
| | Road tolls |
| | Administrative charges |
| Property | Ownership rights |
| | • land titles |
| | • water rights |
| | • mining rights |
| | Use rights |
| | • licensing |
| | • concession |
| Market creation | Marketable emissions permits |
| | Marketable catch permits |
| | Quota systems |
| | Tradable land permits |
| Liability system | Legal liability |
| | Natural resource damage liability |
| | Liability insurance |
| Bonds and deposit system | Environmental performance bond |
| | Land reclamation bond |
| | Deposit refund scheme |

| Fiscal instruments |
| --- |
| Input taxes, Product taxes, Export taxes, Import tariffs, *Tax differentiation*, Royalties and resources taxes, Land use taxes, Investment tax credits, Accelerated depreciation, *Subsidies* |

| Financial instruments |
| --- |
| Financial subsidies, Soft loans, Grants, Location/relocation incentives, Subsidized interest, Revolving funds, Sectoral funds |

*Source:* Markandya et al, 2002.

**economic rent** The sale value of a resource less the cost of harvesting it. The latter should include the full *social costs*, including externalities and a return on the necessary investment. This concept is highly relevant in forestry, where rents collected by concession holders can be a powerful incentive for increasing production, and in the mining of *non-renewable resources*.

**economic sustainability** Economic sustainability can be defined as a situation in which the *capital* stocks which generate an economy's flow of wellbeing are not depleted over time. The different classes of capital stock usually considered in an analysis of economic sustainability are: *human-made capital*, environmental or *natural capital*, *human capital* and *social capital*. Two major definitions of economic sustainability are *weak sustainability*, which requires that the aggregate value of the total capital stock should be non-decreasing, and *strong sustainability*, which requires that each of the different classes of capital stock should be maintained in its own right, at least above *safe minimum standard (SMS)* levels. See also *sustainability; sustainable development (SD); genuine saving index*.

**economically viable** A project or programme is said to be economically viable if it yields more benefits than it costs after a *benefit–cost analysis* has been carried out. Crucially, on the cost side this should include a measure of the benefit which could have been obtained had the resources been used for the next-best project. This is known as the project's *opportunity cost*. It is this factor which distinguishes the concept of economic viability from that of financial viability, which means that a project generates a sufficient net revenue to justify going ahead under prevailing market conditions. The benefit–cost analysis should also include the values of any *externalities*, positive or negative, generated by the project.

**economies of scale** This refers to the increase in output which results from all inputs being increased in the same proportion. If output increases by the same proportion as the inputs, this represents constant returns to scale. If output increases less than proportionally, one has *decreasing returns to scale* and if it increases by more than the proportional increase in inputs one has *increasing returns to scale*.

**eco-radicalism** Radical green movement. The extreme wing of this group dismisses development as a concept because it poses an enormous threat to the *environment* and to society as a whole. (Krishnan et al, 1995.)

**ecosystem** See *ecological systems*.

**ecosystem diversity** See *biodiversity*.

**ecosystem health** *Ecosystem* health is a measure of the ability of an ecosystem to maintain its structure and functions over time. It is difficult to provide a general definition of ecosystem health, since the criteria with which health can be judged vary according to the characteristics of the system. However, in general it refers to *resilience* of a system to shocks, its *stability* and its productivity. Ecosystem health is described in Costanza et al (1992): 'An *ecological system* is healthy and free from "distress syndrome" if it is stable and sustainable – that is, if it is active and maintains its organisation and autonomy over time and is resilient to stress'. The *sustainability* of an ecosystem means that its structure is stable, and that it maintains over time its ability to perform ecological functions. An ecosystem suffers from 'distress syndrome' if it is suffering a level of stress which will lead eventually to a collapse of its structure.

Ecosystem health has traditionally been measured using indicators that consist of, for example, a particular *species* or other aspect of an ecosystem. However, such indices are not now considered to be capable of reflecting fully the state of health of an ecosystem, largely because they do not account for the complexity of ecosystems. Alternative indices have been developed which include: The Index of Biotic Integrity (which consists of 12 characteristics of fish communities) developed by James Karr to appraise freshwater ecosystem health; and the Index of Network Ascendancy which accounts for ecosystem characteristics including the diversity of species and overall activity. (Costanza et al, 1992.)

**ecotage** A term that combines the words 'ecological' and 'sabotage', referring to direct and dramatic action taken by individuals or groups to raise awareness of environmental issues, or to protest against environmental destruction. (Savage et al, 1974.)

**eco-taxation** See *environmental taxation.*

**eco-tone** An area of transition between adjacent ecological communities, usually involving competition between organisms common to both. (IPCC, 1996a.)

**ecotourism** The World Tourism and Travel Environment Research Centre (WTTRC) has defined ecotourism as:

'implying a building of environmental considerations into all tourism and travel products and their consumption. This would suggest that sustainable tourism development is a level of activity at or below the level which will not result in environmental or socio-cultural deterioration or be perceived by tourists as depreciating their enjoyment and appreciation of the area.'

There are various types of ecotourism, including: nature-based tourism, such as walking and hiking in rural areas; agro-tourism, which involves staying in rural farmhouses and eating home-grown produce; bird-watching; and other low-impact sports.

The term ecotourism does not imply the absence of environmental and social impacts. Rather it means that these impacts will be considerably less than those of mass and activity-based tourism, and that they should be of such a level not to result in *depreciation* over time of the *environment* and culture of the visited areas. (Stanners and Bourdeau, 1995.)

**eco-toxicity** The damaging effects on plants, animals and humans of toxic substances, including chemicals and natural substances. (Stanners and Bourdeau, 1995.)

**eco-vests** Investments in ecological protection and *conservation*, where the main purpose is to demonstrate the private profitability of projects involving better wildlife utilization and *ecotourism*. (Pearce, 1991.)

**effective protection rate** This measures the extent to which an economy effectively protects its markets against imports. The effective protection rate is based on Corden's (1966) theory of effective protection, and includes the effect of protection on inputs in the final level of protection of outputs. Protection is measured in terms of the value-added element in production. The implied protection rates can differ significantly from the nominal protection rates as given by tariffs.

**efficiency** See *economic efficiency, energy efficiency, technical efficiency.*

**efficient level of durability** This refers to the fact that products which last longer, and thus yield increased benefits to individuals and society, are also more expensive to produce. Thus, the efficient level of durability is the one which maximizes the product's net benefit (Tietenberg, 1996.) See also *economic efficiency*.

**efficient level of pollution** This concept is used in *environmental economics* to describe a situation in which the *marginal abatement costs (MACs)* of a polluter and the value of *marginal damages (MDs)* of the pollution caused are compared in order to identify the economically desirable level of pollution. This requires the *valuation* of the damages caused by pollution. Figure 5 illustrates this concept: MAC is the marginal abatement cost; MD is the marginal damages and OE the efficient level of pollution. The efficient level of pollution is shown by the level E in the diagram. This is the point at which the marginal abatement costs and the marginal damage of the pollution are equalized. This is the efficient level because if pollution were to be abated any further towards zero, the benefits (MD) would be outweighed by the costs (MAC). This efficient outcome can be obtained through the use of *market-based instruments (MBIs)* or *command and control (CAC) policies*. (Markandya et al, 2002.)

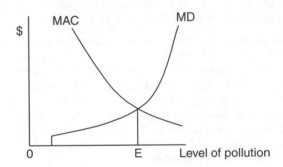

**Figure 5** *The Efficient Level of Pollution*

**effluent** Wastewater, treated or untreated, which flows out of a treatment plant, sewer, or industrial outfall. The term usually refers to wastes discharged into rivers, lakes and streams or directly into the sea. See also *acceptable effluent*.

**effluent charges** See *emissions charges*.

**effluent limitation** Restrictions established by a state or environmental authority on quantities, rates and concentrations in wastewater discharges.

**egoism** Usual meaning of selfishness is interpreted here as pursuit of self-interest. Hohmeyer et al (1997) argue that people prefer policies which lead to an increase in GNP whenever it leads to an increase in their own income. Neoclassical economists, however, argue that such self-interest is compatible with the broader public good as long as an appropriate legal framework is in place and social norms are followed. See also *altruism*.

**elasticity of demand or supply** The responsiveness of the quantity demanded or supplied of a product to a change in price. It is expressed as the percentage change in quantity demanded or supplied of a good as the result of a 1 per cent change in price. Demand or supply is said to be inelastic if elasticity is less than 1, of unit elasticity if elasticity is equal to 1, and elastic if elasticity exceeds 1.

**elasticity of substitution** The elasticity of substitution measures how freely we can vary inputs as their relative prices change but the amount of output produced remains constant. Formally, the elasticity of substitution measures the percentage change in the ratio of the inputs used to produce a given quantity of a good, as the ratio of input prices changes by a given percentage. The elasticity of substitution is important in *resource economics* because it measures the degree to which firms can substitute labour and *human-made capital* for *natural resources* when the latter become increasingly scarce. See also *weak sustainability*.

**electricity co-generation** The combined production of electricity and useful thermal energy. Also referred to as combined heat and power (CHP).

**El Niño/Southern Oscillation (ENSO)** A temporary warming of the Eastern tropical Pacific Ocean associated with changes in atmospheric circulation in the western Pacific. It tends to occur around the end of the year and has disastrous effects on marine life and fishing in Peru and other affected countries. *Climate change* could positively or negatively affect the damages resulting from this climatic phenomenon. (IPCC, 1998.)

**embedding phenomenon** This is a form of bias found in *contingent valuation method (CVM)* studies. It refers to the fact that when respondents are asked to value, for instance, a certain population of bird *species*, their answer will not be proportionately lower than the value that they would give for the entire species, or perhaps for all of the bird species in their country. What this means is that most of the value that would be attached to the more general commodity has been captured in the answer to the first question. This means that the answers to *valuation* questions will depend on which question is asked first, constituting a source of bias. (Dixon et al, 1986.)

**emission banking** Allows firms to store *emissions permits* for subsequent use or sale to others. See also *economic instruments; emissions trading; marketable emissions permits*.

**emission factor** The relationship between the amount of a pollutant and the amount of raw material associated with it. For example, an emission factor for a car could be the level of particulate matter, or other pollutants, emitted per litre of petrol or ton of coal used.

**emissions charges** *Charges* to be paid by polluters on their discharges. These charges are based on the volume of emissions or the concentration of pollutants in the emissions. *Economic instruments* such as this neither *ban* the emission nor dictate the technology for reducing the emission. Rather, they are intended as a *disincentive* to pollute. The polluter can choose to pay the emission charges, treat the *effluent* in order to reduce the charge, or cut back on production. Thus when the emissions have high *social costs*, the emission charge should be high (reflecting the negative *externality* of the pollution), and polluters will be induced to invest in pollution prevention or to desist from the polluting activity.

The revenues raised may be *earmarked* for pollution monitoring, *abatement*, or clean-up. Setting effluent or emission charges high enough to meet revenue requirements may clash with the motive of setting the charges at a level where net benefits are maximized, with the appropriate level of incentive effect. In general, the revenue objective has dominated, but with charges generally being too low for the full incentive effect to operate. Revenues from such taxes are often earmarked to environmental agencies or particular categories of spending. The system has worked well when emissions can be measured at relatively low cost and when the allocation of the revenues is transparent.

Emissions charges have been rated as successful in the field of air emissions in Scandinavia (where a *carbon tax* has also been successfully introduced) and in water pollution control policy in a few countries (eg the Netherlands). They have also been used with some success in discouraging aircraft noise, where they are narrowly applied as a differentiation of landing fees. See also *economic instruments*. (OECD, 1989b.)

**emissions credits** See *emissions reduction credit scheme; emissions trading*.

**emissions permits** See *marketable emissions permits; permits*.

**emission source** Any factory, furnace, or other outlet which discharges pollutants into the *environment*. A point source is a source whose emissions are sufficiently significant to be accounted for separately in a pollution inventory. *Dispersion modelling* techniques are used to estimate the pollutant loads on different areas resulting from the emission from a particular source. See also *non-point source pollution; point source pollution*.

**emissions reduction credit scheme** This scheme was part of the *emissions trading* programme introduced in the US in 1977. They allowed trading between areas which had reached their pollution limit, and which would otherwise have been unable to acquire new industry, and areas which had reduced pollution by more than was required. A polluter who reduced emissions by more than was required could obtain a credit for the excess reduction. This credit could be traded through an *offset policy* system to be used in areas which had not met their pollution-reduction requirements. The object of this system is for aggregate pollution levels to remain unchanged while allowing new industry to be established in regions where current pollution levels exceed permitted levels. (Pearce and Turner, 1990.)

**emissions standards** Set levels of allowable emissions of pollutants. They may be varied by size of plant, according to location and over time. See also *ambient-based standards; command and control (CAC) policies; fixed standard approach; direct regulation; regulation; quantitative controls; standard setting*.

**emissions trading** A system by which polluters trade *emissions permits*. This process is intended to ensure that a given level of pollution reduction is achieved at the lowest possible total cost to polluters. Thus, if permits are held by a polluter who can reduce pollution more cheaply than the market price of a permit, that polluter will sell some permits on the emissions trading market. Likewise, if another polluter finds it more expensive to reduce pollution than to buy permits, that polluter will buy permits on the market. Thus, the trade should be to the advantage of both parties. The equilibrium price of the permit should be equal to the *marginal cost (MC)* of pollution reduction at the level of pollution for which permits have been issued. There are a number of variations on the basic emissions trading model including *bubble trades, netting*, offset, and *banking schemes*. (OECD, 1992a.) See also *emission banking; economic instruments; marketable permits; offset policy*.

**emission taxation** See *emissions charges, environmental taxation.*

**enclosure** Enclosure generally refers to the conversion of communally managed agricultural land into individually owned lots. Specifically it refers to the enclosure of waste (marginal) land and especially of the open fields supposedly characteristic of feudal Europe. The latter involved a rotation between individually farmed arable strips within communally managed fields, and the use of the fields as common grazing. Discussion of enclosure was long dominated by neo-Marxist theories, and it is certainly the case that an unequal distribution of income was often associated with enclosure, as is now often observed with the loss of common-use rights in developing economies. However, improved understanding of the economics of transactions costs and of *common property resources* has enabled a better appreciation and even formal modelling of the *efficiency* and *sustainability* of pre- and post-enclosure farming systems and of their relationship with the level of agricultural technology. (Stevenson, 1991; Dahlman, 1980.) See also *asset conversion; biogeography; global conversion process; opportunity cost.*

**end-of-pipe technology** This is a type of technology which reduces the pollution contained in waste products before they are emitted into the *environment*. An example of such a technology is a filter on power station stacks which remove sulphur dioxide ($SO_2$) and particulate matter from the air which is expelled. It is not clear that end-of-pipe technologies reduce pollution in the most efficient way since often it is more cost effective to reduce the amount of waste generated than to clean it before it is emitted. (Hanley et al, 1997.) See also *direct regulations.*

**endogenous risk** A risk which is the result of human activity, so that the level of risk depends on the *regulations* in place and the policies adopted. It differs from exogenous risk, which is determined by factors outside human control. The distinction between exogenous and endogenous *risks* is not clear-cut. For instance, the risk of extreme weather has hitherto been considered an exogenous risk, but human behaviour, by causing climate change, appears to be affecting this risk, so that it becomes in part an endogenous risk. See also *risk.*

**endogenous variable** A variable whose value is determined within a model or set of equations, rather then being introduced as a predetermined set of values. See also *exogenous variable.*

**endowment** The initial allocation of resources and goods to individuals and nations.

**energy accounting** The use of energy inputs to describe a production process. This can, where appropriate, be compared to the energy content of the output of the production process, for example in the case of food. (Common, 1995.)

**energy efficiency** Energy *efficiency* measures the ratio of energy output from a process to the input into the process. For instance, when applied to cars, it reports how many miles a car can travel on a gallon of fuel. According to Elsworth (1990), the average efficiency of household appliances in the US increased by 20 to 30 per cent over the period 1985 to 1990. In Japan this figure was 50 per cent. See also *eco-efficiency.*

**enforcement** Enforcement is an important issue in the implementation of environmental policy. If a policy is enacted but not enforced by the relevant authorities, then the environmental problem which the policy seeks to address will persist. Lack of enforcement is a particular problem for countries which lack administrative or legal capacity, which have a large black economy or which suffer from corruption. To facilitate the enforcement of environmental policies, *capacity building* may be required, leading to implementation costs.

Enforcement may also be an issue in the design of *international environmental agreements*. Several recent agreements include the potential use of trade sanctions to encourage compliance with the agreement by signatory nations. Where global environmental problems are concerned, an example being *climate change*, enforcement of such agreements may be particularly difficult, given the gains that can be obtained by the nation which reneges on the agreement. This is an example of the *free rider problem*.

**Engel Curve** A representation of the relationship between income and expenditure on a given good. When plotted on a log scale, the slope of the curve at any point represents the income *elasticity of demand* for the good, or the incremental change in demand from an incremental change in income. See also *Engel's Law*.

**Engel's Law** This law states that the proportion of a nation's income spent on food indicates the nation's relative level of welfare. Lower proportions of expenditure on food relative to other consumption imply a higher standard of living, since as income rises, expenditure on food rises less than proportionally. See also *Engel Curve*.

**engineering approach** This is an approach to identifying the costs of implementing environmental measures, in particular the reduction of pollution emissions. This approach, rather than measuring the costs of pollution reduction for each firm, uses standard engineering data. This produces a cost estimate for a typical well-informed firm. This method saves the costs of collecting information about individual firms and avoids the possibility that some firms may inflate their stated costs in the hope of receiving a lower emissions reduction target. The disadvantage of this method, however, is that the typical estimates may be inaccurate for any particular firm. (Tietenberg, 1996.)

**entropy** A measure of the disorder in a system. The lower the entropy in a system, the more order there is and the more energy is available. For instance, compare a piece of wood and the ashes and dispersed heat which remain after it is burned. From the *First Law of Thermodynamics*, the matter and energy in existence after the burning are exactly the same as they were before. However, the entropy has increased; the order and the amount of available energy have both decreased. In *environmental economics* the concept of entropy is relevant via the *Second Law of Thermodynamics*, which states that the entropy of a system must either increase or remain unchanged. This has been used by the economist Georgescu-Rogen to argue that materials should be conserved as far as possible since their complete *recycling* is impossible. See Perman et al (1999).

**environment** Refers to the quantity and quality of *natural resources*, both renewable and *non-renewable*. It includes the ambient environment, which consists of the landscape, water, air and the atmosphere, and is a crucial determinant of human quality of life, as well as supporting human life. The state of the environment is a critical determinant of the quantity, quality and *sustainability* of human activities. (Panayotou, 1993.)

**environmental accounting** The systematic description of interactions between *environment* and economy by means of an accounting framework. This framework is intended to provide information on the effects of the economy on the environment, and the contribution of the environment to economic output, both within a given time period and over time.

The standard *system of national accounts* (SNA) measures *gross domestic product (GDP)*, the most widely used indicator for economic performance and *economic growth*. The SNA framework has three major drawbacks with respect to the environment: the neglect of the depletion of *natural resources;* the inadequate treatment of *defensive expenditure;* and the failure to account for the degradation of environmental quality and its effects on human health and welfare. No consensus has yet been reached on the appropriate form for an adjusted *gross national product (GNP)* – a 'green' national product. There are, however, three major approaches:

1  The adjustment of national (economic) accounts to incorporate environmental effects.
2  The development of *satellite accounts* outside and complementary to the core SNA.
3  Independent natural *environmental and resource account*s linked to the national accounts.

The first two approaches involve the economic *valuation* of environmental damages and the depletion of natural resources. (It has been suggested that environmental services should also be valued, but in practice it would be impossible to value all environmental services.) The net value of environmental damage and depletion can then be deducted from net national product (NNP) to arrive at a measure of *green net national product*. The second approach, in addition to valuing environmental damage and depletion, includes measures of the corresponding physical flows and stocks of resources. The third approach concentrates on keeping inventories of physical and monetary flows and stocks of natural resources. (OECD, 1994a; Markandya and Pavan, 1999.) See also *environmentally adjusted domestic product; green accounting*.

**Environmental Action Programme (EAP)** The main objective of the EAP, an initiative of the OECD, was to help address environmental problems in Central and Eastern European countries which required urgent action. The EAP's goal was to ensure that the urgent environmental problems of transition economies were addressed as cost effectively and efficiently as possible. This involved a combination of policy tools including *market-based instruments (MBIs)*, realistic *regulations* and *enforcement* mechanisms, investment in infrastructure, and *capacity building* of institutions to control environmental damages. For further details on environmental action plans see the OECD EAP homepage: http://www.oecd.org/env/eap/eap.htm.

**environmental assessments** Accurate and scientifically defensible assessments of the impacts of proposed human actions on the *environment* and on human health and safety. They also evaluate the effectiveness of alternative actions and of possible *mitigation* and *restoration activities. See also environmental impact assessment (EIA).*

**environmental assurance bonding system** This system is a variation on the *deposit refund scheme.* It is designed to internalize environmental values into private decision making. The system operates by requiring those seeking to use environmental resources, such as logging or mining firms, to deposit a bond equal to the maximum environmental damage that the project could cause. The onus would be on resource-using firms to demonstrate that environmental damage was less than the value of the bond, in which case the difference and a portion of interest earned would be refunded. This system ensures, in principle, that the funds to repair the environmental damage or to compensate those affected are available. Assurance bonding is an extension of the *polluter pays principle (PPP)* referred to by Cornwell and Costanza (1994) as the 'polluter pays for *uncertainty* as well' or the 'precautionary polluter pays principle'. Also known as *environmental performance bonds. See also performance bonds.* (Cornwell and Costanza, 1994.)

**environmental audit** An environmental audit is an independent assessment of a company's environmental performance with respect to environmental standards. Environmental audits are increasingly used alongside financial accounts to assess the performance of companies. They have been developed in response to demands from consumers and shareholders for measures of companies' attitudes towards the *environment.* Environmental audits can also be extended to measure a company's overall environmental performance, so that additional information on the extent to which it exceeds environmental standards would be provided.

Environmental audits are used as part of the *environmental impact assessment (EIA)* of projects. This can be used to compare the ex-post environmental impacts of a project with the impacts which were projected and, on the basis of scientific evidence, both measure the discrepancy and analyse its causes. (Ledgerwood et al, 1992.)

**environmental collapse** Environmental collapse is said to have occurred where environmental degradation has destroyed the natural regeneration processes in the *environment.* (Barbier, 1993.) See also *absorptive capacity; assimilative capacity; ecological stability.*

**environmental conventions** See *convention, international environmental agreements.*

**environmental convergence theory** A theory which suggests that environmental disruption will tend to be uniform between countries at similar levels of economic development, regardless of their political or institutional characteristics. (Pearce and Turner, 1990.)

**environmental covenants** These are voluntary agreements with specific groups of people to set targets and design instruments for implementation and procedures for monitoring environmental performance. For example, an industry, or a section of an industry, could agree certain environmental targets with the government. The incentive for the industry to agree to these targets is the avoidance of governmental regulation. However, while it may seem that

# environmental double dividends

environmental standards might be lower under such a scheme, in practice it has been shown to be an efficient and low-cost way to meet environmental goals. (OECD, 1994b.)

**environmental double dividends** This refers to the fact that when efforts are made to reduce a certain type of pollutant, emissions of other types of pollutant will be reduced as a by-product. For example, *greenhouse gases (GHGs)* tend to be associated with other pollutants and toxic substances. Action taken to reduce GHG emissions will also reduce the other pollutants. These may also be called *ancillary* or *secondary benefits*.

The environmental double dividend should not be confused with the *double dividend*. This measures the *economic benefits*, in terms of increased *efficiency* of resource allocation, which follow from using the revenue from an *environmental tax* to reduce other distortional taxes such as those on labour. The first dividend derives from reducing the distortion from having unpriced environmental goods, and the second comes from reducing the distortion of taxes on desirable factors, such as labour. (Goulder, 1995.)

**environmental dumping** This occurs when countries with relatively lax environmental standards export goods to countries with relatively stricter standards. The exporting country benefits from a competitive advantage which accrues because the environmental costs of producing goods are not included in the products' prices. There is an effective subsidy to production. (Lang and Hines, 1993; Krishnan et al, 1995.) This is similar to the *pollution haven* debate.

**environmental economics** Environmental economics follows *neoclassical economics* in having as its central concern the efficient allocation of scarce resources among competing uses. This branch of economics brings scarce environmental resources into mainstream economic analysis. It addresses issues of pollution control, the efficient setting of *emissions standard*s, waste management and *recycling*, the industrial activity of *environmental externalities*, the *conservation* of *natural resources*, the *valuation* of natural resources, and so on. The objective of environmental economics is to identify policies which will move the economic system towards an efficient allocation of natural resources.

Environmental economics is distinct from *ecological economics* to the extent that it adheres more closely to conventional, neoclassical economics. That is, it emphasizes the desirability of attaining environmental objectives by means of using market mechanisms, like adjusting price signals, in order to influence the behaviour of households and firms. There is, however, a significant overlap between environmental and ecological economics. (Tolba and El-Khaly, 1992.)

**environment–economy interaction** The interdependence between the *environment* and the economy arises from the fact that the environment provides the raw materials for economic activity as well as directly providing welfare, and because the way in which the economy is managed impacts on the environment. Thus, environmental damage caused by economic activity will in turn affect both welfare and the performance of the economy.

**environmental effectiveness principle** The environmental effectiveness of a policy or instrument used in environmental regulation may be measured by its impacts on the emissions of pollutants and on the use of *natural resources*. (Turner et al, 1994.)

**environmental and energy resources** Environmental and energy resources can be thought of as natural assets which provide valuable services to humans. For instance, *ecological system*s are responsible for providing clean air and water, scenic values, maintaining soil fertility, and regulating flows of water, as well as assimilating and processing waste and regulating the world's climate.

Stocks of natural assets are also responsible for providing natural renewable inputs to production such as timber and agricultural products. Environmental resources include stocks of exhaustible mineral resources. These resources perform many functions including the provision of raw materials for production, and the generation of energy. (Perman et al, 1996.) See also *natural resources*.

**environmental ethics** The set of moral principles that we apply to our actions with respect to the *environment*. Environmental ethics can be described as the ethical foundations of *environmental economics* and *ecological economics*. An important distinction is to be made between humanist ethics and naturalist ethics. Under humanist ethical principals fundamental rights are assigned only to humans. Under naturalist ethical principals rights are also assigned to animals and natural systems. A well-known expression of the naturalist ethic, which underlines its role in appraising behaviour towards the environment, is from Aldo Leopold's 'A Sand Country Almanac' which states 'A thing is right when it tends to preserve the integrity, *stability* and beauty of the biotic community. It is wrong when it tends otherwise.' (Leopold, 1970.) See Perman et al (1999) for a review of the ethical foundations of environmental economics. See also *bio-ethical standpoint; ethics; extended rights; extended stewardship ideology; Kantian ethics; libertarian ethics; naturalism; Rawlsian ethics; stewardship ethic.*

**environmental externalities** See *externalities.*

**environmental funds** see *ecological funds.*

**environmental groups** Pressure groups which aim to draw attention to issues of concern regarding the *environment*. Examples include Friends of the Earth, Greenpeace and WWF, among others.

**environmental impact assessment (EIA)** Environmental impact assessment (EIA) is a systematic process by which the impacts of a planned activity on the *environment* are identified and assessed using both qualitative and quantitative assessment techniques. EIA is undertaken at the earliest stage of an activity, ideally at the planning stage, and the outcome of an EIA usually takes the form of an environmental impact statement (EIS) or environmental statement (ES). The EIS provides the means of conveying to the decision makers the nature, magnitude and significance of the proposed activity's environmental impacts. The information is provided at a point in time when it can materially affect the decision made; that is, at a stage when plans can still be altered, or *mitigation* measures incorporated into the design. The emphasis of the EIA process is therefore very much on anticipation and prevention. EIA is usually represented as consisting of a number of distinct steps. In reality, however, it is more of a cyclical process, with a great deal of interaction and feedback between the steps. It is also necessarily multidisciplinary in nature, and involves input from numerous experts, as well as from statutory consultees and the public. See also *impact assessment*.

**environmental indicators** Environmental indicators both quantify and simplify complex environmental information so its significance is clearer and thus easier to communicate. The general approach is to identify a single measure or a small number of measures of environmental *pressure, state and response* for a limited set of key environmental issues. For example, OECD and UNEP consider selected issues such as *climate change* with *greenhouse gas (GHG)* emissions as a pressure indicator, concentrations of greenhouse gases as a state indicator and energy intensity and environmental measures as response indicators. Indicators are integrated into indices.

Other issues for which indicators have been developed include *ozone* depletion, *eutrophication*, acidification, toxic contamination, urban environmental quality, *biodiversity* and waste. The World Bank categorizes issues into: source indicators (agriculture, forest, marine resources, water and subsoil assets); sink or pollution indicators (climate change, acidification, eutrophication, toxification); life-support indicators (biodiversity, oceans, special lands such as wetlands); and human impact indicators (health, dependence on water, and air quality as well as occupational exposure, food security and quality, housing, waste and natural disasters). (Hammond et al, 1995.) See also *sustainable development, indicators of; environmental indices*.

**environmental indices** These are aggregated *environmental indicators*. That is, indices can be thought of as being at the apex of an information pyramid which has primary data at its base, and the results of increased *aggregation* and analysis as one moves further up the pyramid. The goal of environmental indices is to communicate information about the environment – and about the human activities which affect it – in ways which highlight trends (and thus emerging problems) and draw attention to the effectiveness of current policies. Thus, sink indicators can be summarized in a composite pollution index, and the *sustainability* of resource use for many types of resources can be summarized in a resource depletion index. Indicators for the maintenance of *biodiversity*, an *ecosystem* life-support function, can be summarized in a composite biodiversity measure. Environmental conditions which affect human health and welfare can be summarized in an index of environmental impact on human welfare. (Hammond et al, 1995.) See also *base period*.

**environmental investments** Investments which protect and/or increase an economy's *natural capital* stock. These include investment in clean technology, although it is difficult to separate the environmental protection component from the productivity component. See also *defensive expenditures; eco-vests*.

**environmental Kuznets curve** See *Kuznets curve, environmental*.

**environmental management** Control in the use of *natural resources* and the implementation of measures to ensure their *conservation*, the protection of habitats and the control of hazards. See also *regulations*.

**environmental performance bonds** See *environmental assurance bonding system; deposit refund scheme; performance bonds*.

**environmental policy instruments** See *economic instruments.*

**environmental product declaration** A written statement of all a product's properties, pertaining to its consumption and final disposal, which are important from an environmental point of view. Environmental product declarations are intended to encourage manufacturers to develop products with improved environmental properties. See also *eco-labels; green consumerism; ecological consumerism.*

**environmental and resource accounts** These refer to quantitative accounts of stocks and flows of environmental assets, or environmental resources. These accounts can be recorded in terms of biomass (volume and weight), area, population and diversity, depending on the environmental resource in question. Examples of environmental and resource accounts are forest accounts, water resource accounts, wildlife resource accounts and land accounts.

Environmental and resource accounts can be extended to include qualitative aspects of environmental resources. Qualitative environmental and resource accounts aim to, for instance, measure pollution flows from economic activities to *natural resources* or to draw a picture of the quality of a particular natural resource. They complement the quantitative, physical versions of environmental accounts. (OECD, 1994a.) See also *green accounting.*

**environmental risk internalization through capital markets (ERICAM)** This is a system which environmental regulators may use to force firms who wish to use environmental resources to insure against potential environmental damage. Potential polluters obtain a licence to operate only if they meet the requirements set by the regulator for insurance against (ideally the total potential) environmental damage.

Firms may thus offer payments for risk participation shares on the open market and investors have the opportunity to sign such shares upon accepting the payment. For a given share price, an investor will choose the polluter with the lowest *risk* of liability for damage. The less risk-averse investors may be prepared to trade off increased risk against a higher *risk premium*, or payment for risk participation shares. One of the interesting features of the ERICAM system is that, through trade in risk participation shares, it generates market prices for environmental damage. (Zweifel and Tyran, 1994.)

**environmental shirking** Environmental shirking refers to a situation in which an individual or institution which is responsible for reducing environmental damage reduces the damage by less than is required. An example of environmental shirking is a firm which has been charged by an environmental regulator with reducing pollution to a certain, socially optimal, level, and which devotes too few resources to abating pollution, resulting in pollution which is greater than the required level.

An incentive for environmental shirking is present when the individual or institution charged with reducing damage receives only a fraction of the total benefits of damage reduction to society. This is illustrated in Figure 6 overleaf. The uppermost curve, *BB*, represents the *marginal benefits (MBs)* to society of the reduction in pollution by a particular firm. The lower curve *bb* shows the MB to the firm itself from its own reduction in pollution. The *marginal cost (MC)* to the firm of abating pollution is represented by curve *cc*. The socially

## environmental sustainability

optimal solution is that the firm reduce pollution up to the point $s^*$, since that is the point at which the marginal social benefits of pollution *abatement* equal its marginal costs. However, the firm receives only a fraction of the social benefits, represented by $bb$. The optimal solution from the point of view of the firm is to set its abatement level at $s'$, where the MBs of abatement to the firm are equal to the MCs. Since $s^*$ is greater than $s'$, insufficient resources are allocated to abatement, relative to the socially optimal solution. See also *regulation; direct regulation; efficient level of pollution*.

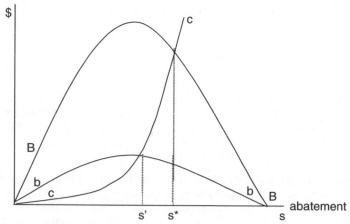

*Source:* After Hanley et al, 1997.

**Figure 6** *The Causes of Environmental Shirking*

**environmental sustainability** Environmental sustainability can be defined as sustainability of the *ecological services* on which humans depend, directly and indirectly. These services include the provision of food and other raw materials, and the ecological services required to support agricultural production including hydrological regulation, production and protection of soils, and the regulation of the climate.

Environmental sustainability can be defined in different ways. A strict version of environmental sustainability would label as unsustainable any conversion of natural *ecosystem*s to alternative uses, eg the conversion of forest land to agriculture, since the ecosystem and its services have been lost. Such a definition would, however, be criticized, even by proponents of *strong sustainability*, as being too rigid. Another, perhaps more useful although clearly anthropocentric way to think of environmental sustainability is to acknowledge that some ecosystem services are not essential to humans, and that economic development which involves depleting some ecosystems can be sustainable. However, environmental sustainability requires that those ecosystems and ecosystem services which are essential to humans be conserved, to an extent that respects *safe minimum standards (SMS)*.

At a local scale, the conversion of a forest to agriculture may be economically and environmentally sustainable, if the ecosystem services required to support the agriculture are maintained. (See *environmental collapse*.) However, if these services are not maintained, for instance if too many ecosystems are depleted in an area prone to *soil erosion*, then the agricultural conversion may be environmentally and therefore economically unsustainable. Environmental sustainability at a global scale includes maintaining the *ecological stability* of the global ecosystem, for instance by limiting the emissions of greenhouse gases to levels which will not lead to catastrophic changes in the climate. See also *sustainability; sustainable development (SD)*.

**environmental systems on small islands** These are mutually dependent ecological subsystems on which economic, social and demographic factors can have a major impact, resulting in serious and *irreversible* degradation if not carefully monitored and addressed.

**environmental taxation** The use of economic, and in particular fiscal, instruments for environmental protection. Taxes are compulsory payments to general government. As defined in OECD (1997) a tax falls into the environmental category 'if the tax base is a physical unit (or a proxy for it) of something which has a proven specific negative impact on the *environment*, when used or released.' This definition addresses the way the tax functions, rather than the reasons for introducing or increasing the tax. A distinction must be made between environmental taxes and environmental charges. Charges are payments made for specific environmental services. Environmental taxation has gained increasing support and a number of practical experiments have taken place in OECD and some developing countries (Ekins, 1999; Serôa da Motta et al, 1999.)

The advantages of environmental taxes are as follows:

- Environmental taxation leads to the internalization of *externalities* into the prices of goods and services which are detrimental to the *environment*, leading to a correction of *market failure* and a shift in consumer behaviour.
- Environmental taxation, like other *market-based instruments (MBIs)*, has an advantage over traditional *command and control (CAC) policy* instruments, in that it enables firms to respond by reducing pollution at least cost (Markandya, 1998a). Taxation policies also negate the need for extensive monitoring of pollution, which may be costly. Thus, particularly for *non-point sources* of pollution, environmental taxes are to be preferred to other instruments (Speck, 1999).
- Environmental taxes may lead to innovation in the productive process, resulting in improvements in *efficiency* and reduced environmental damage.
- Taxation raises revenue, which can be used to reduce the levels of distortional taxation and potentially increase employment (the *double dividend* effect). (O'Riordan, 1997.)

The relative costs and benefits of environmental taxation are often compared in a *partial equilibrium* framework, such as that presented in Figure 7. The value of the internalization of externalities is represented by the area ABCD, while the costs incurred are represented by the area ACD. Hence, a net gain of ABC could be expected. The relative costs and benefits of environmental taxes depend on assumptions regarding the *elasticity of demand* and substitution for

## environmental voluntary agreements

the good being taxed. The potential double dividend from the reduction of distortional taxation (for example labour taxes) is not included in the diagram below, although this would reduce the net costs of the tax policy. However, where the policy reduces the level of consumption of the taxed good to a large extent then the potential for a double dividend falls. *Secondary benefits* may also arise from the implementation of, for instance, *carbon taxes*, where levels of other pollutants will also fall as a result of the tax being introduced.

Potential difficulties may arise in the implementation of environmental taxes in terms of the distributive implications of the environmental tax, or the *equity* issue, and also due to lack of administrative capacity, which may be particularly important in the *enforcement* of such taxes in developing countries.

See also *Pigovian tax; transparency.*

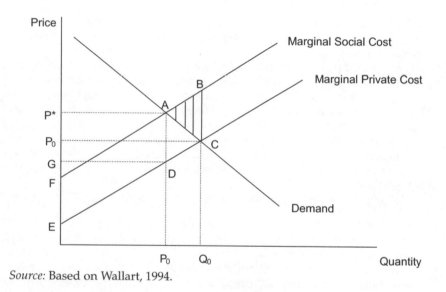

*Source:* Based on Wallart, 1994.

**Figure 7** *Costs and Benefits of Environmental Taxation*

**environmental voluntary agreements** Agreements between private sector businesses or business associations and government environmental authorities which result in businesses undertaking self-regulation in order to meet certain environmental targets. The regulatory frameworks are often established through industry organizations, such as manufacturers' associations. Individual businesses are allowed as far as possible to decide how best to meet the agreed targets. One form of voluntary agreement is the sector-wide covenant; another is the pledge programme which encourages action by individual corporations. Examples of voluntary agreements include energy-savings programmes, pollution prevention programmes, and *eco-labelling* programmes. See also *environmental covenants.*

**environmentally adjusted domestic product** Measure calculated in monetary units by taking the *net domestic product (NDP)* and subtracting a monetary value for all natural resource use and environmental deterioration.

The aim is to arrive at a measure of national welfare which takes account of damage to the natural *environment*. (Krishnan et al, 1995.) See also *environmental accounting; green accounting*.

**epidemiology** The study of the occurrence, distribution and control of disease in a population. In environmental studies it is a key input into *dose–response evaluations and functions* where the link between exposure and health impact is mostly studied by epidemiologists. See also *dose–response valuation technique*.

**equilibrium climate response** The steady-state change in climate which will eventually occur if a given concentration of *greenhouse gases (GHG)* remains in the atmosphere for a sufficiently long period. It takes time to reach this steady state because of lags caused by thermal inertia of the oceans, and other factors. See also *climate change*.

**equity** In broad terms this refers to *justice* or fairness. This concept can be applied both in the present, and over time, where it has particular relevance for the analysis of *sustainable development*. In current terms, equity can be thought of as, for example, fair access to *natural resources* or a trading system which does not systematically discriminate against a particular group. For the purpose of defining SD, equity refers to fairness in the allocation of resources and opportunities between present and future generations. Various interpretations can be given to the *intergenerational equity principle (IEP)*. One of the strictest interpretations is for per capita consumption to be constant over time. This is known as the maximin criterion, after Rawls (1971). Another is for stocks of natural resources to be maintained over time (*strong sustainability*), and a third is for the total (per capita) *capital* stock to be maintained over time (*weak sustainability*). There are serious disagreements as to whether or not these conditions need to hold across all generations, since many economists would argue that the best way to ensure the maximum wellbeing for both current and future generations is to allow the market to allocate resources efficiently rather than imposing limits on their use. Despite this, the notion of equity defined as equality in these terms has broad appeal. Following the *Brundtland Report*, intergenerational equity implies that current generations should manage their *environment* in such a way which future generations have the same (or better) opportunities for using these systems. (Izac and Swift, 1994.)

Equity can also be thought of in terms of the fairness of the tax system. Economists have focused on two principles: *horizontal equity*, which says that individuals who are in identical or similar situations should pay identical or similar taxes; and *vertical equity*, which says that people who are better off should pay more taxes. See also *ethics; maximin principle; discounting*.

**equity principle** Principle that an *economic instrument* should not be significantly regressive, ie the burden should not increase, either in absolute terms or as a proportion of income, as income falls.

**equivalent surplus** In *environmental economics*, equivalent surplus is used to measure the value to an individual of a change in the availability of a pure *public good*, such as the *ozone* layer or air quality. Suppose for example that there is the prospect of a change in an individual's environmental quality. The equivalent surplus is the amount of money that would have to be given to (or taken away from) the individual, in the absence of the environmental change, in order to take her to the level of *utility* at which she would have been had the environmental change taken place. That is, it is equivalent to the environmental change. The distinction between equivalent surplus and *equivalent variation* is that the calculation of equivalent surplus assumes that the individual cannot vary her consumption of the good. That is, it is a pure public good. This measure is thus appropriate for valuing changes in air quality and similar environmental goods. See also *compensating surplus; compensating variation*. (Markandya et al, 2002.)

**equivalent variation** This is a measure of the monetary value of a change in the availability of a good which is not a pure public good. This measure is used to assess projects which result in an increase or decrease in environmental quality. Suppose that a certain project is proposed that will involve an environmental improvement, such as an improvement to a national park. The equivalent variation is calculated as the amount of money which, in the absence of the environmental improvement, would have to be given to the individual in order for him to be as well off as he would have been with the improvement. That is, it is the monetary equivalent, in *utility* terms, of the environmental improvement. The calculation of equivalent variation assumes that the individual can vary his consumption of the good. In this respect it differs from the calculation of *equivalent surplus*. See also *compensating surplus; compensating variation*. (Markandya et al, 2002.)

**erosion effect** Concept whereby imposing an *environmental tax* on final goods causes consumers to switch away from the affected goods. This makes it less likely that the *double dividend* from the taxation will result in an increase in welfare, since the revenue raised may not be sufficient to fully compensate consumers by reducing income taxes. This is because when a consumer switches to another good, her *utility* is reduced relative to her initial position. Because she does not pay the environmental tax, no revenue is gained with which to compensate the utility loss. (O'Riordan, 1997.)

**ethics** A set of moral principles against which behaviour and actions can be measured, and with which issues, including environmental issues, can be analysed. It is important to recognize that the ethical framework on which most economic analysis of the *environment* is based is the utilitarian framework. Let us take as an example the question of the distribution of income and environmental benefits between generations. Under the discounted utilitarian framework, the best outcome is the one which results in the highest level of discounted *utility*. However, this may result in future generations being disadvantaged. Under *Rawlsian ethics* the most desirable outcome is the one which maximizes the position of the least well-off generation. Under this framework, the best solution is a sustainable one, in which future generations are no worse off than the current one.

In the study of environmental issues, it is important to distinguish between two types of ethical frameworks, namely humanist and naturalist moral philosophies. The premise of humanist moral philosophies is that only humans can be assigned rights and be assumed to bear responsibilities. Naturalist moral philosophies on the other hand reject the setting-apart of humans from all other *species*, and hold that rights should not be assigned solely to humans. In this framework values are not defined solely by the consequence which objects have for humans. Rather, natural systems, non-human organisms and non-living objects can have rights as well as *intrinsic value*. (Perman et al, 1999.) See also *bioethical standpoint; environmental ethics; extended rights view; Kantian ethics; libertarian ethics; naturalism; Rawlsian ethics*.

**ethnobotany** The research into the traditional medicines of indigenous peoples. (Swanson, 1994.)

**eutrophication** This is a natural process in bodies of freshwater which can be hastened by the introduction of man-made inputs. Eutrophic bodies of water are those which have a high nutrient content and therefore a high biological productivity. This increases the uptake of oxygen, reducing the oxygen content of the water. (See *biochemical oxygen demand*.) By-products of the high levels of biological activity include animal waste and dead bodies; these accumulate in the water, reducing its depth and promoting the invasion of the water by reeds and shrubs.

    The process of eutrophication is accelerated by the introduction of nutrients into water by humans. The main processes by which humans introduce nutrients to water are in the disposal of sewage and the leaching of animal slurry and chemical fertilizers from agricultural land. Thus, eutrophication tends to be a problem in industrialized countries and those with high concentrations of arable agriculture. An area in which the effects of eutrophication are well documented is England's Norfolk Broads, where many of the lakes are now virtually dead.

    Levels of eutrophication can be reduced by treating (including removing phosphates from) domestic sewage, reducing the levels of phosphates in cleaning products, and by reducing the use of inorganic fertilizers. Eutrophicated waters can also be restored and protected from future damage. (Pope et al, 1991.)

**evolutionary ecology** This discipline studies the ultimate causes of evolution – the historical reasons why natural selection has favoured the particular adaptations we now see. (Barbier, 1989.)

**excludability** A situation where the consumption of a good is restricted to certain people, such as those willing to pay for the good. An example of such a good is satellite television. Television broadcasts have the characteristics of *public goods*, in that one person's consumption of the good does not reduce its availability for other people. However, it is possible to exclude those not willing to pay for the good by coding the transmissions so that they can be received only by those willing to pay for the appropriate equipment. Improved air quality, on the other hand, is not excludable. The absence of excludability is one of the features of public goods. (Schotter, 1997.)

**exhaustible resources** This term is used to mean resources whose extraction and productive use inevitably results in a permanent reduction of their in situ stock. There are several important *natural resources* which are exhaustible in this sense, in particular minerals such as iron, copper and other metals and energy resources such as oil and gas. More recently in the literature the term *non-renewable* has been used interchangeably with exhaustible. This is to distinguish the types of resources mentioned from renewable resources such as forests which can also be exhausted, but which can be regenerated unlike

## existence value

non-renewable resources. (Robinson, 1989.) See also *natural resources, Hartwick rule*.

**existence value** This is a type of *non-use value*. The argument behind existence value is that people care about the *environment* not only because they, or their heirs, can get some benefit by using or preserving environmental assets. People wish to maintain or improve environmental assets for their own sake. The motivation behind this wish may be sympathy for animals and nature or moral conviction. There is therefore an *intrinsic value*, 'a value that resides "in" something and that is unrelated to human beings altogether'. Existence value is part of the *total economic value* of a resource. (Pearce and Turner, 1990; p135.)

**exogenous variable** A variable whose value is predetermined and introduced into a model or set of equations, rather than being determined within the model. See also *endogenous variable*.

**expected utility** This refers to the different, and identifiable, levels of *utility* an individual may enjoy under different circumstances. For instance, a person who has booked a seaside holiday will derive a certain level of utility (say, $U_S$) from the holiday if the weather is sunny and another, presumably lower, level of utility ($U_R$) from the holiday if it rains. The utility which the individual expects from the holiday can be calculated if $U_S$, $U_R$ and the probability of sunny weather, $P_S$, are known. This is related to the concept of *risk*, since $(1 - P_S)$ is the risk of rain. The expected utility of the holiday, assuming that the weather will be either sunny or wet, is:

$$EU = P_S U_S + (1 - P_S) U_R$$

That is, the utilities associated with each set of circumstances are weighted by the probability of that set of circumstances arising. See also *expected value (EV), risk*.

**expected value (EV)** Expected value can be calculated where a situation has an uncertain outcome and the possible outcomes can be assigned probabilities. For example if the set of possible outcomes is {−5, +5 and +10} and the probabilities attached to each outcome are, respectively, 0.1, 0.3 and 0.6, then the EV is:

$$0.1(-5) + 0.3(5) + 0.6(10) = +7.$$

The EV approach is useful in predicting the expected outcome of situations involving *risk*. However, it is less useful as a tool for decision making, since it does not account for the fact that the value of a unit of consumption gained may be lower than the negative value of a unit of consumption lost. In fact, individuals and societies are usually assumed to place more weight on a loss than they attach to a gain of the same size. This is known as *loss aversion*. Moreover, more weight is often attached to losses from certain types of risk. For instance, the negative weight which people place on the *risk* of nuclear accidents is so great that huge resources are devoted to avoiding nuclear accidents. This means that the expected loss of life from nuclear accidents is much lower than the expected loss from other, less dreaded, risks such as car accidents. See also *expected utility*.

**exposure assessment** Part of *health risk assessment*, this quantifies the uptake of xenobiotics from the *environment* by any combination of oral, inhalation and dermal routes of exposure. (Paustenbach, 1995.)

**exposure–response functions** See *dose–response evaluations and functions.*

**extended benefit–cost analysis** Extended benefit–cost analysis uses the framework provided by *benefit–cost analysis (BCA)*, but includes external impacts, or *externalities*, in the analysis. Thus, using *valuation* techniques, such as the *contingent valuation method (CVM)*, the external impacts of a decision are implicitly included in the estimation of the returns from a project. Perman et al (1999) present a framework for the inclusion of such external impacts into the project appraisal decision, calling this environmental cost–benefit analysis, which is essentially the same concept. Under this framework, *external costs* are considered side by side with the financial costs and benefits associated with a project, using the *net present value (NPV)* concept to measure the merits of a project. The NPV calculated under such a framework is in essence the same as that used under conventional benefit–cost analysis, although it includes a factor for the discounted environmental (or external) cost associated with the project. Using the decision rule that a project should proceed if its NPV is greater than zero, the project should proceed if the present value of external costs is less than the discounted net financial benefit from the project. (Perman et al, 1999.) See also *judgemental benefit–cost framework.*

**extended rationality** This represents an extension to the standard framework of rationality usually used in economic analysis. Many social scientists criticize this *neoclassical economic* framework of self-interested rationality, arguing that it is easy to think of examples of purely altruistic behaviour, and therefore that an extended framework of rationality is required to account for this. It is possible to think of extended rationality as an expression of an individual's social priorities, which exist alongside his or her self-interested priorities. This can then be used as a moral framework with which to judge actions and motives. Under such a framework, for instance, altruistic actions and motives could be judged to be morally superior to those based on self-interest. One manifestation of a social, as opposed to individualistic, priority is the case in which groups of individuals, or societies, are willing to hold assets in common rather than attempting to allocate ownership to individuals. Extended rationality can, given its moral connotations, generate obligations on the part of the individual to abide by social norms and laws, which, while they may not be in his or her immediate self-interest, can be seen as promoting his/her broader social preferences and priorities. (Pearce and Turner, 1990.)

**extended rights view** This view is part of the framework of naturalist moral philosophy. This view holds that moral interests, including rights, can be held by non-human beings, and that non-human beings have value in and of themselves, that is, they have *intrinsic value*. This is in contrast to the humanist moral framework, in which rights and responsibilities are held solely by humans, and values are determined solely with reference to humans. See *ethics; environmental ethics.*

**extended and shared responsibility** This refers to producer responsibility for environmental impacts throughout a product's life cycle. This responsibility

## extended stewardship ideology

involves accounting for the environmental impacts of the supply of inputs to production, and the environmental impacts of the use and disposal of the product. (OECD, 1998.)

**extended stewardship ideology** The view that humans should act as nature's stewards and practise careful husbandry of *natural resources*, for their own sakes and to protect the interests of other creatures. (Pearce and Turner, 1990.) See also *stewardship ethic; ethics; environmental ethics.*

**external cost** The difference between private and *social costs*. See also *externalities.*

**external diseconomies** The damages suffered by the party affected by an *externality* problem. (Tietenberg, 1996.)

**externalities** An externality arises when the actions of an individual, firm or community affect the welfare of other individuals, firms or communities. For this effect to be defined as an externality, the agent responsible must not take account of the effect that it has on the other party. Externalities reflect the fact that social and private costs and benefits often do not coincide, so that an action which benefits an individual or firm may harm society in general. For instance, it may be in the commercial interest of a farmer or forestry company to reduce the *biodiversity* in an *ecosystem*, but this imposes an external *social cost*, or externality. Likewise, hillside *deforestation* may increase *soil erosion* and the sedimentation of streams, which may constitute an *external cost* to downstream farmers.

The most commonly used mechanism for ensuring that individuals and organizations account for the effects of their actions is the market. For example an upstream firm generating waste into a river may affect a downstream firm. In the absence of a market mechanism corresponding to this externality, the upstream firm will not be obliged to take account of its consequences for the downstream firm. If such a mechanism were to exist, for instance if the upstream firm were to be charged for its emissions into the river, then this firm would be forced to effectively take account of the costs of its actions for the other firm. When an activity causing an externality has been corrected to the point at which *economic efficiency* has been attained we say that the externality has been internalized.

Externalities may be positive or negative. Environmental pollution is a classic case of a negative public externality which affects a variety of economic activities including industry, fisheries, tourism and urban development, as well as the general quality of life. Positive externalities are fewer but are nevertheless important. An example of a positive externality is the pleasure which neighbours derive from looking at a particularly well-kept garden. A commercial example of a positive externality is the watershed benefit which accrues to farmers from the sound management of upstream forests.

Much of *environmental economics* is concerned with *valuation* of externalities in order that they may be internalized. Methods for doing so include the productivity method, *hedonic pricing*, the *travel cost method (TCM)* and the *contingent valuation method (CVM)* (Markandya et al, 2002; Perman et al, 1999). For a review of the externalities arising from electricity generation and an attempt at valuing these see ExternE (1999). See also *consumption externality; production externality; extended benefit–cost analysis; economic instruments.*

**extinction of species** Extinction occurs when the population of a *species* falls below the level that is viable for reproduction, and the species ceases to exist. Species loss happens naturally, as more successful species take over the habitat of, or hunt to extinction, less successful ones. However, natural levels of species loss are dwarfed by those attributable to human activity. Rates of species loss are estimated in the Global *Biodiversity* Assessment, published by UNEP, to be 50 to 100 times the natural rate. Humans cause species loss in two major ways. The first is by hunting species to extinction. This is particularly likely to happen if harvesting of a species, such as the blue whale, is subject to *open access*. Hunting has been the cause of the extinction or endangerment of many large, high-profile species, but the majority of species are lost due to the loss of their habitat, which is often converted from species-rich land such as forest land or wetland, to agricultural or urban land. (Swanson, 1994.) See also *open access, tragedy of the commons*.

**extraction costs** The costs of removing *natural resources*, for example coal, from the ground. Whether these costs rise or fall over time depends on the relative strengths of two effects, namely the cost-increasing effect of the depletion of more easily accessible stocks, and cost-decreasing *technical progress*.

**extractive reserve strategy, forest management** This is a strategy which attempts to protect the indigenous people of the forest and to prevent *deforestation*. It involves the establishment of extractive reserves, which are reserved for the use of indigenous people to engage in traditional hunting and gathering activities. This restriction of access to the resources thus prevents deforestation. (Tietenberg, 1996.) See also *environmental management*.

# Ff

---

**fabric filter** A cloth filter that extracts dust particles from industrial emissions. (Luken, 1990.)

**factor four/factor ten clubs** A movement of economists and environmentalists who argue that the intensity of material and energy use in industrialized countries should be reduced by a factor of four or ten by about 2025–40, in order to reduce environmental damage to within acceptable levels while allowing for continued *economic growth*. (OECD, 1998; O'Riordan, 1997.) See also *thirty-per-cent club*.

**factors of production** The factors with which the production of goods and services is undertaken. The factors of production that are commonly identified are: *capital*, labour, land and raw materials. (Perman et al, 1999.)

**fair trade** The notion that trade should be to the advantage of all participating parties and in particular that trade relationships should not be exploitative. The two major issues encompassed by fair trade are the prices paid to small independent producers, and the wages and working conditions of employees.
There are two major ways in which the issue of fair trade is promoted. The first is by means of fair trade labels, such as Traidcraft in the UK. Such labels perform a role in promoting social issues similar to that played by *eco-labelling* in promoting environmental concerns. Consumers know that by purchasing such goods they are supporting a trading system that meets certain minimum criteria of fairness. The second means by which fair trade issues are promoted is the more general creation of consumer awareness. Increasing concern in developed countries in recent years has led to demands by consumers for information about the means by which the goods that they purchase were produced – whether or not they involved sweated labour or child labour, and whether workers are paid a fair wage. The possibility of consumer boycotts when the information received regarding these issues is not satisfactory acts as a pressure on companies to increase standards. The criteria of a fair trade commitment are:

- paying a fair wage in the local context;
- providing equal opportunities for all people, with particular attention to the opportunities of the most disadvantaged;
- engaging in environmentally sustainable practices;
- building long-term trade relationships;
- providing healthy and safe working conditions; and
- providing financial and technical assistance to workers whenever possible.

Source: Institute for Global Communications, undated.

**feedback loops** Positive feedback loops are those in which a secondary effect, which follows as a result of a primary effect, reinforces the trend brought about by the original factor. Examples of this are the positive feedback effects between *capital* accumulation and *economic growth*. An increase in investment causes an increase in output, which in turn generates increased profits. Part of these increased profits will be reinvested, reinforcing the effect of the original increase in investment.

Negative feedback loops are those in which a secondary effect, which follows as a result of a primary effect, counters the trend brought about by the primary effect. Thus, negative feedback loops are self-limiting rather than self-reinforcing. An example of a negative feedback loop is the relationship between population growth and death rate. As population growth occurs, the resources required to support human life often become inadequate. This causes disease and starvation, in turn causing an increase in death rate, which retards population growth. From this example, it can be seen that negative feedback loops can provide a tempering influence on the population growth process, although not, in this case, a desirable one. (Tietenberg, 1996.) See also *basic pessimist model*.

**fertility rate** The crude fertility rate is the average number of live births per 1000 people in a population.

**First Law of Thermodynamics** This law states that in a *closed system* the total quantity of energy and matter remains constant. For example, if a piece of wood is burnt in a closed system, the result is ash, escaped gases and heat. However, the total amount of energy and matter in the system is unchanged. See also *Second Law of Thermodynamics*.

**fiscally neutral** A policy instrument is fiscally neutral if the net revenue to the exchequer is zero. Thus, an *environmental tax* can be made fiscally neutral by redistributing the resulting revenue, for instance by reducing taxes on labour and profits. (Turner et al, 1994.)

**fixed standard approach** The fixed standard approach sets an *emission standard* that each firm must meet. The advantage of this approach over those employing *economic instruments* is that it is easier to administer. The role of economic analysis in this approach is in identifying the most cost-effective way for each firm to meet its target reduction. This approach is in contrast to the economic approach to setting environmental standards. The economic approach is to place a tax, or charge, on the emission of pollutants equal to the *marginal damage* caused by the pollutant at the efficient level of emissions. This allows firms to reduce pollution to the extent to which it is cost effective for them to do so, so that each will reduce pollution up to the point at which the unit cost of doing so reaches the level of the tax. This results in the firms that can reduce pollution most cheaply undertaking the highest reductions, so that a given aggregate reduction in emissions is achieved at the lowest total cost. (Pearce and Turner, 1990.) See also *ambient-based standards; command and control (CAC) policies; emissions standards; direct regulation; regulation; quantitative controls; standard setting*.

**flip-flop changes** This type of change is characteristic of linear programming models, and is typified by a situation in which a moderate change in the relative prices of two goods, such as wheat and beef, could cause a wholesale shift in production from one to the other. This is the most extreme example of

**flow conditionality**

a flip-flop change; in less extreme cases a change in relative prices might induce a significant change in the mix of activities. (Dixon et al, 1989.)

**flow conditionality** This is a form of trade restriction designed to promote *sustainability* of resource stocks and of *biodiversity*. The condition would restrict the amount of a natural resource that could be purchased by a given individual or firm to the amount that could be sustainably produced by the supplier. (Swanson, 1994.)

**flue gas desulphurization** A technology that usually uses lime or limestone to remove sulphur dioxide ($SO_2$) from the emissions produced by fossil fuel combustion.

**fly ash** Non-combustible particles which remain after the combustion process, carried by flue gas.

**fly tipping** The illegal dumping of waste, usually in order to avoid paying *charges* for designated waste disposal sites. (Manser, 1993.)

**food species** Food *species* can be defined as species of plants and animals that are edible by humans. There are thousands of plant species that are deemed edible and that could form part of the human diet. However, the vast majority of the world's food is now produced by only 20 of these species, on which humans have thus become reliant for their sustenance. A substantial number of the other edible species are now endangered. (Swanson, 1994.) See also *biodiversity*.

**forest economy** A forest economy consists of the management of the forest for timber, for the grazing of animals and for non-timber products such as game, fruits, mushrooms and so on, either for domestic consumption or for sale. A *sustainable* forest economy is one in which the forest and all of its components are conserved, and are not exploited at a rate faster than that at which they can regenerate. See also *afforestation; deforestation*.

**Framework Convention on Climate Change (FCCC)** This *convention* went into force on 21 March 1994. Reducing *carbon dioxide (CO₂)* emissions to 1990 levels by the end of the decade was specified as a voluntary target within the convention. The convention identifies a set of nations (listed in Annex I) committed to achieving a stabilization of $CO_2$ emissions by 2000. Other nations have subscribed to the general principles of the convention, but are not on the list of nations committed to meeting the stabilization target. See also *climate change; Kyoto Protocol*.

**free rider problem** In the context of negotiations to reduce environmental damage, the free rider problem is the problem of persuading individuals, firms or countries to reveal their true preferences, or *willingness to pay (WTP)* for environmental improvements. By understating the benefit that they would receive from an environmental improvement, a free rider would hope to benefit from an improvement that is largely paid for by others. See also *free riding; international environmental agreements*.

**free riding** In the context of negotiations to reduce pollution, a free rider is defined as an individual, firm or country which benefits from the actions of others in reducing emissions without either compensating the others for the costs they incur in reducing emissions, or reducing their own emissions. In the context of *climate change*, a free-riding country would be one which does not agree to limit its own emissions but that enjoys the benefits of *mitigated* climate change which result from the reduced emissions of other countries.

The incentive to free ride is particularly strong where the benefits of reduced environmental damage are largely external to the individual, firm or country which bears the cost of actions to reduce the damage. This is an example of the problem of *externalities*. See also *international environmental agreements*.

**fuel cycle** A chain of activities by which a fuel or other resource is used to generate electric power. (Hohmeyer et al, 1997.)

**full-cost pricing principle** The principle that the financial costs of production and consumption should reflect their full *social cost*, specifically including their cost to the *environment*.

**full cost resource pricing** This would require that the services of *environmental resources* be paid for in full in order to avoid the inefficient and unsustainable use of those resources. This means, for example, that rather than waste being discharged without cost into the atmosphere, onto land and into water, the waste assimilation services of these *natural resources* would be priced and charged for.

In order for the prices to ensure sustainable as well as efficient use of natural resources, the prices would have to reflect the costs of meeting sustainable environmental standards. Thus, if aggregate emissions were to be limited to within the *assimilative capacity* of natural *ecosystems* in order to avoid the degradation of those systems, the price charged for emissions would be such that, in aggregate, polluters would have an incentive to reduce pollution to below the environment's assimilative capacity. (OECD, 1994c.)

**functional obsolescence** This occurs when a new product can perform a function better or more efficiently that an existing product. Tietenberg (1994) provides an example of the vacuum tube, which became functionally obsolescent when the transistor replaced it. Functional obsolescence is the consequence of the successful search for better products. See also *planned obsolescence*.

**fund pollutants** These are pollutants which can be absorbed and/or recycled by the *environment* up to a certain limit, known as the *absorptive capacity*. Beyond this limit, the pollutant will accumulate in the environment. An example of a fund pollutant is *carbon dioxide ($CO_2$)*. (Tietenberg, 1996.) See also *assimilative capacity; carrying capacity*.

**funds** See *environmental funds*.

**futures markets** A futures contract is a legally binding agreement to deliver or supply a commodity or financial instrument at a specified date in the future. A futures market, or exchange, is thus a market in which such contracts are agreed, which allows the contracts to be re-traded over time. A futures contract will specify the quantity and quality of the commodity as well as the price at which it will be exchanged. Although futures contracts involve an obligation to deliver an instrument or commodity, individual investors can avoid delivery by offsetting purchase deals against sales deals.

## futures markets

Futures contracts provide the prospect of high rates of return; investors who agree to purchase a commodity in a futures contract are in effect betting that the price specified in the contract is lower than the market price of the commodity at the specified time. Likewise, investors who agree to sell a commodity in the future will hope that the price specified in the contract is higher than the market price at the specified time. Futures contracts clearly involve considerable *risks*. (Howells and Bain, 1994.)

# Gg

**Gaia hypothesis** The Gaia hypothesis, named after the Greek for 'Earth goddess', is the notion that the world is a self-equilibrating organism with an internal feedback system that will correct deviations from the optimal ecological state. This contradicts fears that human activities are having a persistent, negative effect on global *ecosystems*. (Tietenberg, 1996.)

**game fish** Game fish are thought of as those which provide sport for the angler, in that they fight when hooked. Game fish commonly refers to fish of the Salmonidae family, which includes salmon, trout, char and whitefish. All other types of freshwater fish are known as coarse fish.

**game theory** Game theory permits analysis of the choices of individuals, firms or countries, known as 'players' in situations in which the outcome of a decision by one player depends on the decisions of other players. Thus, the anticipated decisions of other players will affect the initial decision of each player. Game theory is particularly relevant in situations where legal regulation cannot be used to ensure that the maximum benefit to all players is achieved.

An example of game theory in *environmental economics* is in the analysis of *international environmental agreements* on the reduction of *greenhouse gas (GHG)* emissions. Legal regulation to force countries to reduce emissions to the socially efficient level is not possible in the absence of international government. The analysis in the economic literature of agreements by individual countries to reduce emissions for global rather than national benefits has relied to a large extent on game theory. (Perman et al, 1999.) See also *international environmental agreements; cooperative solutions; non-cooperation; chain-store paradox.*

**GATT and the environment** See *WTO and the Environment.*

**gender-related development index** The gender-related development index (GDI) measures achievements in the same dimensions and variables as the *human development index (HDI),* but captures inequalities in achievement between women and men. It is simply the HDI adjusted downward for gender inequality. The greater the gender disparity in basic human development, the lower a country's GDI compared with its HDI. (UNDP, 1999.) See also *human poverty index.*

**general circulation models (GCMs)** Complex climate models used to estimate the likely impacts of different scenarios for *greenhouse gas (GHG)* emissions and the associated *climate change.* These are based on mathematical representations of the known atmospheric, oceanic and terrestrial processes. GCM-based scenarios are the most credible models to date. These models, however, have yielded a wide range of different scenarios for temperature changes and precipitation levels induced by increased concentrations of greenhouse gases. Thus, *climate change impact assessments* based on GCMs should be treated with caution. (IPCC, 1998.)

**general equilibrium analysis** In economic analysis, the effect of a policy change, such as the increase in a tax on a good, is often analysed using *partial equilibrium analysis*, which means that the effects on prices and quantities of all goods other than the one (or more) of immediate interest are 'assumed away'. General equilibrium analysis, by contrast, involves modelling an entire economy, assuming that markets exist for all goods and services and that these markets clear, so that the effects of a change on the prices and quantities of all goods can be observed. The large information and resource requirements of full general equilibrium analysis means that it is seldom performed. (Perman et al, 1999.)

**genes** Genes determine the particular characteristics of a given organism, including the functions that it performs. They contain the information that is used in the reproductive process to produce a new organism. Genes are one level on which *biodiversity* can be measured; the greater the variety of genes in a given *ecosystem*, the greater the diversity of *species* and the functions that they perform. This, other things being equal, will tend to make an ecosystem more stable. (Swanson, 1994.)

**genetic diversity** See *biodiversity*.

**genetic modification** The scientific process of taking *genes* that represent desirable characteristics from one organism, and introducing them into the genetic make-up of another organism in order to make a new product. The desirable characteristics introduced to plants using this technique include resistance to pesticides and herbicides, and delayed ripening that allows produce to be shipped further. In the case of animals, the characteristics include the introduction of genes which cause animal flesh to be more lean, and genes which cause animals to develop and mature more quickly. While genetic modification has so far concentrated on plants and animals, research has begun on altering the characteristics of bacteria and microbes.

   The process of genetic modification is controversial for a number of reasons. On the one hand, the *biotechnology* companies who develop genetically modified organisms (GMOs) claim that they will lead to the increased food supplies which are required to solve the world's problems of food shortages. However, environmental activists complain that use of genetically modified crops can lead to increased pesticide use and associated environmental problems, and that it is possible that GMOs may cross-pollinate with wild plants, releasing foreign genes into *ecosystem*s with unknown consequences. Genetically modified crops are often developed to be sterile, meaning that farmers are obliged to buy their seed corn each year, increasing both farmers' costs and their dependency on seed companies. This is enforced by the application of *intellectual property rights* to newly developed GMOs. See also *cell fusion*.

**genuine saving index** An index that adjusts the conventional measure of an economy's net savings and investment, ie gross investment minus the *depreciation* on existing *capital* stocks, for changes in the economy's stock of *natural capital*. This extended measure is intended to reflect more accurately the effect of an economy's current activities on its future wellbeing, and to underline the fact that the assets of a resource-depleting economy are decreasing in value over time unless the economy invests at least the value of depleted natural resource stocks in an alternative form of capital. The development of this measure is related to the failure of the standard national accounting framework to account for the value of depleted natural resource stocks, and the development of *green national accounting*.

The genuine savings index is calculated as follows:

$$GS = I - D_M - D_N$$

Where, *GS* is genuine saving, *I* is investment in *human-made capital*, $D_M$ is depreciation of man-made capital and $D_N$ is depreciation of natural capital, which can be positive in the case of renewable resources. (World Bank, 1995.) See also *constant economic value; constant capital rule; weak sustainability*.

**geothermal energy** 'Geothermal' means of or relating to the Earth's interior heat. Thus, geothermal energy is energy which is captured from the Earth's interior heat and either used directly, eg to heat buildings, or transformed into electricity. There are three means by which hydrothermal fluids (steam and hot water) are converted into electricity. Steam is used to directly drive turbines which power generators. High-temperature water can be converted into steam by spraying it onto a low-temperature surface; it is then used to drive turbines. Lower-temperature water (below 200° Celsius) is used to convert a secondary fluid to steam which is again used to drive turbines. Steam resources represent the easiest means by which to convert geothermal energy to electricity, but they are relatively rare. The geysers in Northern California are the biggest single source of geothermal power. However, hot-water plants are more common, and account for most of the world's geothermal power.

**gift values** Gift values are used to explain part of the *total economic value* of a natural asset. They are very similar to *bequest values* but the recipient of a gift tends to be a current person, for example a relative, rather than a future person, and is more likely to directly use the asset than in the case of a bequest. Therefore gift value is thought of as being an aspect of use value that is altruistic in origin, rather than being part of existence value. (Pearce and Turner, 1990.)

**global commons** *Natural resources* that are shared as *common property* by all nations. Examples of assets that comprise the global commons are the Earth's atmosphere, the stratosphere and the world's oceans. (Pearce and Turner, 1990.) See also *tragedy of the commons*.

**global conversion process** This is the process by which *extinctions* result from a failure to invest in the *conservation* of *species*, and the conversion of biologically diverse habitats to more uniform, but more economically productive, states. There are two major reasons for *disinvestment* in a species. The first is if the species is valuable but its growth rate is too low for it to be profitably held as a stock. In this case the species may be exploited to the point of extinction. The second is if the species is not sufficiently valuable for resources to be devoted to its conservation. The process of disinvestment in species at a global level represents one of the major factors behind the loss of *biodiversity*. (Swanson, 1994.) See also *asset conversion; biogeography; enclosure; opportunity cost*.

**global environmental conventions** See *conventions*.

## Global Environmental Facility

**Global Environmental Facility** The Global Environmental Facility (GEF) is a financial body, funded jointly by UNDP, UNEP and the World Bank, that provides grants to support projects in developing countries which help to address environmental problems of a global nature. The four main global environmental problems towards which GEF funding is targeted are: *biodiversity loss*, global *climate change*, pollution of international waters and depletion of the *ozone* layer.

One of the major problems in *internalizing* the *total economic value* of natural assets into the decision-making process is that many of these values are global rather than local. For these values to be accounted for, the value must be appropriated in some way. The GEF is designed in part to provide international subsidy for the *conservation* of global environmental goods. See also *global premium concept*. (See the GEF website for further details: http://www.gefweb.org/).

**global premium concept** The global premium represents the financial equivalent of the *global values* of the natural assets held by individual countries. *CITES* has called for the global premium of natural assets to be paid in the form of *subsidies* to investments in diverse resources which represent the value of the non-appropriable services they render. This system would, by compensating developing countries that are rich in globally valuable natural assets for development opportunities foregone, create the possibility of *alternative development paths* that do not involve the wholesale loss of biologically diverse habitats. (Swanson, 1994.)

**global public goods** *Public goods* have the characteristics of being non-rival in consumption (which mean the consumption of the good by one individual or group does not reduce its availability to others) and non-excludable (which means that no individual or group can be prevented from consuming the good). Some global environmental assets can be described as global public goods, since some of the benefits they provide are non-rival and are global in nature. The global *non-use values* provided by *biodiversity* make it a global public good.

The problem with the efficient use of global public goods is that, while the costs of preserving the assets are borne by the country in which the assets are found, many of their benefits accrue to the citizens of other nations. Thus, the countries in which global public goods are found do not have an incentive to preserve as much of the goods as would be globally efficient. This problem could be resolved by the implementation of, for example, the *global premium*. (Turner et al, 1994.) See also *global premium concept; free rider problem; free riding; tragedy of the commons*.

**global values** See *global public goods*.

**global warming** See *climate change*.

**government failure** There are two main types of government failure. The first occurs when a government fails to correct a distortion which arises due to *market failures* such as environmental externalities. The second occurs when the actions of a government have a distortionary effect in themselves. An example of this is the widespread provision of *subsidies* for the exploitation of timber resources. The fact that forests and the *biodiversity* that they contain have non-market values means that there is already a market failure, since these values are not accounted for in economic decisions. A subsidy to forestry *conservation* would be required to internalize these external values. A subsidy for *deforestation* worsens the misallocation of resources.

Thus, a failure in policy is said to occur when the policy interventions necessary to correct *market failures* are not taken. It also arises when government decisions or policies are themselves responsible for worsening market failures. See also *institutional failure*.

**grandfathering** A system of *marketable emissions permits* requires an initial distribution of pollution rights, the total number of permits being equal to the desired level of pollution under the scheme. A system of grandfathering is one by which pollution permits are distributed to polluters in proportion to their emissions at an agreed date. An alternative system would be the auctioning of pollution permits. (Hanley et al, 1997.) See also *permit allocation*.

**green accounting** Green accounting is the form of *environmental accounting* most closely related to the measures of *gross domestic product (GDP)* and *gross national product (GNP)* under the standard system of national accounts *(SNA)*. Green accounting involves including the value of the negative side effects of economic activity, in particular those of environmental pollution, in the measure of economic progress. It also involves deducting from the measure of net investment the value of depleted natural resource stocks. Pioneering green accounting studies include Repetto et al (1989).

There are two main uses for the information gathered on the welfare effects of environmental pollution and the value of depleted *natural resources*. The first is in the adjustment of GDP to provide an alternative measure of green national income, ie a measure of *green net national product*. However, this has been criticized by official statisticians as having limited policy relevance. The preferred use for economic–environmental information is the compilation of *satellite accounts*, in particular the construction of pollution emissions accounts, which appear to have the most direct policy relevance. Green accounting is still in its relative infancy. Dramatic progress has been made in gathering reliable data and in compiling these data into policy-relevant indicators; see for example Markandya and Pavan (1999). See also *environmental accounting; environmentally adjusted domestic product; green net national product*.

**green belt** An area of land between a city or town and the countryside which is designed to limit the encroachment of urban areas onto rural land. A green belt is designated by the local planning authority, and acts as a *buffer zone* between an urban area and the countryside. Development on the green belt itself is restricted, resulting in very high values of existing developments. (Malcolm, 1994.)

**green consumerism** Consumer behaviour that favours products whose production or transportation is relatively environmentally friendly, and avoids products that are perceived to damage the *environment*. Green consumerism can be organized or ad hoc, but requires consumers to be aware of the relative environmental merits of products. The ultimate aim of green consumerism is to use economic power to encourage firms to improve the environmental performance of their production. See also *eco-labelling, ecological consumerism, environmental product declaration*.

**green national accounts** See *green accounting*.

**green labelling** see *eco-labelling*.

**green net national product** An adjusted *NNP* that includes environmental costs, and the net change in all assets, including *natural resources*. See also *green accounting; environmental accounting; net national product*.

**greenhouse effect** See *climate change*.

**greenhouse gases** See *climate change*.

**grey list** One of three classifications under the *Oslo Convention* for the Prevention of Marine Pollution by Dumping from Ships and Aircraft. Under the Oslo Convention pollutants were classified according to toxicity under the headings *black list*, grey list and *white list*. The grey list forms the middle category, representing less harmful substances. Under Article 6 of the convention, the dumping at sea of grey list materials requires a permit from the national authority, which will be granted subject to consideration of the similar substances that could already be present. Disposal in deep water is required for the substances on the grey list, which means a depth of at least 2000 metres and a distance from land of at least 150 nautical miles. Grey list substances are:

- arsenic, lead, copper, zinc and their compounds, cyanides and fluorides, and pesticides and their by-products not covered by the provisions of Annex I;
- containers, scrap metal, tar-like substances liable to sink to the sea bottom, and other bulky wastes which may present a serious obstacle to fishing or navigation; and
- substances which, although non-toxic, may become harmful in large quantities, or which are liable to seriously reduce the amenity value of beaches and so on.

(Leeson, 1995.)

**gross domestic product (GDP)** The total output, or value added, from economic activity within a country's borders, whether or not it is undertaken by nationals of that country, but excluding production by citizens working abroad. Gross domestic product (GDP) is thus a gross measure of economic activity and does not account for the extent to which *capital* assets depreciate. In order that the measure of economic activity should reflect more accurately the net contribution of current economic activity to the value of the economy, the UN Statistical Office recommends that countries estimate *net domestic product (NDP)*, by deducting from GDP the value of *depreciation*. GDP is distinct from *gross national product (GNP)*, which is the total value added by economic activity of citizens of the country in question, whether the activity takes place within the country's borders or not. (Young, 1992.) See also *environmental accounting, green accounting*.

**gross national product (GNP)** A country's GNP is the total output, or value added, by economic activity of the citizens of that country, whether the activity takes place within the country or not. GNP is a gross measure of economic activity, as it does not account for *capital depreciation. Net national product,* which deducts the value of capital depreciation from GNP, is thus a more accurate measure of the net contribution of current economic activity to the value of the economy. GNP is distinct from *gross domestic product (GDP)*, which measures the value added by economic activity within a country's borders. See also *environmental accounting; green accounting*.

**groundwater** Groundwater collects in porous layers of underground rock known as *aquifers*. Though some groundwater is renewed by percolation of rain or melted snow, most was accumulated over geological time and, because of its location, cannot be recharged once it is depleted. Groundwater is a source of drinking water, which makes its *conservation* and protection from pollution important.

# Hh

**Hartwick rule** This is the original rule for *sustainability* and the extraction of *non-renewable resources*. The rule states that for sustainability 'an economy should invest the *resource rents*, or *Hotelling rents*, from resource extraction'. Hartwick (1977) developed the rule, building on the work of Robert Solow. Solow (1974) demonstrated the theoretical existence of a constant consumption path for a closed economy depleting a non-renewable resource and combining it with man-made *capital*. Hartwick developed the rule for sustainable consumption by demonstrating that along the constant consumption path, the amount that the economy must invest is equal to resource rents. This is essentially a *constant capital rule*, or *constant economic value rule*, and is related to the *genuine savings index*.

   The Hartwick rule has been criticized by economists of the *ecological economics* school because it assumes that human-made capital can be a substitute for natural resources in production. They argue that human-made capital and *natural resources* are more often complements in production, and therefore that the rule is impractical.

**hazard identification** The first and most easily recognized step in *risk assessment (RA)*. It is the process of determining whether exposure to an agent could (at any dose) cause an increase in adverse health effects on humans or wildlife. (Paustenbach, 1995.)

**hazardous air pollutants** A term used in the US Clean Air Act to describe *air pollutants* that are not covered by *ambient air* quality standards, but which may reasonably be expected to cause or contribute to illness or death. (Luken, 1990.)

**hazardous substances and hazardous wastes** These are inputs to production, products, and by-products that pose *risks* to human health and natural systems. Such risks are associated with a very wide range of substances, including infectious, radioactive, flammable, carcinogenic, mutagenic (mutation-causing), climate-changing, and polluting agents. Hazardous substances can present either short-term acute hazards or long-term environmental hazards. Wastes may arise as by-products, process residues, spent reaction media, contaminated plant or equipment from either manufacturing operations or the treatment of toxic substances, and from the disposal of manufactured products. Whether or not a substance is regarded as unacceptably hazardous depends in part on the environmental functions that are regarded as being sufficiently important to protect. Therefore, classifications of hazardous substances vary.

**health risk assessment** A distinct branch of *risk assessment* that uses data from human *epidemiology* studies and animal studies, together with information on the degree of exposure to relevant health *risk* factors, to predict the probability of a particular health problem manifesting itself in a human population. Toxicology data has been used to predict health risks by the US Food and

Drug Administration (FDA), among others, for 40 years. In the last 20 years, however, the use of *exposure assessment* has been incorporated into the analysis.

These more advanced, quantitative methods of health risk assessment have been behind the setting of health and environmental standards since 1980, including allowable levels of pesticide residues and food additives, and the quality of drinking water and air. The vast numbers of environmental factors which pose some risk to human health mean that health risk assessment is essential in distinguishing those risks that are unacceptably large from those that may be considered acceptable, so that appropriate *regulations* may be introduced. (Paustenbach, 1995.) See also *dose–response evaluations and functions*.

**health status index (HSI)** This is a health index widely used as an indicator of quality of life. A person's HSI is compiled by scoring various aspects of his or her health, including mobility, physical activity and social activity. (Nussbaum and Sen, 1993.)

**health threshold** A level used in the setting of *ambient air* pollution standards. This approach presumes the existence of such a level, concentrations above which generate adverse health effects whereas those below produce no, or only minor, effects. The belief that the actual damage function has this shape is not consistent with the evidence; adverse health effects can occur at pollution levels lower than the ambient standards. (Tietenberg, 1996.)

**hedonic pricing** Hedonic pricing is a market-based *valuation* method that is used to value non-market, often environmental, assets. The method can be used to infer the value of *non-marketed goods* by analysing the prices of marketed goods to which the non-marketed goods are related. Houses are often used in hedonic pricing studies to infer the values of environmental characteristics. For instance, if some houses are situated on a lakeside, the values of those houses can be related to comparable houses that are not on the lakeside in order to reveal the premium that people are willing to pay to live on the lakeside. Hedonic pricing studies on house prices have also been used to estimate the value that people place on clean air. Another context in which hedonic pricing is often used is in valuing *risks* to life and health. The wages paid in high-risk jobs are compared to the wages paid in other jobs, in order to infer the premium that people require in order to accept higher risks.

Hedonic pricing is a *revealed preference* method of valuation since it analyses actual market behaviour. This distinguishes the approach from *stated preference (SP)* methods, eg the *contingent valuation method (CVM)*, which analyse the responses to hypothetical questions.

**historical resources** See *aesthetic, historical and cultural resources valuation*.

**horizontal equity** See *equity*.

**Hotelling rents** See *resource rents*.

**Hotelling rule** The Hotelling rule describes the time-path of natural resource extraction which maximizes the value of the resource stock. The rule is so called because it derives from the work of Harold Hotelling (1931). The simplest form of the rule is that 'the resource price must rise at the rate of interest'. More generally, the rule states that the most profitable extraction path available is one along which 'the marginal net revenue from the sale of the resource increases at the rate of return to alternative investments'.

The thinking behind the rule can be explained as follows. For asset markets to be in equilibrium, the owner of the resource must at each point in time be indifferent between extracting the last unit of the resource and investing the proceeds, or leaving that unit in the ground until the following period. For this condition to hold, the value of that unit must rise at the same rate as would the invested revenue, ie the rate of interest. This will be the case if, between the current period and the next, the resource price rises at the rate of interest.

Hotelling analysed three cases in his original article. The first is the perfectly competitive mining industry. He showed that under perfect competition, the profit-maximizing resource extraction path is one along which the resource price (which is equal to marginal revenue under perfect competition) rises at the rate of interest. He showed that where the resource is extracted by the central planner, the extraction and price paths are identical to those under perfect competition. Hotelling then showed that a profit-maximizing monopolist limits extraction in early periods in order to generate a higher price. This means that more of the resource stock will remain in later periods, resulting in the saying 'monopoly is the friend of the conservationist'. Because the monopolist's marginal revenue is less than price, price rises at less than the rate of interest in this case.

If there are *extraction costs*, then price minus *marginal extraction cost* (net revenue) must rise at the rate of interest. If the resource in question is a renewable resource, then the Hotelling rule is that net revenue must rise at the rate of interest minus the rate of growth of the resource.

**household production function** This is an indirect approach to the economic *valuation* of environmental goods. The household production function approach argues that households produce a flow of wellbeing using a production function that demands, as intermediate products, *environmental resources* and private goods. The values of environmental resources are estimated by analysing expenditures on goods that are either substitutes for or complements to the environmental resources. For example, the value of a reduction in *noise pollution* can be inferred from the expenditure of households on double-glazing and other forms of noise insulation. (Markandya et al, 2002.) See also *production function approach*.

**human capital** A form of *capital* stock that consists of human skills and knowledge. This can be thought of as a form of capital since it increases the productive power of the individuals who possess the skills and knowledge. Another characteristic of human capital is that, in common with other forms of capital, investment in the capital stock (ie in education and training) is necessary to maintain or increase the stock, while without investment the stock will depreciate. (Perman et al, 1999.)

**human development index (HDI)** The United Nations Development Programme (UNDP) *Human Development Report* has included the human development index (HDI) as a measure of human development since its inception in 1990. The index is intended to be a relatively simple, broad indicator of human development. It is made up of quantitative measures of each country's standards of living, and the longevity and educational opportunities of its citizens. These factors are measured by *adjusted income*, life expectancy at birth, and educational attainment (as measured by adult literacy and combined primary, secondary and tertiary enrolment). (Common, 1995; UNDP, 1999.) See also *gender-related poverty index; human poverty index*.

**human-made capital** This refers to the productive machinery, equipment, buildings and infrastructure accumulated by means of investment. (Perman et al, 1999.)

**human poverty index (HPI)** While the *human development index (HDI)* measures a country's progress on various aspects of human development, the human poverty index (HPI) highlights the levels of deprivation that still exist. There are two measures of HPI. HPI-1 measures poverty in developing countries. The variables used are the percentage of people expected to die before age 40, the percentage of illiterate adults, and economic deprivation (reflected by the percentage of people without access to health services and safe water, and the percentage of underweight children under the age of 5). The recently introduced HPI-2 measures human poverty in industrial countries, focusing on the same aspects of deprivation as HPI-1 with the additional consideration of social exclusion. (UNDP, 1999.) See also *gender-related poverty index*.

**human rights** Human rights represent the minimum social, economic and political standards that are generally considered to be acceptable. The advancement of human rights and their protection by law is often thought of as one of the requirements of human development. The Universal Declaration of Human Rights, adopted by the United Nations General Assembly on 10 December 1948, was the first multinational declaration to refer to human rights. The preamble of the Declaration makes clear that the its motivation is the recognition that 'disregard and contempt for human rights have resulted in barbarous acts which have outraged the conscience of mankind'. The aim of the Declaration is to proclaim 'freedom of speech and belief and freedom from fear and want… as the highest aspiration of the common people.'

The Universal Declaration of Human Rights calls for the prohibition of slavery, torture, other cruel and degrading treatment, arbitrary arrest, detention, and exile, stating that everyone has the right to life, liberty and security of person. It calls for an end to all forms of discrimination, for fair trials and reasonable punishment, and the universal protection of the law. It calls for the right of persecuted people to asylum in other countries, and for freedom of thought, conscience, opinion, expression, association and religion.

Economic provisions in the Declaration include the rights to: social security; work and just conditions of work, including fair remuneration and paid holidays; equal pay for equal work; and to join trade unions. It also calls for universal education which is free, at least during the elementary stages.

**hypothecation** See *earmarking*.

**hypothetical bias** This is a bias that may arise in *valuation* studies that use the *contingent valuation method (CVM)*, due to the fact that the observations are based not on actual economic behaviour but rather on the answers to hypothetical questions. In particular, respondents are asked to state the amount that they would be willing to pay for a certain good. The fact that the

## hypothetical resources

question is hypothetical means that it is difficult to know whether, in an actual expenditure decision, the respondent would be willing to spend the stated amount of money. Thus observations are less likely to be reliable than in *revealed preference* studies such as the *hedonic pricing* method.

**hypothetical resources** *Undiscovered resources* which are reasonably expected to exist in a known mining district under known geographical conditions. (Tietenberg, 1996.)

# Ii

**immissions** The damage directly attributable to emissions of pollutants.

**impact assessment** A process intended to improve the information on the expected effects of proposed projects or programmes in order to improve the quality of decision as to whether or not projects go ahead. In particular, the social and environmental consequences, as well as the financial considerations, should be considered by impact assessment. The process of impact assessment involves predicting, quantifying, and evaluating potential impacts of a project, in order to make a comprehensive estimate of its net benefits. The term 'impact assessment' covers a variety of techniques, including *environmental impact assessment*, social impact assessment, environmental health impact assessment, *risk assessment (RA)*, cumulative effects assessment and *strategic environmental assessment*. (Roe et al, 1995.)

**impact pathway approach** An approach to the *valuation* of external impacts and associated costs resulting from an environmentally damaging activity. The phrase 'impact pathway' simply refers to the sequence of events linking a burden to an impact, and the valuation of that impact. The methodology therefore proceeds sequentially through the pathway, as illustrated in Figure 8. It provides a logical and transparent way to quantify externalities. First, the emissions level – be it air pollution, noise or any other form of emission – is measured. *Dispersion modelling* may then be used to estimate the incremental level of an *externality* in a given area. This locates the impacts. *Valuation* techniques, such as the *contingent valuation method (CVM)*, *hedonic pricing* or the *travel cost method (TCM)*, may be used to place a monetary value on the *external cost* of the harmful activity. (ExternE, 1995 and 1999.)

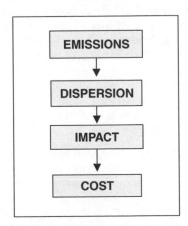

**Figure 8** *The Impact Pathway Approach*

**increasing returns to scale** This describes a level of production at which an equal percentage increase in all inputs (ie with relative shares of input factors unchanged) yields more than an equivalent percentage increase in output. See also *decreasing returns to scale*.

**incrementalism** This denotes the failure to account for the cumulative effects of decisions taken on a project-by-project basis. For example, consider the environmental costs of the extra pollution caused by the introduction of a new factory; or the loss of *biodiversity* and *carbon sequestration* services caused by creating a farm from rainforest land. The environmental costs of these individual projects are minimal, but the aggregate effect of such decisions may threaten *environmental sustainability*. Accounting for the aggregate effects of individual projects would require a national, regional or, in the case of global environmental problems, international plan. (Dixon et al, 1986.) See also *disjointed incrementalism*.

**index-linked charge** *Charges* for pollutants, that account for the effects of inflation, so that the value of the charge rises automatically with the level of inflation. Pollution charges tend to be index-linked in situations of high inflation. (Hammond et al, 1995.)

**index of sustainable economic welfare (ISEW)** A measure, developed by Daly and Cobb (1989) and applied to the US, which attempts to reflect the contribution to human welfare of economic activity more accurately than standard *national accounts* do. Thus, national income is adjusted to account for the welfare costs of environmental pollution, reduced welfare, and reduced economic and personal security. Daly and Cobb found that, according to this measure, welfare had actually declined in the US since the 1970s, after steadily increasing for most of the twentieth century. See also *measure of economic welfare; sustainability; sustainable development (SD)*.

**indirect use values** One of the types of value that make up the *total economic value* of an *environmental resource*. Its definition lies between those of use value and *non-use value*, and can be used to refer to two main types of situation. The first occurs when a person makes direct use of an environmental resource, for example a fishery, but where that fishery benefits from the services of another environmental resource such as a freshwater spawning ground. In this case, the person derives indirect use value from the freshwater spawning ground. The nature and extent of this type of indirect use value is clearly very uncertain, since scientific knowledge of the complex relationships within and between *ecosystems* is incomplete. The second situation in which indirect use values accrue occurs when a resource is used in a way that does not involve depleting the resource, for example recreation. This type of use value is often referred to as *passive use value*. See also *use values*.

**industrial ecology** Industrial *ecology* is a multidisciplinary field of research rooted in the analysis of the interaction between industrial and natural systems. This analysis involves modelling the economy and nature as a series of interdependent systems. It also involves accounting for the circular flows of materials, energy and wastes between economic and *ecological systems*. One of the aims of industrial ecology is to suggest ways in which the use of ecological resources by industry, and its emissions of waste into ecological systems, may be minimized and made sustainable.

**industrial pollution fund** A *fund* that finances *environmental investment*s in the most polluting industries, such as metallurgy, chemicals, pulp and paper, and non-mineral metal products (UN ECE, 1994.)

**information bias** The bias that arises in *contingent valuation method (CVM)* studies from the type of information that is provided to respondents. In particular, increasing the amount of information about the environmental good to be valued tends to increase the amount that respondents will claim to be willing to pay. It has been argued that this is a source of bias, although others have argued that increasing a person's knowledge of an environmental problem would be expected to increase the value that they would place on solving the problem. A final question that has been raised with regard to the information presented to respondents is whether the values stated by well-informed respondents can then be extrapolated to the less well-informed public. (Hanley et al, 1997.)

**input–output technique** The input–output (I–O) technique is a statistical technique used in *environmental economics* to assess cross-sectoral impacts of environmental policy. This modelling technique assumes that there are interactions between changes in price in one sector and the final output of other sectors. By varying different aspects of the model, the implications of different tax policies and other *economic instruments* can be assessed. This technique has been used in assessing the impacts of a *carbon taxation* on different sectors of the economy (Cornwell and Creedy, 1996). See Chiang (1984) for a presentation of technical aspects of this technique and Perman et al (1999) for an application of this technique to environmental economics.

**institutional concordance** The requirement that *economic instruments* used to control environmental damage should be compatible with existing national objectives and legislation, and in the case of EU Member States, with EU legislation. (Turner, Pearce and Bateman, 1994.)

**institutional failure** A situation in which the existing institutions are inadequate to deal with environmental and other problems, or in which the institutions required to deal with an environmental problem are not in place. It is related to the concept of *government failure*. An example of institutional failure within a nation state occurs when a regulatory body required to enforce environmental *regulations* is either insufficiently powerful or does not exist. An example of institutional failure in an international context is the absence of an institution to regulate the exploitation of global fisheries. See also *market failure*.

**instrumental value** This refers to the calculation of the value of an asset in terms of its capacity to fulfil a role, or to act as an instrument, in satisfying the needs of humans. The instrumental value of *biodiversity*, for instance, can be thought of as: its capacity to provide aesthetic and recreational enjoyment; its contribution to supporting, for example, agricultural and forestry economies; and its more general contribution of *ecosystem* services. The *total economic value* of natural assets can be thought of as comprising various types of instrumental values, including *use values* and *non-use values*. (Barbier et al, 1994.)

**intangible benefits** Benefits that cannot be valued in monetary terms. This can be due to a lack of data on the benefit in question; for instance, it might be known that a certain *species* of fish is used for food, but the numbers of people exploiting the fish population might not be known. Benefits can also be intangible if data on the benefit is available but the techniques required to value the benefit are not available. Thus, as *valuation* techniques develop and improve, some benefits previously defined as intangible will become quantifiable. (Tietenberg, 1996.) See also *tangible benefits*.

**integrated pest management (IPM)** An approach to managing pests which combines biological, cultural, physical and chemical tools in a way which minimizes economic, health and environmental *risks*. (See http://aggie-horticulture.tamu.edu/syllabi/cnotes98a/315/ipm.html)

**integrated pollution prevention and control** The IPPC (Integrated Pollution Prevention and Control) Directive 96/61/ EC is an important regulatory development in the European context. The principle behind IPPC is that pollution should be seen in an integrated way so that it is minimized for the *environment* as a whole. Thus the three environmental media of air, water and land are taken into account, in contrast to more traditional approaches used in previous directives which focused on one medium and did not allow for transfers between media. IPPC is also intended to cut bureaucracy by coordinating the actions of authorities responsible for different environmental media, and ideally encourages the establishment of one responsible authority within Member States. The directive applies a source-based regulatory approach by seeking to limit the environmental impacts of specific industrial activities by requiring the use of *best available techniques (BAT)*. See also *best available techniques not entailing excessive costs (BATNEEC); best practicable environmental option (BPEO)*.

**intellectual property rights (IPR)** The rights that people or institutions exert over the manufacture, use and sale of certain items. These rights are usually expressed in the form of patents or copyrights, which allow an individual or institution monopoly rights in the market for a new product for a certain period of time. This system is designed to allow the inventor of a new product to recoup the development costs, while allowing society to benefit from the new knowledge.

One of the most controversial uses of intellectual property rights (IPR) is its application to plant and animal *species*, in particular under the General Agreement on Trade and Tariffs (GATT) agreement on trade-related intellectual property rights (TRIPS), which took effect at the beginning of 1995. Member countries are required to ensure that their IPR laws conform with certain provisions of the agreement, including the provision for 'the protection of plant varieties' either by patents or by another effective system. This is intended to protect the intellectual property rights of firms that develop new plant varieties by means of *genetic modification*. It means, however, that firms can apply for patents on useful plant varieties which are not currently subject to property rights, for example indigenous plant varieties used by communities.

**intensity of use hypothesis** A theory related to the decoupling of *economic growth* and environmental damage. It suggests that a decline in the intensity of use of environmental and energy resources will allow economic growth to continue, at least to a certain extent, without compromising *environmental sustainability*.

# international environmental agreements (IEAs)

**interactive resources** Populations of living, *biological resources* whose stock size is determined by both biological factors, for example relating to its habitat, and human factors. In particular, other things being equal, the more intensively a resource population such as a fish stock is exploited by humans, the smaller it will become. An important issue in the changes in stocks of interactive resources is the economically optimal management strategy – that is, the strategy that maximizes the discounted net benefits of exploiting the resource over time. *Discounting* future costs and benefits will tend to increase the intensity with which the resource is exploited. (Tietenberg, 1996.) See also *biological growth; maximum sustainable yield (MSY); renewable resources; threshold instruments*.

**intergenerational equity principle (IEP)** The IEP is a central principle in the definition of *sustainable development (SD)*. The need for this principle, together with the concerns for SD, has arisen out of a recognition that current generations control the natural and other resources that determine the wellbeing of future generations. Stocks of *man-made capital*, *human capital* and scientific knowledge are likely to rise over time in most, if not all, countries. However, stocks of *natural capital*, including *energy resource* stocks and other resources that are directly consumed or which provide inputs to production, tend to be depleted over time. The concern that rising man-made capital stocks may not be sufficient to compensate future generations for decreased natural capital stocks is one of the major concerns of SD. The IEP requires that sufficient investment is undertaken to compensate for any decreases in natural capital stocks. See also *equity; maximin principle; sustainability; discounting*.

**intergenerational externalities** An intergenerational *externality* arises when current generations affect the welfare of future generations without accounting for this effect. Examples of intergenerational externalities are emissions of *greenhouse gases (GHGs)*, the destruction of *biodiversity*, and the depletion of *natural resource* stocks.

Since future generations do not yet exist and thus cannot be bargained with, it is impossible to internalize intergenerational externalities using market mechanisms. The only means by which intergenerational externalities can be internalized is for current generations to place limits on their behaviour in order to minimize impacts on future generations, or to compensate future generations for external effects, for example by investing in substitutes for depleted stocks of *natural capital*. (Pearce and Turner, 1990.) See also *externalities; intergenerational equity principle; sustainable development*.

**internalizing externalities** See *externalities*.

**international environmental agreements (IEAs)** Agreements that are set up to address environmental problems that have international implications. They involve national governments agreeing to take action to limit environmental damage. IEAs currently number about 180. High-profile examples of IEAs are the Montreal Protocol on Substances that deplete the *Ozone* Layer, which came into force in January 1989, and the *Convention* on International Trade in Endangered Species of Wild Fauna and Flora (*CITES*), which came into force in July 1975.

IEAs rely on signatory governments complying with the standards to which they have agreed, since in the absence of a global environment agency, international environmental standards cannot be enforced by law. The actual structure of IEAs varies considerably. Many agreements have operated without any clear and explicit sanctions and have relied on informal and non-binding mechanisms such as negotiations and consultation, supplemented by conciliation, arbitration and judicial settlements. Trade measures have also been written into some IEAs, including the Montreal Protocol and CITES, but only to be used as a last resort in the event of non-compliance. *Game theory* is often used to model the formation of IEAs. (Jha, Markandya and Vossenaar, 1999; Markandya and Mason, 1999.) See also *cooperative solutions; non-cooperative solutions; prisoners' dilemma; free rider problem.*

**intertemporal externalities** An intertemporal *externality* arises when current actions affect welfare in the future. Intertemporal externalities can affect the future welfare of people currently alive, and they can affect future generations that are not yet alive. In the latter case they are known as *intergenerational externalities*. (Bromley, 1991.) See also *externalities.*

**intrinsic value** An aspect of the value of an asset, for example an *ecosystem* or a *species*, which is separate from its role as an instrument in providing wellbeing to humans. Intrinsic value refers to the value of the object in and of itself, and has been used to justify the *conservation* of, for example, *biodiversity.*

**inverse demand curve** The inverse demand function represents the relationship between the price of a good and the quantity demanded, with price represented as a function of quantity. It is called the inverse demand curve because the standard demand curve measures quantity demanded as a function of price. (Varian, 1996.)

**iron law** Malthus's concept that, because human population has a tendency to grow geometrically (e.g. in the sequence 2, 4, 8, 16, 32, 64…) while the capacity to provide sustenance for human populations tends to grow arithmetically (e.g. in the sequence 2, 4, 6, 8, 10…), disease and hunger are the inevitable consequence of an eventual failure of the economic system to provide sufficient quantities of food. (Barbier, 1989.)

**irreversibility** This refers to the effects of actions that cannot be undone. The *extinction of species* is an example of an irreversible action. Irreversibility applies only to *natural capital*, not to *human-made capital* which, having been created by humans, can be depleted and recreated at will. Irreversible actions reduce future choices and the *intergenerational equity principle* would require that irreversible actions are not undertaken without full consideration of the effects on the future. This has led to calls for the *precautionary principle* to be observed. (Barbier, 1993.)

**isolated system** In thermodynamics, an isolated system is one which exchanges neither energy nor matter with another system. Apart from the entire universe, an isolated system does not exist in nature. See also *entropy, First Law of Thermodynamics, Second Law of Thermodynamics.* (Common, 1995.)

# Jj

**joint implementation (JI)** The JI concept allows countries to fulfil their obligations to reduce *greenhouse gas (GHG)* emissions jointly. It implies crediting the donor's emissions quota with investment in emissions reduction projects in a recipient country. JI projects present specific voluntary agreements between the donor-investor and recipient. Donors invest in the project to achieve additional reduction of GHG emissions or increase carbon sink capacity. These additional reductions are then credited to the quota of donor. Participation in JI projects makes it possible for countries with high costs for GHG reductions to meet their obligations more cheaply. JI projects can only be carried out between countries that have emission reduction targets. This mechanism allows the cost of mitigating international environmental problems to be reduced by exploiting the disparity in pollution *abatement costs* between high-income and lower-income countries.

This concept has been used in several international *environmental conventions*, including the *Kyoto Protocol* (KP) of the *Framework Convention on Climate Change* (FCCC). Three types of flexibility mechanisms have been incorporated into the FCCC. The first, called simply joint implementation, is defined above. It is only permitted between two parties that have emissions reductions agreements under the KP, usually a developed country and/or a transitional country. The second, called the *clean development mechanism (CDM)*, applies when a developed country invests in emissions reductions, as well as the achievement of other *sustainable development (SD)* objectives, in a developing country that does not have emissions reductions targets under the KP. The third is *emissions trading*.

**joint and several liability doctrine** A legal doctrine that can apply in cases where many individuals or organizations may be jointly responsible for a liability. In the context of environmental legislation it can apply to environmental damage such as the damage caused to a river by the pollutants released into the river from a number of sources. Application of the joint and several liability doctrine in a prosecution for damage means that each one of a number of defendants found guilty of the total damage can be liable for the entire value of the damage caused, no matter how large or small their own contribution to the damage. (Tietenberg, 1994.)

**jointness in supply** Products are said to be joint in supply if the production of one good leads to the production of another as a by-product. Examples of *natural resources* that are joint in supply are oil and natural gas. (Hartwick and Olewiler, 1986.)

**judgemental benefit–cost framework** A framework in which gains and losses are compared but are not changed into common units, eg through *monetization*. Under this approach, the monetary costs of pollution control might be compared with an *environmental impact* statement on the effects of pollution, including the distribution of those effects both geographically and over time. (Pearce, 1995.) See also *benefit–cost analysis (BCA); extended benefit–cost analysis*.

**justice** Justice, in an economic context, means that the economic actions and outcomes of economic systems, especially the distribution of benefits, are ethically acceptable. Criticisms of classical utilitarianism, for example, have focused on the fact that measuring the success of an economic system on the basis of the aggregate wellbeing may mask ethically unacceptable, and hence unjust, inequalities. Rawls (1971) outlined a theory of justice with respect to social and economic equality which has been highly influential in economics. Rawls argued that a set of moral principles regarding justice would be best determined under a 'veil of ignorance', so that the principles would be discussed and agreed without people being aware of their standing in society (whether they are rich or poor). From this principle of justice, rules for the organization of society are derived. When these rules are enacted, each person will have equal rights to the maximum amount of freedom possible without infringing upon the freedom of others. When inequalities arise, they can only be justified if they are potentially advantageous to everyone. This principle is equivalent to the *maximin principle,* which implies that each person will opt for the maximum amount of protection possible to avoid the *risk* of being the poorest person in the society.

Rawls's theory of justice has been used to analyse the *ethics* of *sustainability,* in terms of the distribution of economic benefits over time, the depletion of *natural resources,* and the investment that should be undertaken to compensate for depleted natural resources. (Krishnan et al, 1995.) See also *equity; intergenerational equity principle; ethics, Rawlsian ethics.*

# Kk

**Kaldor improvement** This refers to a potential *Pareto improvement*: that is, a resource reallocation which results in a gain that is greater than the losses incurred by any parties damaged by the reallocation. In this situation an actual Pareto improvement results only if compensation is given to the damaged party, so that no party is actually made worse off. (Perman et al, 1996.)

**Kantian ethics** This is a system for deriving rules for ethically sound behaviour. Under a Kantian ethic, the basis of moral behaviour is duty, and the following of rules. Kant's view was that to be ethically just, the motivation for an action must be based on a valid ethical rule. Moreover, *justice* is evaluated by reference to whether or not the motivation of an action is prompted by a valid ethical rule, rather than by reference to the outcome of the action. Ethically valid rules under Kantian *ethics* are defined as those which, if generalized to the population as a whole, would produce desirable results. Under this framework, individual actions that in themselves would be negligible, such as dropping a piece of litter or failing to pay taxes, are ethically unacceptable since they may not be generalized without socially undesirable results. (Perman et al, 1999.) See also *ethics; environmental ethics; Rawlsian ethics; libertarian ethics; utilitarian ethics*.

**Kaya identity** Kaya (1989) noted this identity for *carbon dioxide (CO$_2$)* emissions, which is used in developing strategies to reduce emissions. The identity states the following:

$CO_2$ emissions = $CO_2$ emissions per energy unit x energy per unit of output x output per capita x population

IPCC (1996b) suggests that this identity enables the identification of different approaches to the reduction of carbon emissions. For developed countries, this identity suggests that, with a low population growth, emissions will decline as long as energy per unit of output declines faster than the level of output increases. This implies an increase in *energy efficiency*. The use of different fuels may also permit the reduction of $CO_2$ emissions per unit of energy produced. For developing countries, emissions will increase if there is no offsetting of the impacts of population and output growth against the increased use of energy-efficient technology and changes in fuels used. See also *climate change*.

**keystone species** *Species* without which an *ecosystem* would either collapse or change to a different state, performing different ecological functions or *ecological services*. A change in the ecological functions of an ecosystem may affect the *ecological stability* of surrounding areas. An example of a keystone species is the elephant. It is responsible for creating paths through forests, which are essential for many of the other animals living in forests. This concept can be used to assign priority to the protection of species and habitats. (Barbier, 1993.)

## knowledge societies

The determination of whether or not a species can be considered to be a keystone species is evaluated in De Leo and Levin (1997) and subsequent responses by Khanina (1998), Vanclay (1999), and Piraino and Fanelli (1999). See also *biodiversity*.

**knowledge societies** Societies in which materials and energy-intensive industries have been replaced with information and skills-based industries tailored to suit situations and problems specific to the local area. (Rich, 1994.)

**Koopsman efficiency** An allocation of productive resources to products is Koopsman-efficient if, for a given environmental quality, the output of one of the products cannot be increased without decreasing the output of any other product. This concept is related to the concept of *Pareto efficiency*. (Siebert, 1987.) See also *efficiency; economic efficiency; eco-efficiency*.

**Kuznets curve, environmental** An example of an environmental Kuznets curve (EKC) is shown in Figure 9. The theory of EKCs suggests that the intensity of the per capita environmental impacts of production falls after per capita income passes a certain threshold level, represented by $Y^*$. The fundamental implication of this theory is that *economic growth* may be seen as favouring environmental protection. This is contrary to the general belief that economic growth leads to environmental degradation.

There are, however, problems with EKCs. The first is that the relationship depicted in the figure is not observed for all types of pollutant. While it has been observed for pollutants whose effect is felt locally and currently, it tends not to be observed for *transboundary* pollutants, or those whose effect will be felt in the future. Energy use, for instance, seems to have a linear relationship to income, rather than an EKC relationship. Thus, it is not clear that the EKC indicates that economic growth is compatible with *environmental sustainability*. Borghesi (1999) presents a survey of the literature on the issue of EKCs, concluding that there is as yet little clear-cut evidence to support the existence of an EKC. (Perman et al, 1999.) See also *sustainability*.

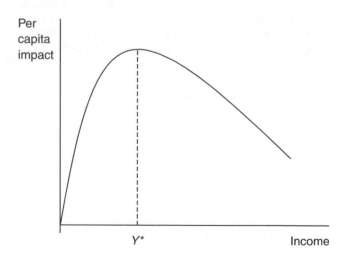

**Figure 9** *An Environmental Kuznets Curve*

**Kyoto Protocol** The first substantial agreement to set *greenhouse gas (GHG)* emission limits. Adopted in 1997, the Kyoto Protocol established carbon emission targets for developed countries, with an average target reduction of 5 per cent by 2008–12. Switzerland, the EU, and most Central and Eastern European (CEE) countries agreed to reductions of 8 per cent, while the target for the US was 7 per cent. Some countries were allowed net increases in emissions of the 6 GHGs under consideration, notably Australia which was allowed an 8 per cent increase. The protocol included a degree of flexibility in meeting targets with the official endorsement of *emissions trading* and the establishment of *joint implementation* and the *clean development mechanism (CDM)*. The Kyoto Protocol is an important step towards achieving the aim of the United Nations *Framework Convention on Climate Change (FCCC)*: that of preventing 'dangerous anthropogenic [human-made] interference with the climate system'. (For more information see UNFCCC website: www.unfccc.org). See also *international environmental agreements (IEAs), climate change.*

# Ll

$\mathbf{L}_{Aeq}$ See *dB scale*.

**landfill sites** Areas in which refuse and other waste matter is buried for disposal. See *waste disposal*.

**Learned Hand formula** This formula is commonly used in US courts in deciding whether a defendant, for example in a case concerning environmental pollution, exercised due care. Named after the judge who developed it, the test concludes that a defendant has been negligent if the loss caused by the pollution, multiplied by the probability of the pollution occurring, is greater than the cost of preventing the pollution. (Tietenberg, 1992a.)

**least-cost theorem** This theorem suggests that the *abatement costs* associated with reducing pollution by a certain amount are minimized if the emissions of all polluting firms are taxed at the same rate. This follows from the fact that profit-maximizing firms whose emissions are taxed at a given rate will reduce pollution up to the point at which the *marginal abatement cost* is equal to the tax rate. All firms, regardless of their *abatement* cost structure, will have the same marginal abatement cost, so that the cost of the aggregate abatement achieved could not be reduced by changing the allocation of abatement between firms. However, although *market-based instruments (MBIs)*, such as *pollution taxes*, are more efficient than *command and control (CAC) policy* instruments in terms of total abatement costs, the latter have other advantages, including the fact that they can achieve a predetermined level of pollution abatement. (Common, 1995.) See also *regulation; direct regulation*.

**liability insurance** See *environmental liability insurance; environmental risk internalization through capital markets (ERICAM); liability roles*.

**liability rules** Rules that award damages to those who have suffered as a result of another's actions, for example as a result of environmental pollution. The amount of the award tends to correspond to the value of the damage. Liability rules are relevant to *environmental economics* in that they create legal precedents which affect the perceived costs of economic decisions which in turn affect the *environment*. For instance, the incentives to invest in improved safety for oil tankers would be increased if the firm were responsible for restoring environmental damage and for compensating those affected. (Tietenberg, 1996.)

**libertarian ethics** Libertarianism asserts the fundamental inviolability of individual rights. To libertarians, the rights of individuals are paramount and actions cannot be judged in terms of their outcomes, but rather in terms of whether or not they violate individual rights. Libertarianism tends to be associated with a belief in minimal government intervention, since any redistribution is unlikely to have the consent of all individuals concerned, and therefore is likely to violate individual rights. (Perman et al, 1999.) See also *ethics; environmental ethics; Kantian ethics; Rawlsian ethics; utilitarian ethics*.

**life cycle approach or analysis** An analytical tool which estimates both the environmental effects (for example emissions, discharges and waste generation), and energy and resource use, from the creation to the disposal of products. Sometimes it is called cradle-to-grave analysis. It typically deals in physical units, not monetary costs, and aims to estimate the size and probability of future environmental impacts. Companies use this information to evaluate the expected alternative outcomes of different strategies. See also *best environmental practice; deposit refund schemes; eco-labelling*.

**life support functions** The functions performed by some *ecological systems*, without which human life would not be possible. They include the provision of food and shelter and the maintenance of a habitable atmosphere and climate. The ecological systems that perform these functions are also known as critical *natural capital*. The fact that their removal could cause major harm to mankind has led to suggestions that the substitution possibilities between *man-made capital* and environmental capital are limited. (Barbier, 1993.) See also *sustainable development (SD)*.

**limited altruism** A situation in which an individual is concerned with the wellbeing of a limited group of people. For instance, it could describe the concern of an individual to see *justice* done for the poor and unemployed of his or her own nation. This could reflect an *option value* for those who consider the possibility of becoming poor or unemployed themselves. It could also reflect a *use value* for those who consider themselves to be part of the group in question and who believe they have not received their fair share. (Hohmeyer et al, 1997.) See also *altruism; disinterested altruism*.

**limits to growth** The title of a book by Meadows et al (1972), which has given its name in turn to the position that *economic growth* is ultimately constrained by the availability of *natural resources*. Meadows et al used *systems analysis* to predict that trends in industrialization and rapid population growth, and their effect on resource use and pollution, would lead to the eventual collapse of environmental, and thus economic, systems.

Encapsulated in the limits to growth theory is the view that *environmental resources* are ultimately finite, as is the residual *carrying capacity* of the environment. The theory suggests that economic growth cannot be indefinitely sustainable, since there are limits to the availability of environmental resources and to the ability of the *environment* to assimilate waste.

The limits to growth theory, and the results of the Meadows analysis, have been largely dismissed by economists because the model did not include a *price system*. Thus, the model did not account for the fact that as natural resources become scarce, they become relatively more expensive. This induces producers to substitute away from those resources, as well as encouraging the development of substitutes for natural resources. (Perman et al, 1999.) See also *man-could-master-nature attitude*.

**local pollutants** Pollutants that cause damage near to the source of an emission. (Tietenberg, 1994.)

**locally available capacity** The part of local ecological capacity whose use by humans is compatible with *sustainability*. The remaining part should be left untouched for preserving *life support functions*, including those associated with *biodiversity*. The *Brundtland* Report suggests the calculation of the available capacity by subtracting 12 per cent from the existing capacity.

**logrolling** This is a concept in decision making. Logrolling occurs where one individual agrees to support another on an issue about which he has little concern, in return for reciprocal support on another issue. Also known as vote trading. (Cullis and Jones, 1998.)

**loss aversion** Barbier (1993) suggests that there is strong evidence in economics and psychology for a high degree of aversion to environmental losses. This may be because people feel that they have a natural right to their existing *endowment* of natural assets. See also *cognitive dissonance*.

**Loury's theory** This theory concerns the extraction of oil in an oligopolistic market (that is, a market with relatively few producers.) Loury's proposition was that the rate of oil extraction increases as reserves increase, but at a decreasing rate, and that extraction declines as the cost of extraction increases. The theory was largely validated by Polansky's (1992) *econometric* analysis. (Loury, 1986; Hanley et al, 1997.)

# Mm

**major groups** Major groups of people identified in *Agenda 21* and adopted by the *Earth Summit* include NGOs, women, youth, local authorities, trade unions, business and industry, and the scientific and technological community.

**Man and the Biosphere Programme** Programme established by UNESCO which aims to encourage the rational use and *conservation* of resources in the *biosphere*. Under this programme, 357 *biosphere reserves* have been established around the world. See http://www.unesco.org/mab/home.htm for more details. See also *biosphere homogenization; biosphere reserve*.

**man-could-master-nature attitude** The belief that anthropogenic activities can overcome natural barriers to development, for example natural resource *scarcity*. This can be thought of as the opposite of the *limits to growth* position.

**man-made capital** See *human-made capital*.

**marginal abatement cost (MAC)** This is the *marginal cost* of reducing pollution. Different firms may have different marginal *abatement costs*, depending on the goods they produce, the technologies used, and the potential for the application of less pollution-intensive technologies. The existence of differing MACs is cited as a reason for the preference of *market-based instruments (MBIs)* over *command and control (CAC) policies*. The marginal cost of abatement is assumed to increase as pollution decreases, because increasingly sophisticated and expensive technologies have to be used. (Markandya et al, 2002.) See also *abatement; abatement cost; efficient level of pollution; defensive expenditures*.

**marginal benefit (MB)** The additional benefit gained from the last unit of a good or service consumed, or a resource used in production. In consumption this is also known as *marginal utility*. For *economic efficiency* to be achieved, an activity such as production or consumption should be carried out until its *marginal cost (MC)*, which tends to increase with levels of the activity, is equal to its marginal benefit (MB), which tends to fall as levels of the activity increase.

**marginal cost (MC)** The cost corresponding to the last unit of an output produced, or any other activity carried out. For example, the MC of pollution *abatement* is the cost of the last unit of pollution avoided. See also *marginal abatement cost (MAC)*.

**marginal cost pricing** A pricing system in which the price charged for a product or service, for example a natural resource or electricity, is determined by the cost of producing the last unit. Since lower-cost production techniques are used first, *marginal costs (MCs)* tend to increase as production increases. Thus, under marginal cost pricing, expenditure rises more quickly with increased consumption than it does under *average cost pricing*, providing a better incentive to limit consumption and conserve resources. See also *declining block pricing; peak load pricing*.

## marginal damage

**marginal damage** The damage caused by the last unit of a damaging activity carried out; for example, the damage caused by the last ton of emissions of a polluting substance, or the last hectare of land converted from natural habitat to an alternative use. The value of marginal damage must be established using a *valuation* method in order to establish, for example, the efficient level of pollution, or to decide, using *benefit–cost analysis (BCA)*, whether *conversion* of a piece of land from its natural state should go ahead.

**marginal discovery cost** The cost of finding an additional unit of a *natural resource*. This cost, which is observable, can be used as a proxy for the *resource rent* of a natural resource, which is not observable and which is an indicator of the true *scarcity* of the resource stock. Marginal discovery cost can be used as a proxy for scarcity rents because profit-maximizing firms should undertake resource (for example, oil) exploration up to the point at which marginal discovery cost and marginal resource rent (the *marginal benefit (MB)* to the firm of exploration) are equal. (Tietenberg, 1996.) See also *marginal extraction cost*.

**marginal expected penalty curve** This is the marginal expected penalty for breaking a regulation, for example an environmental regulation. The marginal expected penalty increases with both increases in the level of the penalty and increases in the probability of prosecution. Thus, increased incentives for, for example, consumer groups to prosecute firms for breaking environmental *regulations* will increase the expected penalty for doing so. This, in turn, will decrease the likelihood of regulations being broken. (Tietenberg, 1992b.) See also *cheapest available technology not involving prosecution (CATNIP)*.

**marginal extraction cost** The cost of extracting the last unit of a natural resource in each period. This is an indicator of resource *scarcity*, since the closer to depletion a natural resource stock is – other things being equal – the greater the cost of extraction. This is used particularly as an indicator of the depletion of fish stocks and other *common property resources*. Marginal extraction cost is of limited use as an indicator of resource stock scarcity, however, since it casts little light on future resource scarcities, and thus does not provide governments and firms with the information necessary to prepare for resource scarcity. (Tietenberg, 1996.) See also *marginal discovery cost; extraction cost*.

**marginal user cost** An *opportunity cost* imposed by *scarcity*. Greater current use of scarce resources reduces the future opportunities for exploitation of the resources. The marginal user cost is the present value of these foregone opportunities at the margin. (Tietenberg, 1996.) See also *user cost*.

**marginal utility** The additional *utility*, or wellbeing, gained from the last unit of a good or service consumed. See also *marginal benefit (MB)*.

**market alternatives to direct regulation** See *market-based instruments (MBIs)*.

**market-based instruments (MBIs)** An approach to environmental policy which modifies the market signals received by producers and consumers in order to induce more environmentally friendly behaviour or a movement towards the *efficient level of pollution*.

Examples of MBIs are *pollution charges, subsidies* for pollution *abatement, marketable permits, product charges,* and *full-cost resource pricing*. Governments can also improve firms' incentives to reduce environmental damage by removing environmentally harmful subsidies, that is, by reducing *government failure*. MBIs can be used to achieve the *Pareto-efficient* level of emissions. Figure 10 shows that *charges* and subsidies can be used to yield the efficient level of *abatement*. Note that it is possible to over-regulate and under-regulate. The *efficient level of pollution* is OP, which can be achieved using MBIs or *command and control* (CAC) *policies*. In this case possible policy measures involving the use of MBIs include setting a charge equal to OT, the implementation of a subsidy for the removal of pollution to a value of OT, or the issuing of OP *marketable emissions permits*. (Markandya et al, 2002.) See also *least-cost theorem; economic instruments*.

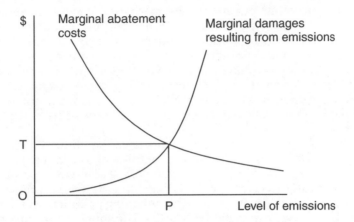

**Figure 10** *Market-Based Instruments*

**market distortions** Market distortions occur when government intervention results in *market failures* which are more serious than any previously existing. (Panayotou, 1993.)

**market failures** Market failures result from the failure of market prices to reflect the full value to society of a commodity. For example, most of the economic values of ecological resources and *ecological services* are not reflected by markets, and therefore their increasing relative *scarcity* is not readily captured by price signals. An upstream polluter has no incentive to account for the costs he imposes on a user of the river downstream. This is an example of market failure and results from the failure of the market to include the costs of the pollution to the downstream user in the costs of the upstream polluter. These non-market costs represent an *externality*.

There is a distinction between local market failure and global market failure. The former relates, for example, to the inability of markets to capture some of the local or national benefits of an environmental asset such as *biodiversity*, or the local or national costs of pollution. Global market failure relates to the failure of markets to account for the benefits of environmental assets such as biodiversity to people outside the boundaries of the nation faced with a choice, for example whether to conserve *ecosystems* or to develop the land. (Markandya et al, 2002.) See also *government failure; institutional failure*.

**market interest rate** The sum of the real interest rate and the expected inflation rate. (Dixon et al, 1989.)

**marketable catch permits** A type of *economic instrument* used particularly to protect certain fish *species* from excessive exploitation. The *permit allocation* is based on a scientific assessment of the maximum catch which the fish stocks in question can sustain. The permits represent the right to extract a given quantity of fish, and the total number of permits distributed represents the maximum total allowable catch. These permits can either be used by the holder or be sold to other users of the resource. (Perman et al, 1996.) See also *quota systems*.

**marketable emissions permits** An approach used to reduce pollution levels, involving the creation of a market in which firms can buy and sell the right to emit certain quantities of pollution. Under a marketable, or tradable, permit system, the responsible authority sets the environmental standard and identifies the total pollution emissions compatible with the achievement of this standard. Permits that allow firms, in aggregate, to emit this level of pollution are then distributed, either by means of an auction, or by *grandfathering* (a *permit allocation* in proportion to the firms' emissions at an agreed prior date.)

   Emissions permits may be traded between polluters. Polluters will minimize *abatement* costs by reducing pollution as long as the *marginal cost (MC)* of treatment is less than or equal to the cost of buying a permit. Once a firm's *marginal abatement cost (MAC)* is greater than the market price of permits, it will buy permits to cover its excess of remaining pollution over the permits it holds. This creates a demand for permits. The supply of permits is created when a firm's MACs are lower than the market price of permits. Such a firm will increase profits by reducing pollution further, and selling its spare emissions permits. The market for emissions permits will be in equilibrium when the MACs of each firm are equal to the market price of emissions permits, so that there is no further potential for profitable trade. The fact that the MACs of all firms are equalized means that the reduction in pollution is achieved at the lowest possible cost. (Markandya et al, 2002.) See also *least-cost theorem; market-based instruments (MBIs); economic instruments; permit allocation; emissions trading; emission banking*.

**Marxism and ecology** Martinez-Alier and Schlupmann (1995) provide a review of the environmental views of Marxists. Under the Marxist framework there is no commitment to market-determined prices or *market interest rates*, and there is some suggestion of capitalism misusing *natural resources*. However, there is no analysis of either *exhaustible resources* or the problems of intergenerational equity in Marxist writing.

**material levy** An example of an input tax. It would be imposed on the raw materials used to manufacture packaging, with due account being taken of existing rates of *recycling* and re-use. (Turner et al, 1994.)

**material resource accounts** See *environmental and resource accounts*.

**material resources** *Natural resources* whose economic value is typically defined by their use as inputs to economic activities. Examples of material resources are minerals and fossil fuels. The fact that the value of such resources stems from their use as inputs means that their exploitation tends not to affect non-market uses such as recreation, in contrast to other natural resources such as forests. However, their use can involve the non-market costs associated with pollution. (OECD, 1994a.)

**maximin principle** The principle of *equity* that results from Rawls's analysis of social *justice*. The name derives from the words 'maximum' and 'minimum', and refers to a situation in which the position of the least well-off person in society is maximized. The relevance of the maximin principle to *environmental economics* stems mainly from its use in the economics of *sustainable development (SD)*. In analysing SD, the maximin principle is used to describe a distribution of resources over time such that the position of the least well-off generation is maximized. In the absence of population growth, this in effect results in an equal distribution of resources across generations. The maximin principle underlies the *Hartwick rule* for *sustainability* and *non-renewable resource* depletion. See also *justice; Rawlsian ethics; decision theory*.

**maximum net-present-value criterion** A criterion used to compare the costs and benefits of different projects. The *net present value (NPV)* of a project is calculated by adding the discounted value of the net benefits (ie benefits minus costs) in each period during the lifetime of the project. The maximum NPV criterion suggests that the projects with the highest NPV of benefits should be funded. Because *discounting* involves placing less weight on costs and benefits in the future, this criterion tends to favour projects with short-term rather than long-term benefits. (Tietenberg, 1996.) See also *benefit–cost analysis (BCA)*.

**maximum sustainable yield (MSY)** This refers to the maximum yield that can be harvested from a renewable resource stock without reducing the size of the stock. *Renewable resources* such as fish stocks usually grow at an increasing rate as the stock size increases, and then reach a maximum before falling again to zero once the stock level reaches the *carrying capacity* of its habitat. The MSY corresponds to the stock level at which the growth rate of the resource is maximized.

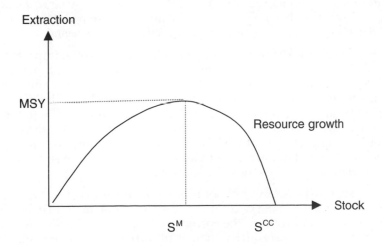

**Figure 11** *Maximum Sustainable Yield*

## measure of economic welfare (MEW)

Figure 11 shows the growth function of a renewable natural resource stock. The net growth rate initially increases with the stock size, reaching a maximum at $S^M$ and falling to zero at $S^{CC}$, the *carrying capacity* of the resource's habitat. *MSY* indicates the maximum sustainable yield of the resource stock. (Perman et al, 1999.) See also *biological growth; ecological species–area relationship; interactive resources.*

**measure of economic welfare (MEW)** A measure that attempts to adjust standard measures of output, such as *net domestic product*, so that they yield a more accurate measure of wellbeing. An early example of a measure of economic welfare was developed by Nordhaus and Tobin (1972). It consists of net domestic product less an estimate of the cost of pollution. Under this measure the value of the services of consumer durables are spread over their lifetime, and expenditure that does not contribute to welfare, such as the costs of commuting, are deducted. The value of leisure time is added, as is the value of government services. The study found that wellbeing grew between 1929 and 1965 at around only half the rate at which net domestic product grew. A more recent measure of economic welfare was compiled by Daly and Cobb (1989), who found that welfare has actually fallen since the 1970s. (Tietenberg, 1996.) See also *index of sustainable economic welfare (ISEW); sustainable development (SD).*

**measured emissions taxes** This is a type of *market-based instrument (MBI)* involving tax payments that are linked to measured quantities of a polluting substance. (O'Riordan, 1997.) See also *emissions charges, environmental taxation.*

**media, environmental** Environmental media are specific areas of the natural environment – air, water, and soil – which can be the subject of regulation concern and activity. See also *medium-by-medium approach; cross-media approach.*

**medium-by-medium approach** The traditional approach to solving environmental problems, which targets each component of the *environment* – air, water and soil – independently. The disadvantage of this approach is that it does not account for the interconnectedness of the different environmental media, and thus involves the *risk* that in solving an environmental problem in one medium, a problem relating to another medium may be worsened. An alternative approach that accounts for the interdependence of environmental media is the *cross-media approach*. See also *media, environmental.*

**meta analysis** This is a technique by which environmental impacts may be estimated. It applies a methodology similar to the *benefit transfer* technique to yield estimates for *willingness to pay (WTP)* and other measures of environmental welfare based on studies previously carried out. This technique applies coefficients taken from regression analysis in previous studies to the socio-economic and other data available for the area in which the estimate is required, to yield a rough estimate of the WTP in that area. A more accurate estimate would be obtained by carrying out a primary study, for example using the *contingent valuation method (CVM)*. See also *valuation.*

**mineral accounts** An example of *material resource accounts*, these involve compiling estimates of the value of a country's mineral stocks. This is difficult, as there is no consensus on the correct method for estimating the value of mineral assets. Some argue that there is no supply constraint evident in the market for certain resources and that more exploration will yield new reserves.

However, Harrison (1993) argues that the existence of auctions for prospect rights means that mineral deposits do have a market value. Three methods of evaluating mineral deposits are proposed. The first considers mineral deposits as fixed *capital*, meaning that exploitation reduces the value of *net domestic product* but leaves *gross domestic product (GDP)* unchanged. The second method is to treat mineral deposits as raw material; exploitation then leads to intermediate costs and subsequent reductions in income and both net and gross domestic product. The third, and Harrison argues most preferable, option is to reclassify the extraction of minerals from a primary to a tertiary industry.

**minimum environmental stock** The minimum stock of environmental attributes that provides a viable basis for sustained economic activity. (Barbier, 1993.)

**mitigation** Measures taken to reduce human impacts on the *environment*, and thus the associated costs to humans. Generally, mitigation strategies involve reducing environmental damage, for example by reducing the emissions of damaging pollutants.

There has been a large amount of research into mitigation policies for *climate change* as there is considerable scope for reductions in greenhouse gas *(GHG)* emissions. Strategies for mitigation include the introduction of incentives for the use of fewer GHG-producing technologies in the production process, and the planting of forests to increase the *carbon sequestration* potential of the *environment*. The IPCC has produced a series of reports investigating the issue of mitigation (IPCC, 1996a and 2001). See also *abatement; abatement cost; adaptation; defensive expenditures.*

**monetization of environmental impacts** The conversion of impacts of polluting activities into monetary terms. This permits direct comparison of the costs and benefits of pollution *abatement* strategies. For health impacts the *value of a statistical life (VOSL)* is often applied to facilitate project evaluation. Monetization forms part of the *impact pathway* methodology. *Benefit transfer* may be used to allow the estimation of damage costs for areas for which detailed valuation studies are impractical. (ExternE, 1995 and 1999; Markandya et al, 2002.) See also *valuation.*

**monocropping** This occurs when a farm or another agricultural enterprise produces only a single crop. This reduces soil fertility, and thus productivity. (Manser, 1993.)

**moral suasion** Manipulation of the social environment. Moral suasion may include the generation of publicity to place pressure on polluters, or the education of those affected by pollution. It may be used to influence consumer choices, and is seen by some environmentalists as one of the most important instruments for the promotion of *sustainability*. (Common, 1995.)

**multicriteria analysis** A technique designed to quantify the impact, whether economic or environmental, of a process or action. It is used in situations in which the information necessary to perform a *benefit–cost analysis (BCA)* or a *cost-effectiveness analysis* is not available, for instance when it is not possible to express environmental impacts in monetary terms. Impact analysis thus does not convert impacts into monetary units in order to identify an optimal policy. Rather, the aim is to provide policy-makers with relatively raw information,

## multilateral environmental agreements (MEAs)

which will indicate the various consequences of different courses of action, and to allow the policy-maker to decide the relative importance of each of the consequences. (Tietenberg, 1996.)

**multilateral environmental agreements (MEAs)** See *international environmental agreements (IEAs)*.

# Nn

**national accounts** The compilation of a set of statistics which measure a country's output. National accounts include different measures of annual productivity such as *gross national product (GNP)*, which is the total value added, or output, by the citizens of a country, regardless of location. *Gross domestic product (GDP)* is the total value added within the borders of a country, whether by citizens of the country or by foreigners. The standard framework for national accounting is the UN system of national accounts (SNA). (UN, 1993a.)

National accounts have been used widely since the 1950s, both as a tool of demand management and to indicate relative progress – over time and among countries. Their relevance to *environmental economics* stems from the criticisms that have been made of the SNA regarding its failure to account for changes in many factors that influence both current wellbeing and the economy's long-term productive capacity. In particular, the SNA does not account for the welfare costs of environmental damage such as pollution. Moreover, under the SNA, while *depreciation* of *human-made capital* is deducted in the calculation of net national product (NNP), the depletion of natural resource stocks, which are a form of *natural capital*, is not accounted for. Thus, if an economy's growing NNP is boosted by the sale of depleted *natural resources*, then there could be concerns for the *sustainability* of that economy, in that its NNP may decrease once the natural resource is exhausted. These problems are being addressed by the development of a framework of *green national accounts* to estimate the levels of environmental damage attributable to different sources and to account for the damages caused by certain productive processes. See Markandya and Pavan (1999) for an example of the application of *green accounting*. See also *environmental accounting*.

**National Oceanic and Atmospheric Administration (NOAA)** This is the US body responsible for setting *regulations* regarding the *valuation* of damages from oil spills. In the aftermath of the Exxon Valdez oil spill in 1989, the Exxon company conducted a series of studies which attempted to discredit the *contingent valuation method (CVM)* of environmental valuation, in an effort to render it impossible to value the measured *non-use values* as a basis for the calculation of damages that could be charged to the company. The NOAA panel consisted of a group of distinguished economists, namely Robert Solow, Kenneth Arrow, Edward Leamer, Roy Radnor, Paul Portney and Howard Schuman. The panel concluded that the values calculated using the CVM could be used in calculating legal liability for environmental damage. However, they made a series of recommendations intended to ensure that the estimates are as accurate as possible, and to avoid the charge that CVM overstates the true value of damages. The most important of these recommendations include:

- the use of *willingness to pay (WTP)* as the measure to be estimated, rather than *willingness to accept (WTA)*;
- the use of the dichotomous choice format;

## natural assets

- the use of in-person interviews rather than postal or telephone ballots; and
- the insistence on a minimum response rate of 70 per cent from the sample.

*Source:* Hanley et al, 1997.

**natural assets** See *natural capital.*

**natural capital** Natural capital consists of a nation's environmental and *natural resource* reserves. Natural capital thus includes the stock of life-supporting systems, *biodiversity*, and *renewable* and *non-renewable resources*, but excludes both human capital and human-made capital.

This concept is useful for two major reasons. Firstly it highlights the extent to which *environmental resources* contribute to economic productivity and welfare. For instance, the *environment* provides waste-disposal services for the productive process, absorbing and, as far as its capacity allows, *recycling* waste products and pollutants. Stocks of environmental resources, including energy, raw materials, and agricultural outputs, provide inputs to the productive process. Secondly, the concept of natural capital highlights the implications for the future of the depletion of environmental resources and damage to the *environment*'s capacity to provide valuable services. It is clear that if an economy's stock of *human-made capital* is depleted over time, the wealth of the economy and its capacity to produce and provide wellbeing in the future is diminished. The concept of natural capital underlines the fact that if stocks of productive environmental resources are depleted over time, without investment in an alternative capital stock that truly compensates for the lost natural services, this will reduce the economy's wealth.

Natural capital is particularly relevant to *green national accounting*, which is intended, among other things, to reflect the effect on an economy's aggregate wealth of changes in stocks of *natural resources*. The depletion of natural resources and its effect on future wellbeing is also central to the problem of *sustainability*. (Perman et al, 1999.) See also *capital; weak sustainability; strong sustainability.*

**natural resource accounts** These are quantitative and qualitative accounts of stocks and flows of environmental assets, or *environmental resources.* Two main categories of natural resource accounts can be distinguished: material resource accounts, and environmental and resource accounts. Material resource accounts describe, primarily in physical terms, the stocks and flows of resources within the economy. These accounts can be recorded in terms of biomass (volume, weight), area, population, and diversity, depending on the environmental resource in question. Examples of environmental and resource accounts are forest accounts, water resource accounts, wildlife resource accounts and land accounts. Qualitative environmental and resource accounts aim, for instance, to measure pollution flows from economic activities to *natural resources* or to draw a picture of the quality of a particular natural resource. They complement the quantitative, physical versions of *environmental accounts.*

The aims of natural resource accounting are to provide policy-makers with an information base on natural resources and to contribute to the environmental awareness of both policy-makers and the general public. (OECD, 1994a.) Natural resource accounting is seen as a tool that demonstrates linkages between the environment and the economy and which helps to correct distortions in standard measures of national growth and welfare. *Green net national product* measures are based on quantitative indicators of natural and environmental resource stocks and flows. (OECD, 1997.) See also *environmental accounting; pollution accounts; mineral accounts; green accounting.*

**natural resource management** See *environmental management.*

**natural resource tax** A tax on the extraction of *natural resources* such as oil, gas and timber. Governments often levy such taxes, also known as severance taxes, to compensate local communities for the environmental damage caused by resource extraction, and to compensate, by means of investment in alternative *capital* stocks, future generations for the loss of a *natural capital* stock. The extent to which natural resource extraction is taxed depends on whether or not the government holds the *property rights* to the resource stock. If it does not, then the government arguably does not have a moral right to tax as profits revenue that represents the reduction in value of a non-renewable capital asset. This has led to depletion allowances in the taxation of natural resource extraction. If the government owns property rights in the resource stock, then arguably the government should attempt to recover as tax that portion of revenue which represents the depletion of the resource stock. One form of *government failure* occurs when governments, in granting concessions to resource-extracting firms, fail to recover the value of the depleted natural resource stocks.

**natural resources** Assets and flows of goods which are produced by nature rather than being human-made. Natural resources can be divided into several categories. Renewable resources include solar power, wave power, and geothermal power; their availability is unaffected by the amount exploited at any given moment. Renewable resources also include those with a *biological growth* potential such as forests and fish stocks. These resources can be exploited up to a certain point without reducing the stock available in the following period. However, if exploitation is greater than the regenerative capacity of the resource, then the stock will decrease. Thus, these resources, as well as being renewable, can also be called depletable. *Non-renewable resource* stocks are those that are reduced by any extraction. Oil, gas, coal and metals are examples of non-renewable resources.

*Resource economics* involves analysing the optimal and efficient use of natural resources. The economically optimal management strategy will depend on the relationship between the growth of the resource stock and the *market interest rate* (the return that could be obtained by depleting the resource and investing the revenues in an alternative asset.) When interest rates are higher than the growth rate of the resource it will often mean that it is optimal to deplete the resource unsustainably. However, this leads to concerns as to *environmental sustainability.* Moreover, the non-market values of natural resources, including their *global values,* are usually not accounted for in the identification of the optimal management strategy. (Young, 1992; Perman et al, 1999.) See also *natural resource accounts; environmental and energy resources.*

**naturalism** A philosophy that finds the controlling influence of humans over nature morally unacceptable. The naturalist concept of value, unlike the concept of *total economic value,* is not anthropocentric. Rather, under this framework, natural systems and organisms have value in themselves. This can be described as *intrinsic value*. Under humanist value systems, rights and responsibilities lie only with human beings. Under naturalist value systems, rights, for example to be treated with respect, should be accorded to non-human beings also. (Perman et al, 1999.) See also *ethics; environmental ethics; bioethical standpoint; extended stewardship ideology; stewardship ethic.*

**neoclassical economics** Neoclassical economics is the conventional, mainstream economics on which much of *environmental economics* is based. It is founded on the concepts of *economic efficiency* and optimality, using the tools of marginal analysis. Thus, the theories of the optimal depletion of *natural resources*, eg the *Hotelling rule*, are based on neoclassical economics. Neoclassical economics is distinct from Keynesian economics, which stresses the government's role in stabilizing the economy. Neoclassical economics disputes that the government's role in macroeconomic stabilization can be positive. Environmental economics extends the framework of neoclassical economics to account for the role of *natural resources* in contributing directly to human welfare, and in contributing to the production of goods and services. However, the assumptions used in neoclassical *environmental economics*, for instance regarding the substitutability between natural and man-made resources, have been criticized as leading to unrealistic conclusions as to the extent to which natural resources can be depleted and substituted for by alternative investments. See also *classical economics*.

**net domestic product (NDP)** The value of domestically produced goods and services (*gross domestic product (GDP)*) less the value of *depreciation* of *human-made capital*. This measure is calculated under conventional *national accounts*. NDP does not account for the depletion or degradation of *natural resources*. This measure can be adjusted using the techniques of *green national accounting* to estimate the *environmentally adjusted domestic product*. (Young, 1992.)

**net national product (NNP)** The value of goods and services produced by a country's citizens (*gross national product (GDP)*) less the value of *depreciation* of *man-made capital*.

**net present value (NPV)** An integral part of *cost–benefit analysis*, this concept involves the *discounting* of a stream of net benefits over time. A common algebraic formulation for this is as follows:

$$NPV = \sum_t (B_t - C_t)/(1+r)^t$$

where $B_t$ is the benefit at time $t$, $C_t$ is the cost at time $t$ and $r$ is the discount rate. A test of whether a project is *economically viable* is whether or not its NPV is greater than zero. For the NPV to include a project's full *social costs* and benefits, benefits must include environmental improvements and costs must include environmental degradation. (Perman et al, 1999.)

**netting** This concept is used in systems of *marketable emissions permits*. It allows different emissions sources which belong to a single plant to be considered as one source. Thus if a plant expands, the firm can avoid subjecting the new facility to a *new source* review, and the possibility of being set new standards, by ensuring that the net increase in emissions is negligible. This involves earning emissions-reductions credits by reducing emissions elsewhere in the plant to offset any expected increases in emissions from the new facility. Thus, netting relies on internal trade within a plant. This system is intended to provide greater flexibility in meeting environmental standards. If a firm is not able to comply with the emission limits through netting, it must follow the *offset* rules. (Pearce and Turner, 1990.)

**new source performance standard (NSPS)** These are *emissions standards* that apply specifically to new facilities. Under some regulatory systems, existing pollution sources face less stringent emissions standards than do new facilities. This has two consequences that are undesirable from the point of view of *economic efficiency*. Firstly, when demand in an industry is growing, the increased profits of existing firms will attract new firms into the industry, increasing supply to meet the increased demand and limiting price increases. However, if new firms are subject to higher pollution-control costs than existing firms are, then the entry of new firms will be delayed, allowing existing firms to enjoy increased profits while consumers pay higher prices. The second consequence is that when, by retiring an existing facility and introducing a new one, a firm is subject to the NSPS and therefore increased pollution-control cost, this creates an incentive to prolong the life of older, more polluting, facilities. (UN ECE, 1994.) See also *direct regulations*.

**no-regrets options** No-regrets options for *climate change* are greenhouse gas *(GHG)* emission-reduction options which have negative net costs, because they generate direct or indirect benefits which more than offset the costs of implementing the options. These benefits, by definition, do not include the impacts associated with avoided climate-change damages. The potential for no-regrets was discussed at length in IPCC 1996a and 1996b. The potential for no-regrets options depends on the relative potential for emissions reductions and expansion in economic activity. Figure 12 illustrates this trade-off with a production frontier $F$. Where the economy is below this frontier, emissions reductions can be made without reducing the level of economic

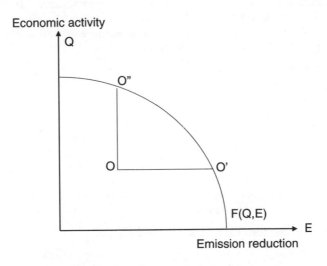

**Figure 12** *The Potential for No-Regrets Options*

activity in the country. Thus, the potential for no-regrets is illustrated by the area $OO'O''$; within this area emissions reductions are possible without loss of activity. For a recent review of these issues see IPCC (2001).

**no-regrets policy** The introduction of a technical innovation that is both cost effective and environmentally friendly. An example is the introduction of an energy-saving technology (eg domestic double-glazing or energy-saving lightbulbs) that decreases the cost of heating a home by more than the cost of the technology. (Helm, 1991.)

**noise abatement zones** Zones established in the UK within which a council may control noise from fixed premises and, in certain circumstances, secure a reduction in the noise level. In a noise *abatement* zone a noise source can be subject to control without the need for a sufferer to show that the noise is creating a nuisance. The fact that noise abatement zones apply only to permanent noise sources means that other measures are required to control mobile noise sources, which often have acute impacts. The principal application of these zones would appear to be in controlling noise in predominantly residential areas. However, procedural complexity has meant that noise abatement zones have not been applied much in practice. (Leeson, 1995.) See also *noise pollution, valuation of*.

**noise pollution, valuation of** The discomfort and annoyance from noise pollution can be valued using various techniques. Studies in this area include the application of the *hedonic pricing* technique to value the impact of differential noise levels on the prices of property. Techniques to value damages resulting from noise pollution are presented in ExternE (1995), where an *impact pathway approach* is used to model the impact of noise emission as an *externality* in the production process. Using noise *dispersion modelling* techniques, the impact of an increase in noise can be measured and the value of the externality applied to estimate the damages accruing from the generation of noise. Two main approaches have been used in the *valuation* of noise, the *dB(A) costing approach* and the *annoyance costing approach*, although ExternE (1995) suggested that the best estimate of noise disamenity is yielded by the dB(A) costing approach. Maddison et al (1996) present some estimates of the value of disamenity brought about by traffic noise.

**non-attainment area** This is defined under the US Clean Air Act (CAA) as an area that has not met a specified deadline for the attainment of a certain standard of *air quality*.

**non-compliance fees** Fees which are imposed if polluters do not comply with environmental *regulations*; a type of *enforcement* incentive. Fees can be imposed to recoup either the environmental damage inflicted, or the benefits to the polluter from not complying. Non-compliance is penalized either ex ante, through the taking of a payment returnable upon compliance, or ex post, through the imposition of a fine when there is non-compliance. (OECD, 1989b.) See also *disincentives; economic instruments*.

**non-consumptive use value** See *passive use value*.

**non-cooperation** This term is used in *game theory* to describe a situation in which two or more players could be made better off by cooperating, but where a failure to coordinate results in a sub-optimal solution. Non-cooperation in an environmental context can be illustrated by a situation in which two countries emit a pollutant, and each country's emissions result in reduced welfare in both countries. A technology is available, at a cost, that reduces emissions by a certain proportion. The issue that leads to the possibility of non-cooperation is the fact that each country bears the entire cost of its own *abatement* while part of the benefit accrues to the other country.

Since each country has two possible strategies, to abate or to pollute, there are four possible outcomes. The actual outcome under non-cooperation will depend on the pay-offs to each player under each of the outcomes. The pay-off matrix in Table 3 represents a situation in which the outcome is non-cooperative.

**Table 3** *A Non-Cooperation Pay-Off Matrix*

|  |  | Country A | |
|---|---|---|---|
|  |  | Abate | Pollute |
| Country B | Abate | A : 4<br>B : 4 | A : 5<br>B : 1 |
|  | Pollute | A : 1<br>B : 5 | A : 2<br>B : 2 |

The table shows the options of countries A and B – to either pollute or to abate their pollution – and the pay-offs of those options, which depend both on each country's own action and the action of the other country. Clearly it is better for both countries if both abate than if both pollute. However, the pay-offs show that each country, whichever strategy the other country chooses, improves its pay-off by polluting. Thus, the non-cooperative solution is for both countries to pollute, resulting in a pay-off of 2 for both countries. This type of situation is an application of the *prisoners' dilemma*. It represents a case in which an *international environmental agreement (IEA)* could result in an increase in welfare for both countries. See also *cooperative solutions*.

**non-exclusion** Non-exclusion occurs when it is impossible or very costly to deny access to an environmental asset. Non-exclusion may result in overexploitation of an asset. For example if a fish stock is non-excludable it is likely to be exploited unsustainably. This is also known as a situation of *open access*. (Hanley et al, 1997.)

**non-incentive taxes** The use of *environmental taxes* to raise revenue, rather than as an incentive to reduce pollution. This type of tax is sometimes used to raise funds for particular environmental expenditures, for instance a publicly funded pollution-reduction scheme. (O'Riordan, 1997.)

**non-marketed goods** Non-marketed goods are often environmental goods such as *ecosystems* and *biodiversity*, or environmental *bads* such as pollution and noise. They are goods which do not have a market price, due to their position outside the market system. Ecosystems and biodiversity are examples of resources which have no market price. The *valuation* of non-marketed goods is a major aspect of *environmental economics*. The main techniques of non-market valuation include the *contingent valuation method (CVM)*, the *travel cost method (TCM)* and *hedonic pricing*. (Hanley et al, 1997.)

**non-point source pollution** This refers to pollution that is emitted into the environment from a variety of sources, with no single point of origin. This type of pollution is difficult to regulate, owing to the difficulties in measuring pollution from different sources. Examples of such pollution include pesticide run-off and the leaching of nitrates into water. Due to the difficulties in measuring emissions of non-point pollutants, controls must focus on the productive process itself (ie inputs of polluting substances and engineering technology), rather than on attempting to monitor emissions. (Hanley et al, 1997.) See also *point-source pollution*.

**non-renewable resources** Non-renewable resources are *natural resources* that are available in fixed quantities. These are sometimes referred to as *exhaustible resources*. However, *reserves* of non-renewable resources, which are defined as known stocks of resources whose extraction is *economically viable*, can be increased in two ways. Firstly, exploration can increase known stocks of the resource, and secondly, *technical progress* can reduce *extraction costs*, so that resources that were previously uneconomical to extract become economically viable. Classic examples of non-renewable resources include fossil fuels such as coal and oil, as well as minerals. (Hartick and Olewiler, 1998.) See also *marginal discovery cost; marginal extraction cost; resource rent; renewable resources*.

**non-use values** Values that individuals derive from natural resources without using them either directly or indirectly. The term is usually used synonymously with *existence values*. Sometimes a *bequest value* is also added to non-use values. However, other authors consider bequest value to be part of use value. (Markandya et al, 2002.) See also *use values*.

# Oo

**objective valuation approaches (OVAs)** A general term for a group of approaches to the objective valuation of environmental damages, through the use of physical relationships. Such techniques include the *alternative cost, change in productivity, cost of illness (COI), opportunity cost* and *replacement cost* approaches. Through the use of *damage functions*, OVAs relate a level of environmental damage to the degree of physical damage to a natural or human-made asset, or to the degree of health impact. These techniques attempt to measure the gross benefits, or losses avoided, of actions to prevent or reduce the impact of environmental damage. They therefore estimate the cost of the environmental damage itself. (Dixon et al, 1986.)

**occupational hazards** Occupational hazards are the *risks* of mortality (death) or morbidity (injury or illness) associated with certain jobs. ExternE (1995) presented a review of the literature on the *valuation* of occupational health hazards, and estimated values for morbidity and mortality impacts arising from the *fuel cycle*. These applied the *value of a statistical life (VOSL)* to estimates of the risk of death. The value of morbidity impacts such as breathlessness and coughing is estimated using approaches such as the *contingent valuation method (CVM)*, the *costs of illness approach* and *avertive expenditures*. Wage-risk studies have also been conducted in this area, in an attempt to measure the willingness of individuals to accept risk in the workplace in exchange for higher wages.

**odd nitrogen theory** A theory to explain the fluctuations in *ozone ($O_3$)* levels. Major proponents of this theory have suggested that $O_3$ destruction is being catalysed by abnormally high levels of 'odd' nitrogen, which is produced by blasts of particles from the sun. The solar particles tend to penetrate at the poles, where the resistance of the Earth's magnetic field is weakest. It is suggested that during the polar night the odd nitrogen sifts down into the stratosphere and aids in the depletion of $O_3$. (Roan, 1989.)

**offset policy** A policy applied in the use of pollution *permit* trading systems to reverse the conflict between *economic growth* and environmental standards. The aim of the policy is to allow new firms to set up in areas in which the environmental quality standards are not met, and in which the environmental *regulations* would not otherwise permit another enterprise to be established. Under an offset policy, a new firm can acquire emission reduction credits from existing firms, ie they effectively pay for existing firms to reduce their emissions further. The offsets acquired are usually required to exceed the expected emissions of the new facility, so that in effect economic growth, in the form of the establishment of new firms, becomes a vehicle for improved environmental standards. (Markandya et al, 2002.) See also *emission reduction credit scheme*.

**open access** A resource is said to be open access when it is not excludable, ie when access to the resource cannot be restricted to a limited group of people.

The best-known examples of open access resources are international fisheries. Because *property rights* over international fisheries are not in place, and there is no international organization to negotiate limited use of the resources, access to the fisheries is unlimited. Unlimited access means that such resources may suffer from overexploitation and the so-called *tragedy of the commons*. See also *non-exclusion*.

**open system** An open system is one that exchanges energy and matter with its environment. Individual organisms, *ecosystems* and planets are examples of open systems. The concept of open and *closed systems* is relevant to the *Second Law of Thermodynamics*. In practice, all systems are open, and the closed system is a theoretical abstraction. (Common, 1995.)

**opportunity cost** The opportunity cost of an activity that uses scarce resources is the value of the next most economically productive use to which those resources could have been put. The concept of opportunity cost is widely used in economics in identifying the most efficient use of scarce resources. Rational consumers and producers, by definition, choose activities whose private benefits outweigh their costs. If costs do not include opportunity costs of the resources used, and an activity's benefits outweigh the costs, then this indicates that an activity is financially viable. If the costs include opportunity costs and an activity's benefits outweigh its costs, this indicates that as well as being financially viable the activity is economically efficient. If an activity's benefits do not outweigh its costs, including the opportunity costs, this indicates that although the activity may be financially viable, an alternative use of the resources would be more economically efficient. For instance, in the case of forest land, the opportunity cost of preserving the forest stock may be the *net present value (NPV)* of profits from deforestation and conversion of the land to crops or *pasture*. If the opportunity cost exceeds the profits from forestry then although forestry may be profitable, it is not economically profitable given the alternative opportunity, and *economic efficiency* would require the *conversion* of the forest land.

As with all cost concepts, opportunity costs depend on the variables included and the individuals and groups considered. In the forestry example above, the social opportunity cost of forest conversion may be higher than the private opportunity cost if one considers the non-market services of forestry, including watershed protection, *carbon sequestration*, aesthetic beauty and so on. See also *asset conversion; global conversion process; economically viable; resource-user cost*.

**opportunity-cost approach** This is an *objective valuation approach*, used to estimate the value of an environmental asset. It estimates unpriced goods and services by measuring the foregone benefits of using the same resource for alternative objectives. For example, the benefits of preserving forests for a national park rather than harvesting them for timber will be measured by using the foregone income from selling timber, rather than by estimating directly the benefits of preservation. That is, this approach measures those things which have to be given up for the sake of preservation. This method measures the cost of preservation and can be used when a choice must be made between a proposed development project with positive net benefits without preservation, or the preservation alternative. In this case, if the preservation alternative is chosen it is implicitly assumed that its benefits are at least equal to the foregone benefits. When using this method, careful consideration should be given to the *option values* and *existence values* of the environmental asset in question, as well as to the irreversible impacts of the development project. The opportunity-cost approach is a very useful technique when the benefits of certain assets, such as natural habitats and cultural or historical sites, cannot be directly estimated. (Markandya et al, 2002.)

**optimal level of pollution** See *efficient level of pollution*.

**optimal resource allocation** This refers to the allocation of resources in both consumption and production, and is distinct from the concept of efficient resource allocation. An allocation of consumption goods is said to be *Pareto efficient* when it is impossible to re-allocate resources so as to make one person better off without making any other person worse off. However, this says nothing about the desirability of a given distribution of resources. Indeed, it has been suggested, for example by Perman et al (1996), that the fact that the *efficiency* concept lacks ethical implications is one of its attractions for the discipline of economics. The identification of an optimal resource allocation requires an objective function, or a *social welfare function*, which allows different, efficient outcomes to be ranked in terms of desirability. For instance, under a strictly egalitarian social objective function, the optimal solution would be the highest possible level of consumption such that consumption is distributed equally across individuals. Note that efficiency is a prerequisite for optimality, but the reverse is not true. (Perman et al, 1996.)

**optimist model** This model was developed by Kahn et al (1976) to counter the *limits to growth* model (Meadows et al 1972) which suggests that, after a point, population will fall due to factors such as insufficient food and energy to provide the required production levels. The optimist model suggests that the natural future path of population growth approximates an S-shaped logistic curve, and that intervention in population growth is both unnecessary and unethical. It sees food and energy production rising as a result of technological progress, which is itself stimulated by population growth. (Tietenberg, 1996.)

**option price (OP)** A measure of *willingness to pay (WTP)* to preserve an environmental good for future use. It consists of the expected *consumer surplus* from the future use of the good, and the *option value*. (Pearce and Turner, 1990.)

**option value** The additional value placed on a natural resource by those people who want to have the option of using goods and services in the future. This concept is based on two premises: *uncertainty* with respect to the future availability of environmental goods, and the *irreversibility* of the loss of many environmental assets. Option value can influence the decision regarding the most efficient allocation of natural assets. (Markandya et al, 2002.)

**Oslo Convention** The Oslo *Convention* for the Prevention of Marine Pollution by Dumping from Ships and Aircraft came into force in April 1974 following its ratification by signatory states. A major feature of the convention was the creation of the Oslo Commission to overview the convention, which classifies pollutants into three grades of toxicity – the *black list*, the *grey list* and the *white list* – and provides *regulations* for the disposal of these pollutants. (Leeson, 1995.)

**output taxes** Taxes levied on products whose production and/or consumption involves environmental damage. The tax rates can be based on a characteristic of the product, for instance on the carbon content of fossil fuels, or they can be levied on the product itself, an example being a tax on petrol or on packaging materials. Output taxes can be differentiated so that the more environmentally friendly products incur lower rates. Output taxes are sometimes confused with *Pigovian taxes*, the difference being that they are levied on the output whereas Pigovian taxes are levied on emissions.

**overlooked natural resources** This term refers to *natural resources* whose stocks and flows are not accounted for in standard measures of *national accounts*; that is, they are overlooked in the compilation of national product measures. Natural resources that are not traded, and so do not have a market price, are usually overlooked by national accounting measures. A large number of natural resources that provide services which are economically valuable but *non-marketed* fall into the category of overlooked resources. (Dixon et al, 1989.) See also *natural resource accounts; green accounting*.

**ozone ($O_3$)** A type of oxygen molecule found predominantly in the stratosphere, (the atmospheric layer immediately above the troposphere, which is the 10km-deep layer immediately above the Earth's surface.) The stratosphere contains the *ozone layer*. The ozone layer performs the positive function of reducing the damaging effects of sunlight. Ozone can also accumulate in the troposphere as a result of the burning of fossil fuels. Tropospheric ozone is a pollutant associated with serious health *risks* as well as damage to crops. (Perman et al, 1999.) See also *chlorofluorocarbons, legislation against; global environmental fund; international environmental agreements; odd nitrogen theory; volatile organic compound*.

**ozone layer** See *ozone ($O_3$)*.

# Pp

**paradox of aggregation** The paradoxical result of the aggregate effect of individual optimizing behaviour. If all individual countries attempt to maximize their own profits, the result for all is lower profits than would be the case under a coordinated policy. For example, in the case of an *open access* resource, the maximum profitability for all those exploiting the resource would be ensured if, in aggregate, the efficient extraction path were followed, involving limits on individual extraction. In the absence of coordination, individuals will usually extract greater amounts, leading to lower profits for all, and often to the unsustainable exploitation and ultimate destruction of the environmental resource. This situation is often the cause of the *tragedy of the commons*.

**parallel compensations** Financial support from developed countries to developing countries for the improvement of their environmental policy.

**Pareto efficiency** A criterion used to determine the *efficiency* of markets in allocating consumption goods. An allocation is Pareto-efficient when there is no possible reallocation that would make one person better off without making any other person worse off. Pareto efficiency is very difficult to achieve in reality, since it requires perfect information and the absence of *externalities*. It is often pointed out that the measure of efficiency does not allow a distinction on the grounds of distributive *justice*. For instance, it does not allow a very unequal distribution to be ranked relative to an equal distribution, as long as both are efficient. Pareto efficiency can be illustrated using an Edgeworth Box, as shown in Figure 13. Individuals have preferences represented by their

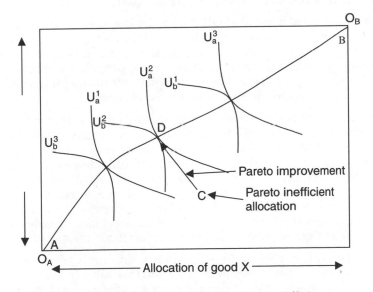

**Figure 13** *Edgeworth Box Showing Pareto Efficiency*

# Pareto improvement

*utility* curves, $U_a$ and $U_b$. The set of Pareto-efficient allocations is represented by line *AB*, representing the points of tangency between the utility curves. Any allocation off this line, for example point *C*, is not Pareto-efficient, and is said to represent a Pareto-inefficient allocation. A movement from an allocation such as this, say from point *C*, to point *D*, represents a *Pareto improvement*, in which it is possible to make the overall utility level gained from an allocation of assets greater without reducing the level of utility of any individual. See also *economic efficiency; efficient level of pollution*.

**Pareto improvement** A reallocation of assets that makes at least one person better off (increases his or her *utility*) without making anyone else worse off. Pareto improvements are only possible if an economic system has not reached *Pareto efficiency*.

**Pareto-irrelevant externality** A Pareto-irrelevant *externality* is one whose removal leads to no net gain in social benefits.

**partial equilibrium analysis** This refers to the analysis in isolation of the market for a particular good, assuming that the markets for all other goods allocate resources efficiently. Thus, partial equilibrium models constitute highly detailed, sector-based models that focus on the impact of a tax or policy change in one sector, and assume that all other sectors are held constant. Partial equilibrium models have been used for modelling, for example, impacts on the energy sector of changes in policies. These models have been used in *cost–benefit analysis (CBA)* in policy formation, and are mainly useful in the analysis of impacts on certain industries, and the consequences of policies where there are no major interactions.

Where there are significant interactions between markets, *computable general equilibrium (CGE) models* are likely to be appropriate to model the wider impacts of policies. *General equilibrium analysis* accounts for effects of a policy change on all markets. (Perman, 1999; IPCC, 2001.)

**participatory rural appraisal (PRA)** A technique used for the evaluation of rural projects and a step towards the attainment of sustainable rural development. It involves both local people and multidisciplinary teams of researchers in gathering information on existing projects, identifying priority needs for further projects, and preparing plans for future projects which are appropriate to the specific area. (Krishnan et al, 1995.)

**particulates** A general term used to describe tiny pieces of matter (technically between 0.1 and 25 thousandths of a millimetre) in the atmosphere. Sources of particulates include certain types of smoke (eg diesel smoke), fine ash, dust and sulphates. Particulates are believed to increase the incidence of asthma attacks and breathing problems, and to aggravate lung and heart conditions. Particulate emissions also cause damage to buildings and materials, through the deposition of particulate sulphur dioxide ($SO_2$) and other corrosive chemicals. ExternE (1995) presents methods for the modelling of the deposition of particulates, and techniques for their *valuation* based on the *impact pathway approach*.

**passive use value** This is the value that individuals place on the *non-consumptive use* of a natural resource. It is a *direct use value*. Examples of passive use of *natural resources* include bird-watching and whale-watching. See also *total economic value*.

**pasture** Grazing land for livestock. Most pasture is significantly less productive – in terms of its conversion of solar energy into biomass – than arable land. Moreover, the limited conversion *efficiency* from plant matter to animal products reduces the energy available to humans, typically by a factor of ten. The conversion of forest land to pasture is a significant cause of *deforestation*. See also *asset conversion; global conversion process*.

**patents** See *intellectual property rights (IPR)*.

**patrimony accounting** A form of *natural resource accounting* used in France, aimed at analysing and describing the natural *environment* in the three basic dimensions that are relevant to humans: economic, social and ecological. (Dixon et al, 1986.)

**payment vehicle bias** A type of bias that may arise in estimating the *willingness to pay (WTP)* for an environmental good using the *contingent valuation method (CVM)*. There is some evidence to suggest that the means by which people might pay for an environmental good (eg a tax or a one-off charge), as well as the proportion of the population who would be required to make the payment, may influence the size of stated WTP. Some have suggested that this is indicative of bias as it suggests irrationality, while others have suggested that there may be rational explanations for the relationship between the WTP expressed and the payment vehicle, involving, for instance, notions of fairness. (Perman et al, 1999.)

**peak load pricing** The costs of supplying electric energy are determined not only by the total quantity demanded, but also by the pattern of that demand, and in particular by the levels of peak demand. This is because the levels of peak demand determine the required capacity of the generating system, so that increased peak demand creates the need for expensive capacity expansion; and because the peak demand is satisfied using all, including the most expensive-to-run, capacity, meaning that *marginal costs* are higher. Peak load pricing is a pricing system that captures the higher marginal cost of peak power supply by charging higher prices during the peak period. It also serves the purpose of reducing peak load demand by encouraging consumers to switch their demand to less expensive periods, reducing the required capacity and thus reducing costs. (Tietenberg, 1996.) See also *marginal cost (MC) pricing; average cost pricing; declining block pricing*.

**perceivable pollution** Public perception of pollution is important in the development of pollution control policy. Barde and Button (1990) note that pollution resulting from the use of petrol by cars is toxic, yet is not much perceived, while engines of cars using diesel produce very noticeable levels of fumes, smells and *particulates*. The negative image of heavy goods vehicles is in part due to public awareness of the damage resulting from their use.

**performance bonds** A type of *enforcement* incentive that can be used in the field of environmental pollution policy. *Non-compliance fees* are the most widely applied variation of this bond. In general, performance bonds are payments to authorities which take place prior to an activity that is potentially environmentally harmful. These bonds are refunded if environmental *regulations* are met, and forfeited if they are not. These are used less frequently than other *economic instruments*, due to difficulties in monitoring environmental damage and legal restrictions in setting up contracts, and have been applied mainly where there is a clear potential for environmental damage, such as surface mining. Australia, Norway, Sweden, Canada and the US use slightly different variations of these instruments in controlling environmentally harmful production. (OECD, 1989b.) See also *assurance bonding system; deposit refund scheme.*

**permit allocation** In a system of *marketable emissions permits,* the aggregate level of pollution is limited by the number of *emissions permits* in existence. The ability to trade permits means that firms whose *abatement* costs are high can buy pollution permits from firms whose costs are lower, minimizing the overall cost of achieving a given reduction in pollution. Permit allocation is the process by which the initial allocation of the permits, prior to trading, is determined. The most common means by which permits are allocated is by auction, or by *grandfathering,* whereby permits are distributed in proportion to emissions at an agreed date.

**permits** Official authorizations to engage in particular activities, particularly to operate a facility within specified limits of pollution. *Marketable emissions permits* allow permit holders to trade their permits with others. See also *allowance.*

**perverse incentives** An incentive that encourages behaviour which is socially inefficient. For example, consider a forest that provides *non-marketed* social benefits, such as the *indirect value* of *biodiversity* and of watershed protection, and the *direct use value* of using the forest for recreation. The private owner of the forest will not account for these social benefits, and may find it financially efficient to convert the forest to agricultural land. This is an example of *market failure.* An efficient government policy would be to subsidize the *conservation* of forestry by the amount of the external social benefit.

A perverse incentive resulting from government policy would arise when a government provides a subsidy for conversion of forest land to agriculture, which re-enforces the effect of the market failure. Such perverse *subsidies* have been responsible for significant *deforestation* in recent years. See also *policy failure.*

**pH scale** This scale measures the degree of acidity of a particular substance, on a 0 to 14 scale. A measure of 14 on this scale indicates that the substance is extremely alkaline, while at the opposite end of the scale 0 indicates pure acid.

**physical depletion** Physical depletion occurs when a stock of a resource is physically exhausted, in the sense that the stock is reduced to zero. This is distinct from *economic depletion,* which means that although the stock is not exhausted, it is no longer profitable for extraction to continue. This is the point at which *extraction costs* exceed the revenues from selling the extracted resource. (Perman et al, 1999.) See also *asymptotic depletion; depletion; natural resources.*

**Pigovian tax** The *environmental tax* paid by the polluting party; it is equal to the marginal *external cost* born by the victims of pollution. The polluter is thus informed about the full *social costs* (ideally including local, regional and global costs) of his or her operation, and the victim can be fairly compensated.

**planned obsolescence** The deliberate production of products with a short lifespan in order to increase the frequency with which they need to be replaced, and thus increase revenue. (Tietenberg, 1996.) See also *functional obsolescence*.

**point source pollution** A type of pollution that emanates from identifiable sources. An obvious example of a point source is a factory with a smoke stack. Pollution from point sources can be modelled using *dispersion modelling* and valued using a number of techniques, based around the *impact pathway approach*. ExternE (1995) presents a review of techniques to value pollution from point sources. See also *non-point source pollution; air quality, valuation of*.

**policy failure** The failure of government policy to correct *market failures*. An example of policy failure occurs when a market failure, such as the *non-marketed* social benefits of *environmental resources*, exists, and government policy does not address the problem. Another example of policy failure arises when a policy instrument is put in place but is insufficient to correct the market failure. Further examples of policy failure are *institutional failure* and *perverse incentives*.

**policy instruments** See *economic instruments*.

**polluter pays principle (PPP)** The principle that the price of a good or service should include the *cost of environmental damage* that results from the production process. This can be achieved by charging polluters for the *environmental externalities* of the production of a good or service.

The PPP was introduced by the OECD in 1973. The idea was put on the international stage by OECD Recommendation C (72)128 in 1982. Countries within the OECD reaffirmed this principle in 1985, seeking to introduce 'more flexible, efficient and cost-effective pollution control measures through a consistent application of the Polluter Pays Principle and *economic instruments*'. (Pearce and Turner, 1990.) See also *victim pays principle (VPP)*.

**pollution accounts** Part of the *natural resource accounts* framework. They measure emissions of pollutants into water and air, taking stock of the source. Pollution accounts do not value stocks and flows of pollution in monetary terms, which means that their use in adjusting economic indicators, eg *national accounts*, is limited. (Krishnan et al, 1995.)

**pollution charges** See *pollution taxes*.

**pollution, efficient level of** See *efficient level of pollution*.

**pollution haven** A country with relaxed environmental standards. These lower standards provide incentives for companies to operate in these countries because the pollution resulting from the productive processes is less controlled, resulting in lower production costs. Many empirical studies have shown little or no evidence to support the theory that lower production costs of this type affect the polluting activities of companies. For a review of the impact of *international environmental agreements* on the establishment of pollution havens see Jha, Markandya and Vossenaar (1999). See also *environmental dumping; uniform minimum environmental standards*.

**pollution permit system** See *emissions trading*.

**pollution taxes** A type of *economic instrument* with two purposes, namely to raise revenue and to provide an incentive to reduce pollution. The ultimate

position goods

objective of a pollution tax is to correct the *market failure* which exists because the *social costs* of pollution are not reflected in production costs, and therefore in the market price of the resulting good. Pollution is taxed so that production costs, and therefore market prices, reflect true social cost.

Charging for pollution will provide firms with an incentive to reduce pollution. The revenue raised from pollution taxes can be used to reduce the taxes on socially desirable items, such as labour. This is known as the *double dividend*. Pollution taxes are imposed relatively infrequently because in practice they are difficult to design. This is because it is difficult to estimate both the true social costs of pollution (although methods for doing this, such as the *contingent valuation method (CVM)*, are available) and the true *abatement costs* of polluting firms. It is thus difficult to know the effect a tax might have on the level of pollution and output of the good. There is thus a possibility that taxes may be set at the wrong level, resulting either in insufficient abatement of pollution or in the imposition of excessive costs on industry. See also *disincentives; environmental taxation; Pigovian tax.*

**position goods** The satisfaction gained by consumers of position goods depends on the position in society associated with such goods. That is, if the consumption of a certain good indicates that a person is socially or economically successful, then the total *utility* provided by the good is greater than it would be otherwise. An example of a position good is an expensive car. (Perman et al, 1999.)

**positive feedback loops** See *feedback loops.*

**precautionary principle (PP)** The PP has been included in numerous international documents, including the European Bergen Declaration of 1990, the UN Rio Declaration on Environment and Development, and the *Framework Convention on Climate Change (FCCC)* of 1992. Upholding the PP means that states agree to act with care when taking actions which may harm the *environment*. The PP is defined in the Rio Declaration as follows: 'where there are threats of serious or irreversible damage, lack of full scientific certainty shall not be used as a reason for postponing cost-effective measures to prevent environmental degradation'.

The practical applicability of the PP has been questioned, given the qualitative descriptions used in its definition, such as 'serious and irreversible environmental damage', and 'scientific certainty'. However, the PP implies the 'institutionalization of precaution, which would itself entail the shifting of the burden of proof from those opposing environmental degradation to those engaged in the challenged activity' (O'Riordan and Cameron, 1994). See also *absorptive capacity; ecological economics; irreversibility; safe minimum standards (SMS); uncertainty.*

**pressure, state, response (PSR) indicators** Means of communicating environmental information and trends in a format that is easy to interpret. The PSR framework has been developed in work on *environmental indicators* by the OECD, World Bank and the World Resources Institute (WRI). The framework seeks to develop indicators that highlight the environmental pressures resulting from human activities, changes to the state of the *environment* arising from these pressures, and societal responses to these changes. Pressure indicators can relate to individual companies, industrial sectors and underlying national or international trends. State indicators relate to environmental quality, economic performance and societal impacts. Response indicators include government policy, regulation, financial instruments (taxes and *subsidies*), research, business strategy and NGO actions.

**preventative expenditure** Expenditures aimed at averting the damages associated with pollution and other *externalities*. Estimates for these are sometimes used as measures of the lower bound of the costs of the environmental damages. Expenditures to mitigate damages to the *environment* can be seen as a surrogate demand for environmental protection. (Dixon et al, 1986.) See also *mitigation; abatement costs*.

**price system** The prevailing set of prices for goods and services in an economy. The price system plays a central role in economic theory, particularly classical and neoclassical theory, because of the importance of prices in establishing the returns on particular investments. A crucial premise of mainstream economics is that when the price system sends accurate signals about the demand for and *scarcity* of goods and services, investment will be directed into the most productive economic activities, these being the most profitable activities. However, the prices of some goods and services, in particular those of *public goods* and activities that produce positive or negative affects on others (positive or negative *externalities*), will not reach their optimal levels through market forces alone, and may require government intervention.

**prisoners' dilemma** A model used in *game theory*. This has several applications in *environmental economics*. The prisoners' dilemma illustrates a situation in which a superior solution can be achieved if two players cooperate, but where both are worse off in the absence of cooperation. The model consists of two prisoners who are being held in separate cells. The authorities require confessions to secure convictions, but will convict on a lesser charge if both prisoners remain silent. Each prisoner can receive a minimal sentence if he confesses while his accomplice remains silent; in this case the accomplice will receive the full sentence. If both confess, moderate sentences will be passed on both. Table 3 illustrates these pay-offs.

**Table 4** *The Prisoners' Dilemma*

|  |  | Prisoner A | |
|---|---|---|---|
|  |  | Confess | Remain silent |
| Prisoner B | Confess | A : 2 years<br>B : 2 years | A : 4 years<br>B : 6 months |
|  | Remain silent | A : 6 months<br>B : 4 years | A : 1 year<br>B : 1 year |

Clearly, if the prisoners could cooperate, they could agree to remain silent and limit their sentences to 1 year. This would be the *cooperative solution* to the problem. However, in the absence of cooperation, the *non-cooperative solution* will hold. An examination of the pay-offs shows that for both prisoners, confession is the best strategy whatever the other prisoner does. Prisoner A's pay-offs if he confesses are 2 years or 6 months, while if he remains silent they are 4 years or 1 year. Prisoner B is in the same position and thus self-interest

# private economic efficiency

will lead both prisoners to confess. This is the non-cooperative solution to the problem.

This framework can be used to model the formation of *international environmental agreements (IEAs)*. If two countries implement an IEA to reduce pollution, then both countries can benefit. However, if one were to abate pollution while the other does not, then the other country would benefit from the reduced pollution while avoiding the costs of abatement. Thus, the prisoners' dilemma can be used to model the decision-making 'game' when IEAs are agreed. (Stead, Curwen and Lawler, 1996.)

**private economic efficiency** A situation in which, on the basis of market prices, resources are allocated to production and consumption so as to maximize the *utility* that they provide. This criterion does not account for the external, social costs and benefits of production and consumption. Thus, an economy could exhibit private *economic efficiency* while being socially inefficient. (Bromley, 1991.)

**producer surplus** A monetary measure of the benefit to a firm of producing a good. It is the excess of the price received for a given quantity of a good over the costs of producing that quantity. An economically efficient allocation of resources is one in which the sum of *consumer surplus*, producer surplus and *external benefits* are maximized. See also *economic efficiency; Pareto efficiency.*

**product charge** A type of *economic instrument*, in which a charge is levied on the final product in relation to the level of damage caused by its production, manufacture or consumption. Hence it is a type of *pollution charge*. Product charges are introduced in order to discourage the consumption of products harmful to the environment (OECD, 1989b.) Product charges have been levied on batteries, used tyres and packaging, among other goods. See also *charges.*

**product standard** This specifies the physical and chemical requirements which a product must satisfy before it can be marketed.

**production externalities** Production *externalities* occur when a firm, in producing a given good, affects other agents, either other firms or individuals, but does not account for this effect in its production decisions. The most common example in *environmental economics* of a negative production externality is pollution of water, air or land.

**production function approach** This is an approach to valuing *non-marketed goods* which serve as inputs to the production of marketed goods. The approach relates the output of particular marketed goods or services (eg agricultural production, timber, fish catches) to the inputs necessary to produce them. These include marketed inputs such as labour, *capital* and land, as well as non-marketed environmental goods or services such as soil stability, water quality or air quality.

The production function that describes the contribution of all of the inputs to production can be expressed as follows:

$$Q = f(X,v)$$

where $X$ is the environmental good or service to be valued, and $v$ is a vector of other inputs.

Likewise, the minimum cost of producing a given output can be expressed as a function of the quantity, the prices of marketed inputs, and the availability of the environmental good or service. A change in the availability of the good or service is likely to change both the amount of the good produced and the price at which this amount can be produced. An accurate measure of the change in welfare brought about by a change in the availability of an environmental good would be the changes in *consumer surplus* and *producer surplus*. In practice these are difficult to measure, and therefore the change in welfare can be approximated by the marginal contribution to production of the environmental good or service times the price of the product. (Markandya et al, 2002.) See also *household production function*.

**property rights** These signify the right to put resources to certain uses, to prevent others from using the resources, and to sell the resource. Resources can be interpreted broadly, and can include both man-made goods and natural assets such as land, forests and fisheries. Property rights can be held by an individual, by the state, or in common – that is, by a limited and identifiable group of people. Property rights to produced resources are usually well-defined. However, this is not always the case for natural assets. An absence of property rights to an environmental asset means there is *open access* to the resource. This often leads to overexploitation of the resource, sometimes resulting in the *tragedy of the commons*, whereby the asset is degraded and/or depleted due to uncontrolled access.

The concept of property rights is particularly important to the proper functioning of markets and to the efficient management of *environmental resources*. For instance, consider the problem of air pollution. This can be considered as a problem of incomplete property rights, in that rights to clean air do not exist. The existence of an *externality* means that the market does not produce either the socially efficient level of the good or the socially *efficient level of pollution*. Consider also the problem of ill-defined property rights to land. In this case, the user of the land has no incentive either to invest in improving the land, or to use the land sustainably. (OECD, 1992a.) See also *non-exclusion*.

**prospect theory** A theory proposed by Kahnemann and Tversky (1979) relating to the way in which individuals value *risk*. Kahnemann and Tversky found that there is a difference between actual behaviour and the way that *expected utility* theory would predict people to behave. They found evidence of a 'certainty effect' whereby individuals presented with a choice between a certain gain of 3000, or the 0.8 probability of a gain of 4000 (with a 0.2 probability of no gain), preferred the former even though the latter provided a greater *expected utility*. However, when the problem is reversed and respondents are presented with the choice between a certain loss of 3000 and a 0.8 probability of a 4000 loss with a 0.2 probability of a 0 loss, the overwhelming majority choose the latter. Such asymmetric preferences between uncertain gains and uncertain losses have implications for policy decisions regarding expenditure to reduce the risk of future environmental losses. (Bromley, 1991.)

**proximity principle** This states that disposal of waste should occur at the nearest plant offering the most appropriate technologies to guarantee a high level of protection for the *environment* and public health. This aims to control waste flows and to support the development of *best available technologies*, to encourage regional and local self-sufficiency. (Erkki and Marttinen, 1995.)

**public goods** Goods whose consumption by one person does not alter the availability of the good for all other consumers. Such a good is 'non-rival in consumption'. To satisfy the definition of a pure public good, it must also be impossible, or possible only at a prohibitively high cost, to prevent people from consuming the good, so that the existing quantity of the good is consumed equally by all people. Many environmental goods are public goods, clean air and the preservation of a nation's *biodiversity* being examples. Because public goods can be consumed by all, there is no incentive for private individuals or organizations to finance them. Thus the quantities supplied in a pure market economy would be lower than the socially efficient level. They are a form of positive *externality*, or *market failure*, and there is a role for government in providing the socially efficient amount of public goods. Non-environmental examples of public goods are national defence and the police service.

**pure rate of time preference** See *utility discount rate*.

# Qq

**quality-adjusted life year (QALY)** This is used to measure the productivity of health services. QALYs are calculated using a number of parameters including physical disability, social and emotional function, and health problems. The relative values of health states are scored on a scale of zero to one, with zero representing death and one indicating normal health. These values are multiplied by the number of life years gained from a treatment, so that the productivity of the treatment in terms of years of life gained is adjusted for differences in quality of life caused by various states of health. (Holland, 1993.) See Drummond, Stoddart and Torrance (1987) for an application of this approach. See also *disability adjusted life year.*

**quantitative controls** Forms of pollution regulation that set direct, quantitative controls, or standards, on the amount of pollution permitted from each source. These are *command and control (CAC) policy* measures, and are the most common form of pollution regulation, being favoured by policy-makers over other forms of regulation, such as *pollution taxes* and *marketable emissions permits.* This is despite the fact that, at least in theory, such *market-based instruments (MBIs)* allow given reductions in pollution to be achieved at the lowest cost, as well as providing incentives to reduce pollution further over time, which pollution standards do not. (Perman et al, 1999.) See also *ambient-based standards; emissions standards; fixed standard approach; direct regulations; regulations; standard setting.*

**quasi-option value** The value of preserving a natural asset, such as an ancient woodland, that accrues because of an expected increase in knowledge that will increase the use that can be made of the asset. For example, increased scientific knowledge may increase the medical use that can be made of the *species* contained in the forest. This is distinct from *option value,* which accrues because of *uncertainty* of the future supply of the *environmental resource* in question. (Pearce and Turner, 1990.)

**quota systems** Quota systems are used in *environmental management* to limit the exploitation of *biological resources* such as fisheries and wild livestock, and thus to prevent the depletion of the resource stock. They involve issuing *permits* to all of the users of the resource, eg fishermen, allowing the extraction of a certain amount of the resource. The total number of permits issued corresponds to the maximum extraction that is considered to be sustainable. Quota systems are widely used in the regulation of fisheries; for instance the European Commission sets total allowable catches (TACs) for stocks within its waters. For the major North Sea Stocks these are set in agreement with Norway, and for the major Baltic Sea stocks they are set in agreement with the Baltic states. See also *marketable catch permits.*

# Rr

**radical uncertainty** This is present when it is not possible to specify all of the potential consequences of a decision. It differs from *risk*, which implies that probabilities can be assigned to the various possible consequences, and from *uncertainty*, which implies that the various possible consequences can be identified but that probabilities cannot be assigned to them. (Common, 1995.)

**rainfed crop management** Method used in the management of crop production in regions where rainfall can be unreliable and hence present problems. Under rainfed crop management the optimal growing strategy may be based on the probability of a given rainfall, which is estimated on the basis of historical experience. A manager might attempt to grow crops and to maximize yield based on the expected rainfall. There are, however, problems in the definition of expected rainfall, as the mean value may underestimate the level of rainfall owing to skewing effects caused by extreme, and unlikely, weather conditions. A more rational strategy, Dixon et al argue, may be to base decisions on the cropping strategy on the most likely conditions of a typical year rather than on a strict averaging procedure. (Dixon et al, 1989.)

**Ramsey rule** This rule, named after the Cambridge economist and mathematician Frank Ramsey, illustrates the relationship between the *consumption discount rate* and the *utility discount rate*. An economy's consumption discount rate is greater than its utility discount rate by a factor related to the rate at which the economy's consumption is growing over time. Thus, in a steady state, when consumption is constant, the two discount rates are equal.

**rate of time discount** See *discounting*.

**rational expectation** The expectation of future conditions based on all the information available. This form of expectation is one of three commonly cited in the literature, the others being *static expectation* and *adaptive expectation*. Under static expectation, current changes in conditions are expected to persist. Under adaptive expectation, changes in conditions over the recent past are extrapolated into the future. Some economists believe that government policies to stabilize the economy are doomed to be ineffective because of rational expectation, since rational economic agents will anticipate the effect of these policies and adjust their behaviour accordingly.

**Rawlsian ethics** Rawls (1971) suggests a view of *justice* that is a challenge to the utilitarian indifference to the distributional impacts of resources. Rawls argues that a 'veil of ignorance' should be employed in decision making, whereby the individual has no idea of their status in a social structure. Perman et al (1999) provide a review of the impacts of Rawlsian *ethics* on *environmental economics*. See also *equity; environmental ethics; maximin principle; Kantian ethics; libertarian ethics*.

**reactive policy responses** Reactive policy occurs when a government institutes environmental regulation or measures to reduce the damages associated with an environmental effect or an environmental change, such as *climate change*. Examples of reactive policy may include the building of larger sea defences in response to rising sea levels and increased inundation. Reactive policy is distinct from *anticipatory policy*, where governments predict changes in the *environment* and respond by taking measures to avoid damages before the event.

**reasonably available control technology (RACT)** This represents the minimum emissions limit that a particular source is capable of meeting by the application of an available, and economically and technologically feasible, control technology. Luken (1990) suggests that this 'is usually applied to existing sources in *non-attainment areas* and in most cases is less stringent than *new source performance standards*'. (Luken, 1990.) See also *best available techniques (BAT)*.

**recycling** The re-use of *natural resources* or products derived from natural resources. Recycling schemes may help to reduce waste levels, *deforestation* and other negative environmental impacts. Instruments to encourage recycling include *deposit refund schemes*. Examples include the re-use of glass bottles and plastics. Panayotou (1998) suggested that a system of *marketable permits* could be used to enable firms to meet targets for recycling at least cost, and that the US was considering such a system to encourage the recycling of old newspapers. Panayotou also presents a review of deposit refund schemes, with the overall conclusion that such schemes are a cost-effective means of both reducing waste disposal costs and conserving inputs. (Panayotou, 1998.)

**reference dose** The reference dose of a *pollutant* is an estimate of the level of exposure to the pollutant that is considered, on the basis of scientific evidence, to be unlikely to cause either short-term or long-term harm to humans.

**regulations** Regulations are government measures that explicitly require or restrict specific actions on the part of individuals or firms in a country. Regulation has been the main instrument of *environmental management*, involving the specification of responsibilities to redress environmental damage. Restrictions have also been placed on actions that may be considered detrimental to the environment, including the location of industry and the dumping of waste.

There is a growing movement towards the use of alternatives to *command and control (CAC) policy* regulations. These alternatives, such as *market-based instruments (MBIs)* and other *economic instruments*, offer opportunities for the reduction of the cost and difficulty of meeting and *enforcing emissions standards* and other environmental regulations (see Panayotou, 1998 for a review of the application of regulation). See also *direct regulations; environmental regulation; environmental shirking*.

**regulatory capture** The capture of a regulatory body occurs when the continued contact of regulators with those firms being regulated leads to the regulator becoming sympathetic towards the regulated firms, which deflects the regulator from their stated purpose. An example of regulatory capture occurs when a regulator leaves the regulation industry to go into the regulated industry. See also *capture theory*.

**relocation cost technique** This is a variant of the *replacement cost technique*. The application of this technique involves the estimation of the potential benefits of avoiding environmental damage, by using the actual costs of site relocation due to a degradation in the ambient *environment*. Dixon et al (1986) cite the case of the *valuation* of the impact of the discharge of wastewater into a stream by an oil-palm mill. Here, it may be necessary to relocate extraction facilities for drinking water in a village to a site which is upstream of the mill; this cost is an indication of (at least a part of) the *economic cost*s of the environmental impact. (Dixon et al, 1986.)

**renewable energy** Renewable energy resources, such as wind, biomass and solar power, are increasingly gaining attention in the field of *environmental economics*. This increase in interest is partly due to potential resource *scarcity* and also *climate change* issues resulting from differentials in the *global warming potentials (GWPs)* of different fuels in the production of energy. See also *backstop technology*.

**renewable resources** Resources that are replenished naturally, including plant resources such as forests, and stocks of animal *species* such as fish. Natural reproduction means that the stocks of these resources can increase over time. However, overexploitation can lead to their depletion. If the harvest of a resource is equal to the maximum natural growth rate, given the productive capacity of the resource stock, then the resource is said to be harvested at the *maximum sustainable yield (MSY)*. Such a yield may be taken indefinitely, all other things being equal. (Perman et al, 1999.) See also *natural resources; non-renewable resources; renewable energy; biological growth; interactive resources, maximum sustainable yield*.

**rent** See *resource rent*.

**rent-seeking behaviour** Rent-seeking behaviour is considered to consist of efforts to retain or acquire *factors of production*. Pearce et al (1990) cite the case of Indonesia in which the government's failure to capture rents from timber extraction resulted in such behaviour. As a consequence, there was an acceleration in *deforestation*, as those holding concessions sought to secure a large share of the rents for themselves.

**replacement cost technique** This approach values the cost of replacing damaged assets, including environmental assets, and takes these costs as estimates of the benefit flow from *avertive* behaviour. This *objective valuation approach (OVA)* is similar to the *preventative expenditure* approach, although in this case the expenditures are based on the actual cost of replacement in the event of damage, and are not a subjective *valuation*. The application of this technique does not measure the benefits of measures to prevent environmental damages as such. This approach makes the assumption that the damage is measurable and that the value of the environmental asset is no greater than the replacement cost. It also assumes that no secondary or *ancillary benefits* arise from the expenditures on environmental protection.

This approach is particularly applicable where there is a standard which must be met, such as a certain level of *water quality*. Here replacement costs may provide a first approximation of the costs or benefits of a given action. See also *shadow project*. (Dixon et al, 1986.)

**resilience** The ability of an *ecosystem* to maintain its structure and behaviour when faced with a change in the *environment*. Common (1995) suggests that resilience means the system remains intact after an environmental change. This does not necessarily require the survival of all of the *species* populations present before the change. A system is considered to be ecologically sustainable if it is resilient. (Common, 1995.) See also *ecological stability; vulnerability*.

**resource accounting** See *natural resource accounting; national accounts; green accounting*.

**resource-adjusted net domestic product (RANDP)** This is the value of a nation's output, adjusted for the *depreciation* of *human-made capital* and the depletion of *natural resources*. The RANDP is a central concept in natural *resource accounting*. This measure has been criticized, however, for its inability to signal the *risks* of *ecosystem* collapse, although it does provide some indication of *sustainability* in that it places a value on the degradation of the *natural capital*. See also *natural resource accounting; national accounts; green accounting*.

**resource economics** A branch of economics related to the exploitation, extraction and regulation of the use of *natural resources*. Resource economics has attempted to build on *neoclassical economics*, with the aim of identifying the optimal and efficient allocation or exploitation of resources. Major topics within resource economics include: *maximum sustainable yield* (MSY) and the fact that extracting the maximum sustainable yield is not necessarily an economically efficient *renewable resource* management strategy; *non-market valuation* of the attributes of natural resources such as *water quality* and *biodiversity* among others; and the *sustainability* of the use of natural resources. Resource economics is linked to *environmental economics*, to the extent that environmental quality can be considered a natural resource. The treatment of *intrinsic value* is a contentious issue in resource economics, as is the treatment of *intergenerational* and intragenerational *equity* in resource use.

**resource intensity** The intensity with which a natural resource is employed in the production of a product.

**resource management** The control of the use of *natural resources* in order to maximize the benefits that the resource provides, while preventing overexploitation or degradation of the resource base. This may include the use of *economic instruments* such as *marketable permits* for the extraction of resources or other forms of *regulation*. Resource management can be used to ensure that *renewable resource* extraction is both efficient and sustainable.

**resource rent** Rents refer to the profits that accrue to a firm, over and above the amount which can be considered a reasonable return on its invested *capital*, the latter being known in economics as 'normal profits'. Resource rents refer to the profits that accrue to a resource-extracting firm due to the fact that part of the price of the resource can be considered to be compensation for the fact that a valuable asset (ie the resource stock) is being liquidated. Thus, resource rents accrue where a *non-renewable resource* is being exploited, and where a renewable resource is exploited unsustainably. Resource rents are also known as *Hotelling rents*.

**resource-use quotas** Quotas established by governments to restrict the exploitation of renewable *natural resources,* thereby limiting pollution and sharing the burden of pollution abatement across different industries. (OECD, 1994d.) See also *quotas.*

**resource user cost** This is the *opportunity cost* of harvesting a natural resource. In the case of *renewable resources,* this is taken to be the *net present value (NPV)* of the return that could have been raised from the resource had the resource been allowed to grow rather than being harvested. In the case of *non-renewable resources* it is the NPV of the depleted resource stock. See also *user cost approach.*

**restoration activities** Activities to counter the environmentally damaging impacts of economic activity, or to prevent a decrease in environmental quality. (Hohmeyer, Otinger and Rennings, 1997.) See also *avertive expenditures.*

**revealed preference** This refers to a class of methods used to estimate the economic value of environmental goods or environmental damage. These methods deploy the fact that there are markets for goods which are related to *non-marketed* environmental goods; consumer behaviour in these markets can be used to infer the value placed on the related environmental goods. An example is the use of the *hedonic price* method to infer from the housing market the value of *air quality.* Another example is the use of the *travel cost method (TCM)* to infer the value that consumers place on visiting environmental assets such as forests. The name 'revealed preference' derives from the fact that these methods use actual behaviour, as revealed in markets, to estimate preferences. These are distinct from *stated preferences (SPs),* which involve asking respondents to state their values for environmental goods. See also *valuation.*

**rights-based approach** An approach that assumes that environmental assets have the right to exist. Under this approach, non-human biota, and sometimes even non-sentient objects, should be conserved regardless of the costs associated with *conservation.* This has been raised in connection with the argument that animals should be considered to have rights. See also *extended rights; ethics.*

**Rio Conference** The United Nations Conference on Environment and Development (UNCED), or *Earth Summit,* was held in Rio do Janeiro in June 1992. It produced the *Framework Convention on Climate Change (FCCC),* the *Convention on Biological Diversity,* a declaration on the *sustainable development (SD)* of forests, and *Agenda 21.* A key part of these policies was an emphasis on the *conservation* of *natural resources.* As a result of this conference, changes have been made in productive processes, and there has been an increased awareness of the need for alternative energy sources – including *renewable energy* – to replace fossil fuel combustion, and the need for public transportation to be expanded. See the UN briefing on the consequences of this conference, available on the web at http://www.un.org/geninfo/bp/enviro.html.

**riparian rights** The riparian water rights doctrine descending from English common law assigns user rights to the landowner whose property borders on a body of water. The presumption made is that one user's consumption of water will not affect the supply available to others on the water body. (Hartwick and Olewiler, 1986.)

**risk** Situations involving risk are those in which the possible consequences of a decision can be completely enumerated, and probabilities assigned to each possibility. Risk is distinct from *uncertainty*, in which the possible consequences of a decision can be enumerated, but probabilities cannot be assigned to these consequences, and from *radical uncertainty*, in which not only can probabilities not be assigned to the consequences of a decision, but the possible consequences themselves cannot be fully identified. See also *expected utility, expected value (EV)*.

**risk assessment (RA)** An assessment to determine the relationship between, say, the concentration of a pollutant in the *environment* and its effect on human health. (Turner et al, 1994.) It is a scientific process of identifying hazards, and estimating risk in qualitative or quantitative terms. This involves four analytical steps: the identification of hazards; the quantification of damaging effects, including the use of *dose–response evelutions and functions*; the quantification of exposure levels; and assessment of the nature of the risk faced, based on evaluation of the factors identified.

**risk assessment policy** This consists of predetermined guidelines for scientific judgements and policy choices which may be applied at specific decision points in the *risk assessment* process.

**risk management (RM)** The development and selection of policy options based on *risk assessment*. Policy-makers may have some risk-balancing standard by which policies can be evaluated, for example using *cost–benefit analysis*. If the important factors relating to a decision cannot be valued in monetary terms, as may be the case for issues relating to the distribution of risk, then *multi-criteria analysis* may be needed.

**risk pooling** Risk pooling occurs when risky outcomes are combined to reduce the overall level of risk. Such pooling can reduce the costs of *risk* and hence can lead to welfare improvements. Examples of risk pooling include the provision of insurance and, in the area of natural resource exploitation, the formation of a syndicate of exploration companies, so that the costs of, and returns from, exploration are shared more widely. (Hartwick and Olewiler, 1986.)

**risk premium** The risk premium is the amount that must be paid to an individual so that he becomes indifferent between the certainty of receiving a sum of money, and a risky outcome the expected value of which is equal to the certain sum. For instance an individual may prefer a certain payment of $100 to the risky prospect of an 0.8 probability of $120 and an 0.2 probability of $20. If an addition of $10 to the risky option meant that the individual was then indifferent between the two options, then this is the risk premium required to take this risk. (Hartwick and Olewiler, 1986.) See also *risk*.

**roll-in pricing strategy** Under this strategy, the price to the consumers is the average cost of the mixture of the depletable resource and the substitute resource. (Tietenberg, 1994)

**rotation period** The rotation period is the period between the planting of a commercial forest and its harvesting. The efficient, or optimal, rotation period is the period which maximizes the *net present value (NPV)* of the revenue from

# rotation period

the commercial forest. This becomes lower as the discount rate increases. However, it is extended if the analysis accounts for the non-timber benefits of forestry, such as recreational and aesthetic benefits, and the habitat provided to diverse *species*.

# Ss

**safe minimum standard (SMS)** Safe minimum standards are usually based on the *precautionary principle*. Common (1995) presents an analytical framework for the evaluation of the SMS, based on the minimax regret criterion whereby one aims to minimize the potential level of regret by adopting the scheme with the lowest level of regret. This concept has been applied to *conservation* of *species* and *natural resources*. (Perman et al, 1999.)

**satellite accounts** Satellite accounts are based on *national accounts* and show how these may be complemented or modified by including the monetary values, or physical measures, of the environmental effects of economic activity, and the effects of changes in the *environment* on the economy. OECD (1994a) suggests that the rationale behind such accounts lies in the fact that changes in the long-established standard national accounting system are unlikely to be accepted or well understood. See also *environmental accounting; green accounting*.

**scarcity** One of the main focuses of economics is on the efficient use of scarce resources. Resources are said to be scarce if demand for them must be rationed by means of a price. Natural resource scarcity is the extent to which *natural resources* are limited. Pearce and Turner (1990) present a review of some measures of scarcity including both physical measures and economic scarcity indices. Physical measures of scarcity are derived from geological estimates of reserves, while economic indices attempt to measure scarcity through an indicator such as price or cost. Three of the measures commonly used are: the real costs of production of a resource; the real prices of goods that are resource intensive; and the scarcity rents of the resource (based on a *shadow price*). Pearce and Turner argue that no one measure of scarcity is generally correct, and suggest that the appropriate use of different indicators depends on the nature of scarcity, based on Hall and Hall (1984), in which scarcity is defined in four ways:

1   Malthusian stock scarcity, where the stock is fixed and there are constant *extraction costs*;
2   Malthusian flow scarcity, where stock is fixed but costs rise with extraction;
3   Ricardian stock scarcity, where stocks are not constrained but costs rise with extraction rate and the extent to which the resource has been extracted previously; and
4   Ricardian flow scarcity, where no stock constraint exists but costs rise with extraction.

(Pearce and Turner, 1990.) See also *absolute scarcity*.

**scrubber** An air pollution device that reduces pollutants in emissions through the use of water spraying or dry processes. (Luken, 1990.)

**Second Law of Thermodynamics** This law states that in any thermodynamic process, the *entropy* of a system plus its *environment* must either increase or remain unchanged. This law has been used to explain the rationale for the lack of *recycling*, since the process of recycling must itself be costly in terms of increased entropy. Thus entropy presents an obstacle to the design of a sustainable system. (Pearce and Turner, 1990.) See also *First Law of Thermodynamics*.

**secondary benefit** Also known as an *ancillary benefit*. A benefit that results from the implementation of a policy, but which is not the principal aim of the policy. An example is reduced health costs arising from lowered air pollution as a result of a *carbon tax* on emissions. These benefits are of particular importance in the *climate change* debate, with the potential for offsetting *mitigation* costs against such benefits, making climate change mitigation more attractive to national governments. Their importance in the climate change debate lies in the fact that many of the key secondary, or ancillary, costs and benefits are short term and local in nature, and as such are quite different from those benefits derived from mitigation policies, which will tend to be global and long term. Krupnick, Buttraw and Markandya (2000) provide a framework for analysing such benefits and costs of climate change policies.

**semi-renewable resources** Resources whose stocks renew themselves to a certain extent, but whose capacity to renew can be compromised by excessive use. Examples of these resources include soil quality, the *assimilative capacity* of the environment and ecological *life support services*. (Barbier, 1993.)

**shadow price** A price that should be used in *cost–benefit analysis (CBA)* and other decision-making frameworks when *market failure* leads to market prices which do not accurately reflect economic values, and thus do not reflect the full *opportunity costs* of an action. Adjustments to market prices to obtain shadow prices are required when there are distortionary taxes and *subsidies*, and when there are monopolies or other market imperfections that lead to the market prices being higher or lower than the economic opportunity cost. Markandya (1998a) suggests that there are two distinct methods for estimating the shadow price of a resource, depending on whether a resource is tradable or not. Where a resource is tradable, the international price can be used. Assuming well functioning markets, the export or import price of a good can be used after a correction for taxes and subsidies. Where a resource is not traded, the shadow price should be estimated from the cost of producing the good when inputs are valued at the economic opportunity cost. The latter method was developed by Little and Mirrlees (1974), Squire and van der Tak (1975) and Ray (1984) and has been applied to estimate shadow prices in a number of countries. (Markandya, 1998a.)

**shadow project method** An application of the *strong sustainability* criterion, whereby if a development threatens a component of the *natural capital* stock such as a rare habitat, a shadow project must provide a substitute for the asset. The possible alternatives are: asset reconstruction (ie, providing an alternative habitat site for a threatened wildlife habitat); asset transplantation (ie, moving the existing habitat to a new site); or asset restoration (ie, enhancing an existing degraded habitat). The cost of the chosen option is added to the basic cost of the proposed development project in order to estimate the full cost. Inclusion of shadow project costs gives an indication of how great the benefits of the development project must be in order to outweigh the losses it causes. The development project will be accepted if the benefits are at least equal to the development project costs plus the shadow project costs. (Markandya et al, 2002.)

**shallow ecologists** Shallow ecologists frame ecological arguments in human terms. Deep ecologists criticize such groups for failing to move to a more biocentric position. (Krishnan et al, 1995.)

**shelter belt** Trees planted to protect crops against storm damage and to protect soils from erosion. (Schramm and Warford, 1989.)

**sickness impact profile (SIP)** Measure of the impacts of a number of health effects on the quality of life. Developed by Bergner and colleagues, this measure examines such issues as sleep and rest, eating, and the ability to work and to enjoy non-work activities, as well as a person's physical and psychological condition. (Nussbaum and Sen, 1993.)

**silviculture** A term used for forest cultivation and management. (Hartwick and Olewiler, 1986.)

**sin taxes** Taxes on products or activities that are considered socially harmful, examples being alcohol and tobacco. Governments justify heavy taxation on such goods by citing the *social costs* of their consumption, for example the adverse health impacts of smoking. (O'Riordan, 1997.)

**social capital** In the analysis of *sustainability* and *sustainable development (SD)*, the various different types of capital, including human-made capital, human capital and natural capital, play an important role. Social capital is now included in this analysis, as being one of the factors that contribute to social wellbeing. There are many competing definitions of social capital but most of them incorporate the following features: relations of trust, reciprocity and exchanges between individuals which facilitate cooperation; and common rules, norms, and sanctions mutually agreed or handed down within societies, networks and social groups. *Cultural resources* such as traditions are another aspect of social capital. The fact that allowing social capital to deteriorate, or *depreciate*, over time will lead to reduced wellbeing, other things being equal, underlines its relevance to sustainability. See also *capital; human capital; human-made capital*.

**social cost** The social cost of an activity is calculated as the sum of the private cost and the *external cost* resulting from the activity. The difference between social cost and private cost is important, as the private cost may over- or underestimate the true cost of an activity. This difference is brought about by *market failure*, and *internalization* of the difference requires the use of *economic instruments*. (Perman et al, 1999.) See also *externality*.

**social time preference rate of discount** See *discounting*.

**social welfare function** This relates the welfare of society to the *utility* levels of individuals and is used in evaluating the effects of changes in the quality or quantity of environmental goods. Johansson (1987) notes that this welfare function is generally assumed to have three major properties. First, an increase in the utility of one individual, when the utility of all other individuals remains constant, increases social welfare. Second, if there is a reduction in the utility

# soft financing

of one individual, there must be an increase in the utility experienced by another for social welfare to remain constant. Third, the weight given to the welfare of an individual is linked to his or her utility level – that is, weights can be applied to account for distributional considerations. (Johansson, 1987.) A social welfare function is necessary to identify the *optimal resource allocation* from among the *Pareto-efficient* allocations (PEAs).

**soft financing** The giving of loans on preferential terms to encourage *environmental investments*.

**soil erosion** The stripping of topsoil by rain and wind. This is a common problem in developing countries and has serious impacts on crop productivity. Erosion has long-term implications, as it may take centuries for the soil to replenish itself. (Schramm and Warford, 1989.)

Perman et al (1999) argue that economic activity is leading to the *desertification* of large tracts of land. Desertification is particularly likely to be a problem where land tenure is insecure, so that the incentives for those using the land to use it sustainably are weak.

**solid waste** Waste products ranging from municipal refuse to industrial wastes. Solid waste also refers to sewage sludge, agricultural waste, demolition wastes and mining residues. Luken (1990) suggests that solid waste also refers to liquids and gases in containers.

**Solow–Hartwick model** See *Hartwick rule*.

**sovereign guarantees** Guarantees by the state to pay the creditor of a company which defaults on a loan. These are required to gain access to IMF funding. The lack of sovereign guarantees has been seen as a stumbling block for development.

**spaceman economy** A term popularized by Boulding (1966) as a metaphor representing the limits to the supplies of *natural resources* and to the capacity of the Earth's *environment* to assimilate wastes. Also known as the 'economics of spaceship Earth', this concept suggests that under conditions of resource *scarcity*, priority should be given to the maintenance of stocks of, for example, natural resources and human knowledge, and the minimization of the throughput of natural resources. See *environmental sustainability; sustainable development (SD); cowboy economics*.

**species** Organisms that are capable of interbreeding, and which comprise distinct populations. Common (1995) argues that *biodiversity* and evolutionary potential may be lost where isolated populations of a species become extinct, even when other populations of the species continue to exist.

**species diversity** See *biodiversity*.

**species trade restrictions** *Regulations* on the use, production and trade of *species* of plants and animals to discourage the unsustainable exploitation of wildlife and to encourage the sustainable use of a species. An example of species trade restrictions is *CITES*. (OECD, 1996.)

**stability** See *ecological stability*.

**standard setting** This is a *command and control (CAC) policy* instrument that requires the level of pollution not to exceed a certain set level. Standards are often set on the basis of a health-related criterion. A major problem with this type of control is that it is unlikely to result in pollution being reduced in the least-cost way, and is therefore likely to be economically inefficient.

*Ambient-based standards* establish *restrictions* on the concentration of a pollutant in a given *environmental medium*. *Emissions standards* establish restrictions on emissions from a given plant or machine, sometimes according to the potential offered through the use of the *best available technology*. Standards may vary according to location, or they may be uniform. (Pearce and Turner, 1990) See also *fixed standard approach; direct regulations; regulations; quantitative controls*.

**stated preference (SP)** A means by which the economic values that people place on non-market goods or *bads* can be measured. SP refers to the fact that respondents are asked to state a value for a non-market good, eg a change in *air quality*. The *contingent valuation method (CVM)* is an SP *valuation* method. SP is distinct from *revealed preference*, which refers to the gathering of data on consumer behaviour in markets that can be related to a *non-marketed good*, in order to infer the value placed on the non-marketed good.

**static efficiency** Static *efficiency* requires that the allocation of resources in any one period is the one that maximizes the measured net benefit from their use. For instance, in extracting a natural resource such as timber or fish, the effort allocated to resource extraction should be such that the *marginal benefit* of resource extraction is equal to its *marginal cost*. See also *dynamic efficiency*. (Tietenberg, 1994.)

**static efficient sustained yield** This refers to the steady-state growth of a *renewable resource* stock at which the net annual return from exploiting the resource is maximized. Unless the costs of exploiting the resource are zero, this growth level is less than the stock's *maximum sustainable yield (MSY)*.

**static expectation** The belief of individuals that today's economic and environmental parameters are likely to continue into the future. See also *adaptive expectation; rational expectations*.

**stationary economy** According to Dasgupta and Heal (1979) this condition may represent a situation in which population and consumption levels are both constant, and where net *capital* accumulation is nil. This is also known as a *steady-state economy*.

**stationary source** A fixed source of pollution. An example often cited is that of a chimney stack or other industrial waste outlet. *Dispersion modelling* techniques can be used to estimate the resulting pollution levels in nearby locations.

**steady-state economy** A steady-state economy is one in which there is a constant stock of *capital* and a constant population. In such an economy, stocks of natural and *man-made capital* are maintained, ideally at such a level as to provide an adequate standard of living while remaining within the limits of environmental and *ecological sustainability*. (OECD, 1997; Daly, 1973.)

**stewardship ethic** The view that humans should act as nature's stewards and conserve *natural resources* and the *environment* for their own sakes, and to protect the interest of other creatures. (Pearce, 1991.) See also *bioethical* *standpoint; extended rights; ethics; environmental ethics; extended stewardship ideology.*

**strategic bias** A form of bias arising in *contingent valuation method (CVM)* studies whereby the respondent attempts to influence either the result of the study, or their own contribution to the cost of the programme being valued. This may lead to over- or underestimation of the *willingness to pay (WTP)* for an *environmental resource*. For instance, if an individual believes that she will not be required to pay a share of the costs of the programme, she may overstate the true value in order to increase the chances of the programme going ahead. If she believes that she will be required to pay the value that she states, then she may state less than the true value in order to reduce her contribution. This would be an example of the problem of *free riding*. Various techniques have been developed to minimize this type of bias, including an examination of the determinants of WTP. (Markandya et al, 2002.)

**strategic environmental assessment** A comprehensive *environmental impact assessment (EIA)* of a policy or programme for use in publicly accountable governmental decision making. (Therivel et al, 1992.)

**strong sustainability** An economy is said to be strongly sustainable if the stocks of each of its *capital* assets, including its *natural capital* assets, are non-decreasing. This contrasts with *weak sustainability*, which allows decreases in the value of one type of capital, for example natural capital, to be compensated for by increasing stocks of another type of capital, for example *human-made capital* or *human capital*. (Perman et al, 1999.) See also *sustainable development (SD)* .

**stumpage fees** *Charges* imposed by governments in return for the granting of logging rights. They may be levied by either local or national government.

**stumpage value** The *economic rent* embodied in a standing stock of trees. This is the difference between the sale value of the timber and the costs of harvesting it. (Pearce, Markandya and Barbier, 1990.)

**subsidiarity** A concept used in the context of EU debates, referring to the principle of delegating decision making to the lowest appropriate level of a political body. This concept is also used in relation to trade, whereby the principle that the least trade-restrictive option for achieving policy goals is preferable, other things being equal. (IISD, 1992.)

**subsidies** Type of *economic instrument*. Subsidies take a number of forms, and may consist of direct transfers or pricing and tax policies that are favourable to certain economic activities. *Neoclassical economics* suggests that subsidies are only justified when economic activities that would produce positive externalities require an additional incentive. The subsidies must be less than the value of the positive *externality*. Otherwise, subsidies distort prices and thereby lead to inefficient allocations of investment. (OECD, 1989b.)

**substitute cost method** This is also known as the *alternative cost approach*, and is used to estimate the monetary value of a *non-marketed good*. The non-priced good can be either a consumer good (eg a park, a substitute for which might be a leisure centre) or an input factor (eg, non-priced forage for livestock, a substitute for which might be sorghum). In both cases, if the two substitutes provide an identical service, the value of the non-priced good is the saved cost of using the marketed substitute.

The validity of this approach depends upon three main conditions being satisfied:

1    that the substitute can provide exactly the same function as the good or service substituted for;
2    that the substitute is actually the least-cost alternative; and
3    that evidence indicates an actual demand for the substitute.

It should be noted, however, that often *natural resources* and the *environment* also provide other services in addition to the one that substitutes for the marketed good or service. In this case the substitute cost should be considered as the lower bound of the value of the environmental asset. (Markandya et al, 2002.)

**sulphur triangle** Phrase used to describe what was once the most polluted part of the world. At its core were parts of Lower Silesia, northern Bohemia and Saxony. In reality it was not a triangle, since neighbouring areas were equally degraded. (Manser, 1993.)

**sunk costs** Costs that are incurred in investment which cannot be recovered, or costs that would have been paid out in any case. Thus, they are distinct from *opportunity costs*.

**super responsibility argument** This relates to the fact that, in making policy decisions using the *net present value (NPV)* criterion, a higher rate of discount tends to favour projects whose benefits are felt in the present or near future, and whose costs are borne in the distant future. The super responsibility argument suggests that governments, having responsibility for the welfare of both current and future generations, should use a discount rate that is lower than the *market interest rate*. (Pearce and Warford, 1993.) See also *discounting*.

**surrogate market techniques** These techniques involve studying consumer behaviour in markets for goods and services that are related to a non-market, environmental good, in order to infer the value that consumers place on the environmental good. The environmental good is often a complement to or substitute for the marketed good. This is a form of *revealed preference*. Policy-makers sometimes prefer these techniques because they rely on actual choices rather than the hypothetical choices involved in the *direct valuation* approaches. Surrogate market techniques include *hedonic pricing* and *household production function* techniques, including the *travel cost method (TCM)*.

**sustainability** A broad definition of sustainability is that the economic, social and environmental systems that generate human wellbeing are being maintained over time, to the extent that human wellbeing can be at least maintained over time. There are many different aspects to this concept, and a more precise definition of sustainability depends on the context in which it is being sought.

Sustainability can best be thought of in terms of the various different types of *capital* stock that contribute to human wellbeing. Some of these are: stocks of *human-made capital*, which are used, together with *natural resources* and *human capital*, to provide consumption goods and services; stocks of *social capital*, which contribute directly to wellbeing; and stocks of *natural capital*, which provide both flows of natural resources as inputs to production, and the ecological *life support functions* on which all human and other animal life depends.

The potential for unsustainability lies in the fact that each of these types of capital stock can be depleted in order to increase current wellbeing, but at the expense of future wellbeing. In particular, the reason that there is concern regarding sustainability is that many people fear that stocks of natural resources (eg *energy resources* and forests), as well as the *environment*'s capacity to provide life support services such as climate regulation, are being depleted over time, so that the environmental basis of the human economy, and thus the economy itself, is unsustainable.

This has led to suggestions of rules for sustainability, which fall mainly into the categories of *weak sustainability* and *strong sustainability*. Weak sustainability rules, broadly speaking, require that the value of the overall capital stock, or the per-capita capital stock, be at least maintained. Strong sustainability rules require that each type of capital be maintained in its own right.

In the 1990s there have been major global debates on *sustainable development (SD)* (United Nations Conference on Environment and Development (UNCED), and for people-centred SD (World Summit for Social Development). These debates have emphasized that *environmental sustainability* is only one aspect of overall sustainability. They have focused on the need for people-centred development, with concerns for human empowerment, participation, gender equality, equitable growth, poverty reduction and long-term sustainability, thus highlighting that there are social, as well as economic and environmental, aspects to the problem of SD. (http://www.undp.org, 'What is Human Development?'.) See *economic sustainability; environmental sustainability; strong sustainability; weak sustainability; sustainable development (SD); sustainable development, indicators of; sustainable economic growth.*

**sustainability indicators** See *sustainable development, indicators of.*

**sustainable agriculture and rural development (SARD)** The FAO criteria for SARD are:

- the meeting of the basic nutritional requirements of present and future generations, qualitatively and quantitatively, while providing a number of other agricultural products;
- the provision of durable employment, sufficient income, and decent living and working conditions for all those engaged in agricultural production;
- the maintainance and, where possible, enhancement of the productive capacity of the natural resource base as a whole, and the regenerative capacity of renewable resources, without disrupting the functioning of basic ecological cycles and natural balances, destroying the socio-cultural attributes of rural communities, or causing contamination of the *environment*; and
- the reduction of the *vulnerability* of the agricultural sector to adverse natural and socio-economic factors and other *risks*, and the strengthening of self-reliance.

(FAO, 1995.) See also *sustainable development (SD).*

**sustainable development (SD)** The term sustainable development (SD) is often used synonymously with *sustainability*. However, while sustainability implies that wellbeing can be at least maintained over time, sustainable development implies in addition that the factors that determine quality of life, such as literacy and education in general, health, *human rights* and so on, improve over time. Thus, the term 'sustainable' implies that the *capital* stocks that generate human wellbeing should not be depleted over time. The use of the term 'development' in conjunction with sustainability requires that the issues crucial to human development must be taken in to account. See also *alternative development paths; economic sustainability; environmental sustainability; sustainability; sustainable development, indicators of; sustainable economic growth.*

**sustainable development, indicators of** Measures that establish the extent to which development is following a sustainable path. In 1995, the Commission on Sustainable Development adopted a work programme on an initial 130 indicators. These include social, economic, environmental and institutional factors which all facilitate *sustainable development (SD)*. Social indicators include poverty, population demographics, education, health, and human settlement. Economic aspects of SD include national income measures (such as *gross domestic product (GDP)* per capita), consumption patterns, measures of aid received, debt servicing, environmental expenditures, and measures of technology transfer and *capacity building*. *Environmental indicator*s considered important for SD include measures of water, land, natural resource, and atmosphere use, as well as measures of waste generation. Institutional aspects considered under this framework include measures of the integration of environment and development in decision making, scientific capacity, legal mechanisms, information dissemination, and the use of NGOs. For more information on these measures of SD see the UN homepage: www.un.org/esa/sustdev/.

**sustainable economic growth** This is experienced when real GNP per capita rises over time and the increase is not threatened by negative feedback from either biophysical or social impacts. (Pearce et al, 1989.) See also *economic sustainability, environmental sustainability, sustainability, sustainable development (SD), economic growth.*

**sustainable economic welfare** See *index of sustainable economic welfare (ISEW)*.

**sustainable shock** A sustainable shock is one which can be absorbed without degrading a resource necessary for the survival of the *ecosystem* to the extent that the ecosystem itself collapses. (Barbier, 1993.) See also *ecological stability, resilience, vulnerability.*

**sustainable tourism** Tourism can, in any part of the world, involve environmental risks, since it involves relatively large numbers of people visiting what are often fragile *ecosystems*, such as coastal ecosystems. There can be social problems too, as local communities may find the presence or the behaviour of tourists disturbing, resulting in social destabilization. Sustainable tourism requires integrated policy and planning to maximize sustainable visitor expenditure and not the short-term number of visitors. It requires that the environmental assets (for example beaches) which attract tourists are not degraded by the effects of tourism, and it can require the acceptance of local communities, for example by ensuring that the *economic benefit*s are shared as widely as possible (e.g. by maximizing the employment created). (Barbier, 1993.) See also *sustainability; sustainable development (SD); environmental sustainability*.

**systems analysis** A tool developed during the 1970s which has been used to analyse the interactions over time between physical and economic systems, and the effects of these interactions on the future prospects for *economic growth*. One of the earliest and best-known studies using the systems analysis tool is *Limits to Growth* (Meadows et al, 1972), which used the tool of systems analysis to simulate economic and environmental trends, concluding that the course of economic development was environmentally unsustainable. See also *limits to growth*.

# Tt

**take-it-or-leave-it experiments** In this type of experiment, respondents are randomly divided into groups. The same *valuation* question is posed to each group, but with a different value. Each person is asked either to take the sum or leave the sum involved, with the sums of money offered being randomly distributed across the surveyed population. The answers for groups can be analysed using econometric techniques to estimate the average *willingness to pay (WTP)* for the average consumer. This value can then be multiplied by the number of people affected (the affected population), in order to yield an estimate of the aggregate WTP. The advantage of this technique is that it more closely simulates an actual market than other valuation methods do. (Dixon et al, 1986.)

**tangible benefits** Benefits to which a monetary value can be reasonably assigned. (Tietenberg, 1992a.) See also *intangible benefits*.

**tax differentiation** A type of *economic instrument*, this involves the use of positive or negative taxes to give incentives to change the consumption pattern of goods and services associated with environmental effects (UNEP, 1993). An example of tax differentiation is car fuels, where different levels of taxes are applied on different types of fuels to encourage the use of cleaner fuels. Tax differentiation systems are relatively easy to implement from an administrative point of view, since they are embedded in existing tax systems. (OECD, 1989a.) Tietenberg (1994) suggests that taxes may also be spatially differentiated, whereby the rate paid is determined by the location of the consumption or production of pollution.

**taxation** See *environmental tax; eco-taxation; environmental taxation* and *economic instruments*.

**technical efficiency** Technical *efficiency* requires that, given the available inputs, no more of any output can be produced without leading to a reduction in another output. See also *economic efficiency, eco-efficiency, Pareto efficiency*.

**technical progress** Technical progress occurs when the productive capacity of an economy is expanded through advances in, for example, technology or scientific understanding. This may be important in determining the *scarcity* of natural resource stocks (since technical progress may increase the *efficiency* with which they are used, or may lead to the development of substitutes for them) and therefore the *sustainability* of *economic growth* and other important measures in *environmental economics*. Uncertainties as to the potential impacts of technical progress also affect the estimation of costs and *baselines* for *climate change mitigation* strategies (IPCC, 2001). Technical progress can be an important factor in the sustainability of a path.

**technological lock-in** Expenditures by firms to reduce pollution (*abatement expenditures*) tend to consist of fixed *capital* costs. This means that new capital investments are required to increase the level of *abatement*. Pearce and Turner

## technology-based standards

(1990) argue this 'lumpiness' in expenditures means that *charges* are likely to be inefficient unless they are pre-announced and stable. Otherwise, firms will not be able to efficiently adapt their production processes to changes in the level of charges, nor will they necessarily trust that the charge will hold, and hence many delay expenditures.

**technology-based standards** Standards that are based on the availability and affordability of technology. See also *best available technology (BAT); best available technology not entailing excessive cost (BATNEEC); command and control policies (CAC); standard setting.*

**thermal efficiency** The thermal efficiency of an energy-generating process may be defined as the ratio of the energy content of the electricity generated to the energy content of the fuel burned. (Common, 1995.)

**thirty-per-cent club** Term used to describe countries that have signed the Protocol to the 1979 *Convention* on Long-Range Transboundary Air Pollution on the reduction of sulphur emissions or their transboundary fluxes. This convention calls for reductions of at least 30 per cent in such emissions. (Helm, 1985.) See also *factor ten/factor four clubs.*

**threshold instruments** Designed to restrict exploitation of endangered species, these instruments restrict the harvesting of renewable natural resources such as fish stocks and whales. Recently, these instruments have been used to attempt to protect ecosystems and biodiversity, in particular where the sensitivity of ecological functions means that overexploitation may lead to irreversible damage. (Barbier et al, 1994.) See also *bioeconomic equilibrium; carrying capacity; ecological species–area relationship; interactive resources, renewable resources.*

**time preference** Time preference is related to the fact that, generally speaking, people prefer to enjoy a benefit in the present rather than to delay it into the future. The rate of time preference is the rate at which the present value of *utility* declines as the time at which it is enjoyed moves further into the future. This is an important issue in *environmental economics* because it is the rationale behind *discounting* the net benefits of projects in *cost–benefit analysis (CBA).* See also *Ramsey rule; consumption discount rate; utility discount rate.*

**top–down modelling** A modelling approach used in *environmental economics*, particularly in the analysis of *climate change*. Top–down models evaluate a system using aggregate economic variables. Modellers using this technique apply macroeconomic theory and econometric techniques to historical data on consumption, prices, incomes and factor costs to model final demand for goods and services. Supply is modelled using data from major sectors like the energy sector, transportation, agriculture and industry. These models are often used to construct demand functions for household expenditures by aggregating individual demand functions, which can facilitate a reasonably detailed assessment of *economic instruments* and distributional impacts of policies for the *mitigation* of *climate change*. Critics of this technique suggest that aggregate models applied to climate policy do not contain adequate detail, and they recommend the use of *bottom–up modelling* techniques. See IPCC 1996b and 2001 for a discussion of this issue. See also *climate change, estimating costs of.*

**tort** An injury to another person or to property, which can be compensated under the law. Examples of tort include negligence, gross negligence, and intentional wrongdoing. The premise underlying tort law is that every person is expected to conduct him-or herself without injuring others. Compensation is probably the most important social role of tort law, since it serves as a deterrent to damaging behaviour. See the World Wide Legal Information Association website for more detail: http://wwlia.org/tort1.htm.

**total economic value** The economic value of environmental assets has various components. It is widely accepted that two broad categories of values exist: *use values* and *non-use values*. Use values are defined as those benefits that derive from the actual use of the *environment*. Use values also include *option values*, ie the additional value placed on a natural resource by those people who want to have the option of using the goods and services in the future. Non-use values are also described as *existence values* by many authors. The argument behind existence value is that people care about the *environment* not only because they, or their heirs, can get some benefit, or can avoid some sort of loss, by using or preserving environmental assets. See also *bequest values; consumptive use values; direct use values; gift values; indirect use values; instrumental values; passive use values.* (Markandya et al, 2002.)

**total reduced sulphur** A gaseous *air pollutant* consisting primarily of hydrogen sulphide, methyl mercaptan, dimethyl sulphide, and dimethyl disulphide. (Luken, 1990.)

**total suspended particulates (TSP)** A solid *air pollutant* consisting of particulate matter measuring up to 25–45 micrometres. See also *particulates.*

**total suspended solids (TSS)** A measure of the suspended solids in waste water, *effluent* or water bodies.

**toxic pollution** See *hazardous waste.*

**tradable emissions permits** See *marketable emissions permits.*

**tradable pollution rights** See *marketable emissions permits.*

**tradable procreation permits** Tradable policy instruments for population control. Common (1995) presents a potential framework for the design of such instruments. The determination of the desired level of population growth would lead to the desired number of permits, which would be freely tradable. Those unable, or unwilling, to have children would be sellers of permits while couples wishing to reproduce in excess of the level of permits allocated would be buyers. The price level of permits would be determined by the permits market. This concept is related to *marketable emissions permits.*

**trade-off games** Trade-off games are used to analyse choices between bundles of goods, commonly a mix of money and different levels of an environmental good. First a *baseline* case is provided, and an alternative is then offered with a higher level of the environmental good but with a lower sum of money, ie with a price. The price is then varied until the respondent is indifferent between the two options.

Dixon et al (1986) provide the example of the determination of the *willingness to pay (WTP)* for a local park. Here the choice may be between no payment and the original park, or a payment after which a larger park is created. This choice would be offered until the respondent says he or she feels indifferent between paying no money and keeping the original park, or paying $x and receiving the improved park. This result can be interpreted as the marginal compensated demand price for the environmental good, or the WTP. (Dixon et al, 1986.)

**tragedy of the commons** This occurs where incomplete *property rights* lead to the overuse of renewable *natural resources*. Hardin (1992) provides the example of herdsmen using a common grazing area. Individual rationality suggests that an individual should aim to maximize his gain from the use of a resource. Hence, each individual is compelled to increase the level of the herd without accounting for the environmental limits, or *carrying capacity*, of the system, leading to overgrazing and environmental degradation. Hardin suggests some possible policy measures to avoid such overexploitation and degradation of the resource, including privatization or *allocation of permits* for access to the resource. See also *Clark model of extinction; extinction of species; global commons; open access; paradox of aggregation; property rights.*

**transboundary impact** A transboundary impact can be defined as any significant adverse effect on the environment that occurs across the borders of different states. Such effects on the *environment* include effects on human health and safety, the natural environment, and physical structures including historic monuments. The existence of such impacts has led to the establishment of *international environmental agreements.*

**transboundary waters** Any surface- or groundwaters which mark, cross or are located on the boundaries between two or more states. Wherever transboundary waters flow directly into the sea, they end at a straight line across their respective mouths between points on the low-water line of their banks.

**transformative values** Characteristics of environmental assets which have the property that when individuals become aware of them, their preferences are changed. (Barbier, 1993.)

**transparency** This is, ideally, a property of tax and policy measures. Transparency requires a tax or policy measure to be intelligible, so that full advantage is taken of its incentive effects. See also *environmental taxation.*

**transport, taxation of** The use of *environmental taxation* such as that on transport, including taxation of motor vehicles and fuels (petrol, diesel, etc.), is increasing. Most OECD countries levy heavy taxes on petrol, and many have differential rates on lead-free petrol, which have been used in the phasing-out of leaded fuel. Road pricing is under consideration in some OECD nations, whereby taxes may be levied on road users depending on the degree of congestion. There is an increasing awareness in many countries of the interrelated nature of transport tax decisions, public transport pricing and subsidy decisions, and infrastructure investment decisions.

**transport or tertiary packaging** This type of packaging may be designed to facilitate bulk handling as well as transport from the producer to the sales outlet (eg pallets). (OECD, 1994b.)

**travel cost method (TCM)** This was developed to estimate the recreational demand for a site when market prices are not available. This applies the travel cost methodology, using the cost of travel to a site as a proxy for the entrance price to a site. *Econometric*, or regression, analysis is used to relate visitation rates to travel cost and socio-economic variables, such as income. The demand curve for the site can be derived by applying the assumption that visitors would respond to an increase in price in the same way as to an increase in travel cost. This method works when the site in question is not congested, as congestion reduces demand artificially. Hence, the result would be an underestimate of the true demand if this method were to be used in the derivation of demand for a congested site. (Tietenberg, 1996.) See also *truncation bias; zonal travel cost method (ZTCM); valuation*.

**trickle-down hypothesis** Hypothesis that growth in affluent countries is good for the less-developed countries following an expansion in their export market. Hence, greater *affluence* in the rich nations can be said to trickle down to the poorer nations. This argument is also used in an in-country context, with growth in the incomes of the better-off being cited as benefiting the less well-off. (Common, 1995.) See also *economic growth*.

**tropical forest** Tropical forests have important roles in the maintenance of microclimates, the protection of watersheds, the provision of unique habitats and supporting the economic livelihoods of indigenous peoples. Barbier (1993) notes that when a forest is degraded or converted, these important services may be irretrievably lost. The economic values of these and other functions of a tropical forest are not fully integrated into decisions concerning forest use, partly due to uncertainties in the *valuation* of *biodiversity* and *climate change*.

**truncation bias** A bias that may affect the *travel cost method (TCM)* of *valuation*, and relates to the issue of ignoring non-visitors to the site. The potential bias stems from the fact that if the level of amenity at a site improved, then some of those who do not currently visit the site would change their behaviour. This poses a problem for the application of the TCM for valuation, as tracing these individuals and determining the extent of possible truncation bias is difficult. (Pearce et al, 1989.)

# Uu

**unassisted recovery** The natural ability of the *ecosystem* to renew and regenerate. Simonis (1990) suggests that 'an *ecological system's* ability to renew itself is expressed in terms of compensatory production of and by the system itself, and its ability to absorb and digest pollutants.' See also *absorptive capacity; assisted recovery*.

**uncertainty** Uncertainty in economics refers to a situation in which all of the various possible consequences of an action can be identified, but where probabilities cannot be assigned to these consequences. In this, it differs from the concept of *risk*. The treatment of uncertainty is an important issue in *environmental economics*. *Climate change* impacts are uncertain, partly due to uncertainties over future developments in technology. The workings of complex *ecosystems*, and the effect of pollutants on these systems, are uncertain. The uncertainty relating to ecosystem damage, and its consequences, has led to some calls for the application of the *precautionary principle (PP)* in this field.

The issue of decision making under uncertainty is evaluated in Perman et al (1999). They present a branch of *game theory*, called *decision theory*, to illustrate how decision makers might behave in the case of uncertainty. However, this does not show the optimum solution in the case of uncertainty, as Perman et al argue: 'there is no way of making decisions that can be unambiguously identified as doing the best for the decision maker in the relevant circumstances'.

IPCC (1996b) identifies three principal areas of uncertainty related to *climate change*: scientific, socio-ecological and socio-economic. Scientific uncertainties relate to the relationships between the levels of emissions and concentrations of *greenhouse gases (GHGs)*, the effects on temperature, and impacts on the environment, including those on ecological cycles and sea level. Socio-ecological uncertainties relate to the impacts of climate change on the interaction between humans and the *biosphere*, such as impacts on agricultural production. Socio-economic uncertainties are those related to the impacts on the *valuation* of resources, trade and technological change. See also *radical uncertainty*.

**UNCLOS (United Nations Convention on the Law of the Sea)** *Convention* established in 1982 with the aim of providing a global framework related to the law of the sea. Its objectives include the promotion of peaceful use of the sea, *conservation* and equitable use of marine resources and environmental protection for the seas. See http://www.un.org/Depts/los/ for further details.

**undifferentiated discharge permit (UDP)** This is a type of *marketable emissions permit* that gives an identical right to emit to every polluter, regardless of location. This is distinct from an *ambient permit system*, under which a permit allows different levels of emissions by different firms, depending on their location. (Tietenberg, 1994.)

**undiscovered resources** These are deposits of *natural resources* which are thought to exist on the basis of knowledge and theory of geology. (Tietenberg, 1992a.)

**uniform minimum environmental standards** A policy that establishes international minimum environmental standards, hence preventing the establishment of *pollution havens*. The use of uniform minimum environmental standards constitutes a safety margin approach, which is appropriate when there is a high degree of *uncertainty* regarding the effects of pollution. (Turner et al, 1994.) See also *pollution haven*.

**use values** The values derived from actual or potential future consumption of a good or service. They may be separated into current use, *option* and *quasi-option values*. See also *non-use value; total economic value*.

**user charge** A type of *economic instrument*. User *charges* are intended to recover the costs of public or community provision of a service, such as the treatment of *effluent* (including waste) and the provision of water. They are common with respect to the collection and treatment of municipal solid waste and wastewater discharged into sewers, as payments for such services rather than as *economic incentives*. (OECD, 1989b.)

**user cost approach (national accounts)** A method suggested by El Serafy (1989) for the adjustment of *national accounts* to account for the fact that, while the revenue from *non-renewable resource* extraction should not be counted as income in its entirety, a natural resource *endowment* constitutes part of a country's wealth, and thus yields a certain level of true income. Thus, the total of natural resource revenues should not be deducted from national income. El Serafy's suggestion was to split natural resource revenue (which he assumed to be constant) into two flows. The first is the amount counted as income, and the second is the amount that, if invested at the current rate of interest, would accumulate into a *fund* that would yield in perpetuity the amount calculated as income. The formula by which this is calculated is shown below, where $X$ is the true income from sales of *natural resources* $(R)$, $r$ is the interest or discount rate, and $n$ is the number of years for which current extraction rates could be sustained:

$$\frac{X}{R} = 1 - \frac{1}{(1+r)^n}$$

See also *marginal user cost, resource user cost*.

**user pays principle (UPP)** The UPP states that beneficiaries should pay for the full cost of using resources and their related services, together with the cost of losses for future generations following the *intergenerational equity principle*. Resource pricing often means increased resource prices for the users, forcing them to reduce their use of the service or of the *natural resources*. (Markandya et al, 2002.)

**usufructory right** This type of right conveys a right to use a *natural resource*, as opposed to an ownership right. (Tietenberg, 1992a.)

**utilitarian ethics** Ethical framework whereby the moral worth of an action is determined solely by the consequences or outcomes of the action. There are many forms of utilitarianism, including classical utilitarianism which evaluates actions solely in terms of their effect on the wellbeing of a whole society. Classical utilitarianism asserts that actions should be made with the purpose of yielding the greatest level of aggregate good. For a review of utilitarianism and its impacts on *environmental economics* see Perman et al (1999). See also *ethics; Kantian ethics; libertarian ethics; Rawlsian ethics*.

**utility** A measure of the level of satisfaction or wellbeing. Utility can be derived from a number of sources, including the consumption of produced goods, interpersonal relationships and the quality of the *environment*. The relationship between utility and different patterns of consumption can be represented by a utility function. For a good summary of utility and its applications, see Varian, 1996.

**utility discount rate** This is the rate at which, in calculating the present value of a flow of *utility*, the present value of a unit of utility decreases as the time at which it is enjoyed moves further into the future. This is also known as the *pure rate of time preference*. The relationship between the utility discount rate and the *consumption discount rate* is described by the *Ramsey rule*. See also *discounting*.

# Vv

**valuation** In *environmental economics* this refers to the estimation of the monetary value of an environmental asset, or to a change in the level of an environmental attribute. Two broad approaches exist in the valuation of *environmental resources*: *direct valuation* and *indirect valuation* methods. Direct methods include techniques such as the *contingent valuation method (CVM)* and *contingent ranking*, which attempt to obtain preferences directly via survey and experimental techniques. People are asked to state directly their strength of preference, or *willingness to pay (WTP)*, for a proposed change. Indirect approaches attempt to elicit preferences from actual, observed, market-based information. They include *hedonic pricing techniques, the travel cost method (TCM), avertive behaviour, dose–response* and *replacement cost techniques*. The value placed on an *environmental resource* is revealed indirectly when an individual purchases a marketed good which is related to a given quality or quantity of the environmental good. Indirect techniques can be further divided into two categories: *surrogate market* approaches and conventional market approaches. Surrogate market approaches include *hedonic* techniques and the *household production function* approach. (Markandya et al, 2002.)

**value of a life year lost (VLYL or VOLY)** A measure of the value of an increased *risk* of death, in terms of a year of life lost. It can be used to value the increased risk of death that results from exposure to environmental pollution, and therefore it can be used in the *benefit–cost analysis (BCA)* of measures to reduce air pollution. It is distinct from the *value of a statistical life (VOSL)*, which measures the value of a statistical life lost. While an estimate of the VLYL can be derived from a calculated value of a statistical life, it is now thought more appropriate to measure it directly. (ExternE, 1999)

**value of a statistical life (VOSL)** A measure of the value that people place on a small change in the *risk* of dying. Such measures are often used as an estimate of the amount that people are willing to spend to increase safety and are therefore used in decisions on public spending on safety.

Techniques to measure the VOSL include the *hedonic* wage approach to estimate the *valuation* of an *occupational health risk* faced by workers, and the *contingent valuation method (CVM)* which explicitly asks individuals to place a value on a change in the level of risk of death faced. A third technique is to examine *avertive expenditures* to reduce the risk of death, for example expenditure on air bags for cars. ExternE (1999) presents a review of some of the main studies conducted in the area of VOSL for both Europe and the US, concluding that the best central estimate is €3.1 million for Europe. Studies for the US have estimated values between €2.4 and €3.6 (1995 prices). The application of VOSL to other countries has been attempted by adjusting an estimate of the VOSL for the US using purchasing-power-parity-adjusted GNP. However this is controversial – particularly in relation to *climate change* damage estimation – and some have recommended the use of a single global value, which has been estimated at €1.026 million (ExternE, 1999.)

**vertical equity** The extent to which benefits or costs of environmental measures
are distributed across different income groups. The estimation of the extent to
which a measure is vertically equitable would depend on whether the net
result of the measure is progressive (ie redistributes resources towards poorer
groups), proportional (so that the incidence of cost and benefit is proportional
to income) or regressive (so that it redistributes resources towards richer
groups). See also *equity; horizontal equity*.

**vicarious liability** Vicarious liability involves holding firms liable for the actions
of employees. It has been argued that this form of liability should encourage a
firm to internalize the cost of damages through compensation schemes tied to
worker behaviour. Tietenberg, however, suggests that 'in many cases involving
environmental *risks*, internal sanctioning may not be possible'. Where a
combination of decisions by both employees and executives result in damages,
it may also be difficult to allocate liability. (Tietenberg, 1994.)

**victim pays principle (VPP)** In contrast to the *polluter pays principle (PPP)*,
this principle suggests that victims affected by pollution should pay the
polluter not to pollute. This implies that *property rights* in environmental
resources lie with the polluter rather than with those who suffer from the
pollution. (IISD, 1992.)

**virgin materials tax** An input tax on raw materials used in the production of
packaging. Taxes of this nature are related to the damage done by production
and the consumption of the packaging, with a *scarcity* premium if relevant.
The aim of this kind of tax is to reduce the use of virgin materials and to
provide an incentive to use recycled materials.

**volatile organic compound** Any organic compound that participates in
atmospheric photochemical reactions. Examples include carcinogens and
chemicals which react with sunlight and nitrogen oxides to form ground-
level *ozone ($O_3$)* or smog.

**voluntary eco-labelling schemes** Voluntary schemes for producers to prove
the extent to which their products are environmentally friendly. Such measures
encourage the production and purchase of the least harmfully produced
products through the life cycle. The criteria for eco-labels and compliance
with standards are guaranteed by the relevant authorities or designated
institutions. Participation in the international harmonization of relevant
standards and criteria has been promoted by international bodies. (UN ECE/
UNEP, 1994.) See also *eco-labelling*.

**voluntary instruments** Voluntary instruments, such as *eco-labels*, are
increasingly being discussed in relation to the reduction of energy-related
*carbon dioxide ($CO_2$)* emissions in industrialized countries. It has been argued
that, if firms comply with voluntary instruments, environmental benefits such
as reduced emissions of $CO_2$ can be obtained at a lower cost than under other
instruments such as *regulations* and *market-based instruments (MBIs)*. (Jochem
and Eichhammer, 1997.)

**vulnerability** This illustrates the extent to which a change in the level of
environmental quality may damage a system. This depends on the sensitivity
of a system to change and on the adaptive capacity of that system. An example

is the vulnerability of human health and socio-economic systems, where adaptive capacity may be determined by economic and institutional factors. The impacts of *climate change* are expected to be more acute in more vulnerable areas such as small islands, semi-arid areas and those regions in which population density is high in sensitive areas, for example low-lying river basins. (IPCC, 1996b and 1998.) See also *resilience, ecological stability, sustainable shock*.

# Ww

waste charges Waste *charges* may be levied either on the collection or on the disposal of waste. They are a common form of *user charge*, with revenues used to finance waste collection and disposal. Such charges can, if calculated individually, lead to a reduction in levels of waste. Waste charges should represent any (external) costs not already incorporated in traditional costs of waste collection and disposal. However, to date only the UK landfill tax has been based on estimates of environmental damages arising from waste disposal (Ekins, 1999.)

water quality standards Criteria established for the level of water quality. These standards, if reached, mean that water is suitable for a designated use. These criteria are based on pollutant levels that would render the water unsuitable for consumption, recreational use or production. (Luken, 1990.)

water quality, valuation of The *valuation* of water quality is an important issue, given the impacts of water quality on health and recreation. The *impact pathway* methodology can be applied to water quality. Valuation of water quality changes has been attempted using the *contingent valuation method (CVM)* in a number of studies, including Markandya and Murty (2000) which estimated the value of changes resulting from water quality in the Ganges River. Health impacts can be valued using conventional *morbidity* and *mortality* measures, such as the *value of a life year lost (VOLY)*. ExternE (1999) presents a methodology for quantifying the damages associated with the acidification of freshwater, including the impacts on fish stocks for commercial use, *existence values (XVs)*, *mitigation* costs and recreational values.

waterlogging A rise in the water table due to excessive irrigation. Salinization of the land can also result, as rising water brings salts to the surface. These problems can be reduced by installing adequate drainage. (Dixon et al, 1989.)

weak sustainability A type of rule for sustainability, which requires that the value of aggregate *capital* stocks (including *human-made capital, natural capital, human capital* and *social capital*) must not decline. Thus, reductions in the level of natural capital, for example due to the depletion of a country's oil stocks or from *deforestation*, must, under this rule, be compensated for by investment in an alternative capital stock. This rule has been criticized by *ecological economists* because it implies that increasing man-made capital can compensate for reductions in the natural capital stock. (Hammond et al, 1995.) See also *sustainability; sustainable development (SD); strong sustainability; green accounting.*

white list The *Oslo Convention* classifies pollutants into three grades of toxicity. The white list consists of all types of waste not included in the other categories, representing the least toxic type of waste. Dumping of this category of waste is subject to approval by the appropriate national authority. (Leeson, 1995.) See also *black list, grey list.*

**willingness to accept (WTA)** This refers to the amount of money that an individual would be willing to accept as compensation for suffering a loss, such as an environmental deterioration, or for not receiving a benefit. It has been used in *contingent valuation method (CVM)* studies as a measure of the economic value of environmental costs and benefits. However, the fact that values stated for WTA have tended to be significantly greater than those stated for *willingness to pay (WTP)* has meant that WTP is now the figure usually elicited. The use of WTP rather than WTA was in fact a recommendation of the *NOAA* panel. See also *cognitive dissonance; loss aversion*.

**willingness to pay (WTP)** This is used in the environmental *valuation* literature as a measure of the benefit to a consumer of a change in the price, quantity or quality of a good. The maximum amount of money an individual is willing to pay to obtain a benefit or avoid a loss is usually assumed to reflect the values he/she attaches to the benefit or loss. Thus, this is the figure that environmental valuation studies attempt to estimate.

When an individual buys an asset by paying the market price, the price paid directly reveals a lower bound of his/her maximum WTP. It indeed reveals that his/her WTP for such an asset is at least equal to the price paid. For example, if one observes an individual paying $1 for a kilogram of sugar, this means that he/she is willing to pay at least $1 for each kilogram of sugar of that quality, otherwise he/she would not buy it at that price. When there is no market for an asset, there is clearly no market price that reveals the lower bound of the individual's maximum WTP. In this case, it is necessary to use an alternative method, such as the *contingent valuation method (CVM)*. (Markandya et al, 2002.)

**WTO and the environment** The WTO (World Trade Organization) was created by international treaty. It establishes the procedures that define '*fair trade* practices'. A crucial principle of the WTO is that import barriers cannot be established according to the techniques used in the production of a good. Kahn (1998) cites the case of the US, whose *regulations* required the production of dolphin-safe tuna. The US attempted to ban imports of tuna produced in Mexico that was not dolphin-safe. The WTO ruled that this constituted discrimination and ruled that the US was in violation of *the General Agreement on Tariffs and Trade (GATT)*. The WTO has also conducted much research into trade and *environment* linkages; see http://www.wto.org/wto/environ/environm.htm for more details. (Kahn, 1998.)

# Zz

**zero-cost improvements** Improvements that do not involve additional environmental costs but which improve the state of the environment, such as improved management and maintenance of *natural resources*. (UN ECE, 1994.)

**zonal discharge permits** A type of *marketable permit* that is based on zones, preventing the occurrence of highly localized concentrations of pollutants. Under this type of permit emission trades are permitted within each zone but not across boundaries. Because this strategy restricts trading opportunities, it can be considered cost ineffective in terms of the aggregate reduction in pollution. (Tietenberg, 1994.)

**zonal travel cost method (ZTCM)** A variant of the *travel cost method*. The ZTCM divides the entire area from which visitors originate into a set of zones and then identifies the dependent variable as the visitor rate (ie the number of visits from a particular zone in a period, divided by the population of the zone).

To value an environmental asset using ZTCM the following procedure can be applied:

1   identification of the site;
2   design of a questionnaire, to cover origin, transport and socio-economic features;
3   conducting the survey;
4   counting the number of visits to a site in a period;
5   the subdivision of visitor origins into zones of increasing distance;
6   the determination of the number of visitors by zone and the relative shares over the sample size;
7   the calculation of annual visits by zone;
8   the collection of data on population by zone and zonal socio-economic features;
9   the calculation of the average visit rate in each zone;
10  the calculation of the zonal average travel cost to the site with reference to the distance;
11  the estimation of the demand function;
12  the computation of the average visitor *consumer surplus* by zone;
13  the computation of the zonal annual consumer surplus by zone; and
14  the aggregation of the zonal annual consumer surplus to get the total annual consumer surplus.

In ZTCM the researcher estimates a demand function using the data from each zone. This derived demand curve is assumed to be the same for each zone. The choke point, where demand is zero, is then calculated. The consumer surplus per visit is calculated by calculating the area below the choke point and the travel cost (price) paid by residents of that zone. (Markandya et al, 2002.)

# References

Anderson, F, A Kneese, P Reed, S Taylor and R Stevenson (1977) *Environmental Improvement Through Economic Incentives*, Johns Hopkins University Press, Baltimore

Arrow, K J (1951) *Social Choice and Individual Values*, Wiley, New York

Bain, J (1973) *Environmental Decay*, Little, Brown and Company, Boston

Bannock, G, R E Baxter and E Davis (1991) *The Penguin Dictionary of Economics*, Penguin, London

Barbier, E (1989) *Economics, Natural-Resource Scarcity and Development*, Earthscan, London

Barbier, E (ed) (1993) *Economics and Ecology: New Frontiers and Sustainable Development*, Chapman & Hall, London

Barbier, E, J C Burgess and C Folke (1994) *Paradise Lost?: The Ecological Economics of Biodiversity*, Earthscan, London

Barde, J-P (1999) 'Environmental Taxes in OECD Countries: An Overview', in OECD (1999) *Environmental Taxes: Recent Developments in China and OECD Countries*, OECD, Paris

Barde, J-P and K J Button (eds) (1990) *Transport Policy and the Environment: Six Case Studies*, Earthscan, London

Barnett, H J (1979) 'Scarcity and Growth Revisited' in V Kerry Smith (ed) *Scarcity and Growth Reconsidered*, Johns Hopkins University Press, Baltimore

Barnett, H J and C Morse (1963) *Scarcity and Growth: The Economics of Natural Resource Availability*, Johns Hopkins University Press for Resources for the Future, Baltimore

Borghesi, S (1999) 'The Environmental Kuznets Curve: A Survey of the Literature', *FEEM Nota di Lavoro*, 85. 99, Fondazione Eni Enrico Mattei, Milan. Downloadable from FEEM website: http://www.feem.it

Boulding, K (1966) 'The Economics of the Coming Space-ship Earth', in J Jarrett (ed) *Environmental Quality in a Growing Economy*, Resources for the Future/Johns Hopkins University Press, Baltimore, pp3–14

Bromley, D (1991) *Environment and Economy: Property Rights and Public Policy*, Blackwell, Oxford

Brown, G (1997) 'Benefits of Biodiversity Evaluation: Why Biodiversity Valuation is Imperative', in OECD (1997) *Investing in Biological Diversity*, OECD, Paris

Buchanan, J M (1965) 'Estimating Demand for Public Goods: An Experiment', *Economica* vol 32, no 125, pp1–14

Chiang, A C (1984) *Fundamental Methods of Mathematical Economics*, McGraw-Hill, London

Clark, C (1973) 'The Economics of Overexploitation', *Science*, vol 181, no 630–4

Common, M (1995) *Sustainability and Policy: Limits to Economics*, Cambridge University Press, Cambridge

Corden W. M. (1966) 'The Effective Protective Rate, the Uniform Tariff Equivalent and the Average Tariff', *The Economic Record* vol 42, no 98, June, pp200–16

Cornwell, L and R Costanza (1994) 'An Experimental Analysis of the Effectiveness of an Environmental Assurance Bonding System on Player Behavior in a Simulated Firm', *Ecological Economics*, vol 11, no 3, Dec, pp213–226

Cornwell, A and J Creedy (1996) *Environmental Taxes and Economic Welfare*, Edward Elgar, Cheltenham

Costanza, R (1997) *Frontiers in Ecological Economics: Transdisciplinary Essays by Robert Costanza*, Edward Elgar, Cheltenham

Costanza, R, B G Norton and B Hakell (eds) (1992) *Ecosystem Health: New Goals for Environmental Management*, Island Press, Washington DC

# References

Cropper, M, S K Aydede and P R Portney (1994) 'Preferences for Life Saving Programs: How the Public Discounts Time and Age', *Journal of Risk and Uncertainty*, vol 8, no 243–265

Cullis, J and P Jones (1998) *Public Finance and Public Choice*, Oxford University Press, Oxford

Dahlman, C J (1980) *The Open Field System and Beyond: A Property Rights Analysis of an Economic Institution*, Cambridge University Press, Cambridge

Daly, H (1973) *Towards Steady-state Economy*, W H Freeman and Company, San Francisco

Daly, H and J Cobb (1989) *For the Common Good: Redirecting the Economy Toward Community, the Environment and a Sustainable Future*, Beacon Press, Boston

Dasgupta, P and G Heal (1979) *Economic Theory and Exhaustible Resources*, Cambridge University Press, Cambridge

De Leo, G A and S Levin (1997) 'The Multifaceted Aspects of Ecosystem Integrity', *Conservation Ecology* (online) vol 1, no 1: 3. See http://www.consecol.org/vol1/iss1/art3

Dean, J (1992) 'Trade and the Environment: A Survey of the Literature,' in Patrick Low (ed) *International Trade and the Environment*, World Bank Discussion Paper no 159

Dewalt, B, P Vergne and M Hardin (1996) 'Shrimp Aquaculture Development and the Environment: People, Mangroves and Fisheries on the Gulf of Fonseca, Honduras' *World Development*, vol 24, no 7, pp1193–1208

Dixon, J, D James and P Sherman (1989) *The Economics of Dryland Management*, Earthscan, London

Dixon, J, L Scuba, R Carpenter and P Sherman (1986) *Economic Analysis of Environmental Impacts*, Earthscan, London

Drummond, M, G Stoddart and G Torrance (1987) *Methods for the Economic Evaluation of Health Care Programmes*, Oxford Medical Publications, Oxford

Easterlin, R A (1974) 'Does Economic Growth Improve the Human Lot?' in P A David and R M Reder (eds) *Nations and Households in Economic Growth*, Academic Press, New York

European Commission (1996) EC Council Directive 96/61/EC, September, *Official Journal of the European Commission*, L257/26–38

Ekins, P (1999) 'European Environmental Taxes and Charges: Recent Experience, Issues and Trends', *Ecological Economics* vol 31, no 39–62

El Serafy, S (1989) 'The Proper Calculation of Income from Depletable Natural Resources' in Y J Ahmad, S El Serafy and P Lutz (eds) *Environmental Accounting for Sustainable Development*, World Bank, Washington DC

Elsworth, S (1990), *A Dictionary of the Environment*, Paladin, London

EPIQ/NRM2 (1998) 'Assessment of the Feasibility of Debt-for-Nature Swaps in Indonesia', report prepared for USAID by EPIQ/NRM2, Conservation International, Development Alternatives, December

Erkki J and H-K Marttinen (eds) (1995) *North European Environmental Law*, Hakapaino Oy, Helsinki

ExternE (1995) *Externalities of Energy: Volume 2 Methodology*, prepared for the European Commission Directorate-General XII Science, Research and Development by ETSU and Metroeconomica, Office for Official Publications of the European Communities, Luxembourg

ExternE (1999) *Extenalities of Energy: Volume 7 Methodology 1998 Update*, Office for Official Publications of the European Communities, Luxembourg

Eyre, N, T Downing, R Hoekstra, K Rennings and R Tol (1998) *Global Warming Damages*, final report of the ExternE Global Warming Sub-task, prepared for the European Commission – DGXII

Fankhauser, S (1995) *Valuing Climate Change: The Economics of the Greenhouse*, Earthscan, London

FAO (1995) *Sustainability Issues in Agricultural and Rural Development Policies Vol 1: Trainee's Reader*, edited by F Petry, FAO, Rome

Field, B (1997) *Environmental Economics: An Introduction*, McGraw-Hill, New York

Folmer, H and E van Ierland (eds) (1989) *Valuation Methods and Policymaking in Environmental Economics*, Elsevier, Amsterdam

George, S (1991) *The Debt Boomerang*, Pluto, London

Gildert, R G (1993) *Evaluating the Noise Externality of Wind Power*, MSc thesis, Imperial College Centre for Environmental Technology, London

Goulder, L H (1995) 'Environmental Taxation and the Double Dividend: A Reader's Guide', *International Tax and Public Finance*, vol 2, pp157–183

Griffiths, A and Wall, S (1996) *Intermediate Microeconomics: Theory and Applications*, Longman, London

Gujarati, D (1992) *Essentials of Econometrics*, McGraw-Hill, London

Hall, D C and J V Hall (1984) 'Concepts and Measures of Natural Resource Scarcity in a Summary of Recent Trends', *Journal of Environmental Economics and Environmental Management* 11: (4) 363–379

Hammond, A, A Adriaanse, D Bryant and R Woodward (1995) *Environmental Indicators: a Systematic Approach to Measuring and Reporting on Environmental Policy Performance in the Context of Sustainable Development*, World Resources Institute

Hanley N, J Shogren and B White (1997) *Environmental Economics: In Theory and Practice*, Oxford University Press, Oxford

Hardin, G (1992) 'The tragedy of the commons' in Markandya and Richardson (eds) (1992) *The Earthscan Reader in Environmental Economics*, Earthscan, London

Harrison, A (1993) 'Natural Assets and National Accounting' In Lutz, E (ed) (1993), *Toward Improved Accounting for the Environment*, The World Bank, Washington

Hartwick, J M (1977) 'Intergenerational Equity and the Investing of Rents from Exhaustible Resources', *American Economic Review*, vol 67, no 5, pp972–974

Hartwick, J M (1978) 'Substitution among Exhaustible Resources and Intergenerational Equity', *Review of Economic Studies* vol 45, pp347–354

Hartwick, J M and N Olewiler (1986) *The Economics of Natural Resource Use*, Harper and Rowe, New York

Hartwick, J M and N Olewiler (1998) *The Economics of Natural Resource Use*, 2nd edition, Addison-Wesley, Harlow

Helm, D (ed) (1991) *Economic Policy Towards the Environment*, Blackwell, Oxford

Hohl, A and C A Tisdell (1993) 'How Useful are Environmental Safety Standards in Economics? The Example of Safe Minimum Standards for the Protection of Species', *Biodiversity and Conservation*, vol 2, pp168–181

Hohmeyer, O, R L Otinger and K Rennings (1997) *Social Costs and Sustainability, Valuation and Implementation in the Energy and Transport Sector*, Springer-Verlag, Berlin

Holland, P C (1993) 'Paediatric Audit' in S Frostick, P Radford and W A Wallace (eds) *Medical Audit: Rationale and Practicalities*, Cambridge University Press, Cambridge

Hotelling, H (1931) 'The Economics of Exhaustible Resources', *Journal of Political Economy*, vol 39, pp137–75

Howells, P and K Bain (1994) *Financial Markets and Institutions*, Longman, London

Hughes, D (1986) *Environmental Law*, Butterworth, London

IISD (1992) *Trade and Sustainable Development: A Survey of the Issues and a New Research Agenda*, by D Runnalls and A Cosbey, IISD, Canada

Institute for Global Communications (undated) 'Philosophy Behind Fair Trade', available from the Institute for Global Communications website: http://www.igc.org/lawg/fair.html

IPCC (1996a) *Climate Change 1995: Impacts, Adaptations and Mitigation of Climate Change: Scientific-Technical Analyses*, contribution of Working Group II to the Second Assessment Report of the Intergovernmental Panel on Climate Change, Cambridge University Press, Cambridge

IPCC (1996b) *Climate Change 1995: Economic and Social Dimensions of Climate Change*, contribution of Working Group III to the Second Assessment Report of the

# References

Intergovernmental Panel on Climate Change, Cambridge University Press, Cambridge

IPCC (1998) *The Regional Impacts of Climate Change: An Assessment of Vulnerability*, Cambridge University Press, Cambridge

IPCC (2001) *Climate Change 2001: Mitigation*, Cambridge University Press, Cambridge

IUCN (1980) *World Conservation Strategy: Living Resource Conservation for Sustainable Development*, International Union for Conservation of Nature and Natural Resources, Gland

Izac, A and M Swift (1994) 'On Agricultural Sustainability and its Measurement in Small-scale Farming in Sub-Saharan Africa', *Ecological Economics*, vol 11, no 2, pp105–125

Jepma, C, and M Munasinghe (1998) *Climate Change Policy: Facts, Issues and Analyses*, Cambridge University Press, Cambridge

Jha, V, A Markandya and R Vossenaar (1999) *Reconciling Trade and the Environment*, Edward Elgar, Cheltenham

Jochem and Eichhammer (1997) *Voluntary Agreements as a Substitute for Regulations and Economic Instruments: Lessons from the German Voluntary Agreements on CO$_2$ Reduction*, FEEM Working Papers: Nota di Lavoro, 19.97 (see http://www.feem.it)

Johansson, P-O (1987) *The Economic Theory and Measurement of Environmental Benefits*, Cambridge University Press, Cambridge

Kahn, H, W Brown and L Martel (1976) *The Next 200 Years: A Scenario for America and the World*, William Morrow, New York

Kahn, J (1998) *The Economic Approach to Environmental and Natural Resources*, Dryden Press, New York

Kaya, Y (1989) *Impact of Carbon Dioxide Emissions on GNP Growth: Interpretation of Proposed Scenarios*, Intergovernmental Panel on Climate Change/Response Strategies Working Group, IPCC, Geneva

Khanemann, D and A Tversky (1979) 'Prospect Theory: An Analysis of Decision Under Risk', *Econometrica*, vol 47, pp549–52

Khanina, L (1998) 'Determining Keystone Species', *Conservation Ecology* (online) vol 2, no 2, R2. See http://www.consecol.org/Journal/vol2/iss2/resp2

Kiss, A and D Shelton (1997) *Manual of Environmental Law*, Cambridge University Press, Cambridge

Krishnan, R, J Harris and N Goodwin (eds) (1995) *A Survey of Ecological Economics*, Island Press, Washington DC

Krupnick, A J, D Buttraw and A Markandya (2000) 'The Ancillary Benefits and Costs of Climate Change Mitigation: A Conceptual Framework', paper presented to Expert Workshop on Assessing the Ancillary Benefits and Costs of Greenhouse Gas Mitigation Strategies, 27–29 March, Washington DC

Lang, T and C Hines (1993) *The New Protectionism: Protecting the Future against Free Trade*, Earthscan, London

Larrain, F and A Velasco (1990) *Can Swaps Solve the Debt Crisis? Lessons from the Chilean Experience*, Princeton Studies in International Finance no 69, Princeton University, Princeton

Ledgerwood, G, E Street and R Therivel (1992) *Environmental Audit and Business Strategy*, Pitman, London

Leeson, J (1995) *Environmental Law*, Pitman, London

Leopold, A (1970) 'A Sand Country Almanac', *Essays on Conservation*, Round River, New York (first published 1949)

Little, I and J Mirrlees (1974) *Project Approach and Planning for Developing Countries*, Basic Books, New York

Loury, G C (1986) 'A Theory of "Oil" igopoly: Cournot Equilibrium in Exhaustible Resource Markets with Fixed Supplies', *International Economic Review*, vol 27, pp285–301

Lovejoy, T (1984) 'Aid Debtor Nation's Ecology', *New York Times*, 4 October

Lowe, J and D Lewis (1980) *The Economics of Environmental Management*, Allan, Oxford

Luken, R (1990) *Efficiency in Environmental Regulation: A Benefit–Cost Analysis of Alternative Approaches*, Kluwer Academic Publishers, Dordrecht

MacGarvin, M (1993) 'The Implications of the Precautionary Principle for Biological Monitoring', paper presented to a Conference on The Broad Challenge of the Precautionary Principle, Green College Centre for Environmental Policy and Understanding, Oxford, and CSERGE, University of East Anglia, 31 March–1 April

Maddison, D, D Pearce, O Johansson, E Calthrop, T Litman and E Verhoef (1996) *Blueprint 5: The True Costs of Road Transport*, Earthscan, London

Malcolm, R (1994) *A Guidebook to Environmental Law*, Sweet and Maxwell, London

Manser, R (1993) *The Squandered Dividend: The Free Market and the Environment in Eastern Europe*, Earthscan, London

Markandya, A (1998a) *The Indirect Costs and Benefits of Greenhouse Gas Limitations*, Handbook Reports/UNEP Collaborating Centre on Energy and Environment, Denmark

Markandya, A (1998b) 'The Costs of Environmental Regulation in Asia: Command and Control versus Market Based Instruments', *Asian Development Review*, vol 16, no 1, pp1–30

Markandya, A, P Harou, L Bellu and V Cistulli (2002) *Environmental Economics for Sustainable Growth: A Handbook for Practitioners*, Edward Elgar, Cheltenham

Markandya, A and P Mason (2000) 'The Essentials for Allocating Global Environmental Goods' in H Siebert *The Economics of International Environmental Problems*, Kiel Institute of World Economics, Kiel

Markandya, A and M N Murty forthcoming (2000) *Cleaning Rivers in Developing Countries: A Cost–Benefit Analysis of the Ganga River Action Plan*, Oxford University Press, Oxford and New Delhi

Markandya, A and M Pavan (eds) (1999) *Green Accounting in Europe: Four Case Studies*, Kluwer Academic Publishers, Dordrecht

Markandya, A and M Pemberton (1990) 'Non-Linear Prices and Energy Demand', *Energy Economics*, vol 10, pp27–34

Martinez-Alier, J with K Schlupmann (1995) 'Summary of The History of the Future' in R Krishnan, J Harris and N Goodwin (eds) (1995) *A Survey of Ecological Economics*, Island Press, Washington, DC. Original work published in J Martinez-Alier with K Shlupmann (1990) *Ecological Economics: Energy, Environment and Society*, Blackwell Books, Oxford

Meadows, D H, D L Meadows, J Randers and W W Behrens (1972) *The Limits to Growth: A Report for The Club of Rome's Project on the Predicament of Mankind*, Earth Island, Universe Books, New York

Meadows D H, D L Meadows and J Randers (1992) *Beyond the Limits: Global Collapse or a Sustainable Future*, Earthscan, London

Mintzer, I (1992) *Confronting Climate Change: Risks, Implications and Responses*, Cambridge University Press, Cambridge

Nordhaus, W and J Tobin (1972) 'Is Economic Growth Obsolete?', in *Economic Growth, 5th Anniversary Colloquium of the NBER*, Columbia University Press, New York

Norgaard, R (1990) 'Economic Indicators of Resource Scarcity: A Critical Essay', *Journal of Environmental Economics and Management*, vol 19, pp19–25

Nussbaum, M and A Sen (1993), *The Quality of Life*, Oxford University Press, Oxford

OECD (1989a) *Renewable Natural Resources: Economic Incentives for Improved Management*, OECD, Paris

OECD (1989b) *The Application of Economic Instruments for Environmental Protection*, Environment Monographs no 18, April

OECD (1991) *Fighting Noise in the 1990s*, OECD, Paris

OECD (1992a), *Climate Change: Designing a Tradeable Permit System*, OECD, Paris

OECD (1992b) *Global Climate*, OECD, Paris

OECD (1994a) *Natural Resource Accounts*, Environmental Monographs no 84, OECD, Paris

# References

OECD (1994b) *Life-Cycle Management and Trade*, OECD, Paris

OECD (1994c) *Eco-efficiency*, OECD, Paris

OECD (1994d) *Methodologies for Environmental and Trade Reviews*, OECD, Paris

OECD (1995) *Developing Environmental Capacity: A Framework for Donor Involvement*, OECD, Paris

OECD (1996) *Saving Biological Diversity:Economic Incentives*, OECD, Paris

OECD (1997) *Sustainable Consumption and Production*, OECD, Paris

OECD (1998) *Eco-efficiency*, OECD, Paris

OECD (1999) *Environmental Taxes: Recent Developments in China and OECD Countries*, OECD, Paris

O'Riordan, T (ed) (1997) *Ecotaxation*, Earthscan, London

O'Riordan, T and J Cameron (eds) (1994) *Interpreting the Precautionary Principle*, Earthscan, London

Panayotou, T (1993) *Green Markets: The Economics of Sustainable Development*, Institute for Contemporary Studies Press, San Francisco

Panayotou, T (1998) *Instruments of Change: Motivating and Financing Sustainable Development*, Earthscan, London

Parry, I (1990) *Climate Change and World Agriculture*, Earthscan, London

Paustenbach, D J (1995) 'Retrospective on US Health Risk Assessment: How Others Can Benefit' see http://www.fplc.edu/risk/vol6/fall/pausten.htm

Pearce D (1976) *Environmental Economics*, Longman, New York

Pearce, D (1985) inaugural lecture, University of London

Pearce, D (ed) (1991) *Blueprint 2: Greening the World Economy*, Earthscan, London

Pearce, D (1993) *Blueprint 3: Measuring Sustainable Development*, Earthscan, London

Pearce, D (1995) *Blueprint 4: Capturing Global Environmental Value*, Earthscan, London

Pearce, D, A Markandya and E Barbier (1989) *Blueprint for a Green Economy*, Earthscan, London

Pearce, D, E Barbier and A Markandya (1990) *Sustainable Development: Economics and Environment in the Third World*, Earthscan, London

Pearce, D and R K Turner (1990) *Economics of Natural Resources and the Environment*, Harvester Wheatsheaf, New York

Pearce, D and J Warford (1993)) *World Without End, Economics, Environment and Sustainable Development*, Oxford University Press, New York

Perelet, R (1996) *Economics and Environment: An English–Russian Dictionary* (ed Anil Markandya), Harvard Institute for International Development/Harvard University and OECD

Perman, R, Y Ma and J McGilvary (1996) *Natural Resource and Environmental Economics*, Longman, Harlow

Perman, R, Y Ma, J McGilvary and M Common (1999) *Natural Resource and Environmental Economics*, 2nd edition, Longman, Harlow

Piraino, S, and G Fanelli (1999) 'Keystone Species: What are we Talking About?' *Conservation Ecology*, vol 3, no 1: see http://www.consecol.org/vol3/iss1/resp4

Polansky, S (1992) 'Do Oil Producers Act as "Oil"igopolists?', *Journal of Environmental Economics and Environmental Management*, vol 23, pp216–47

Pope, S, M Appleton, and E-A Wheal (1991) *The Green Book*, Hodder and Stoughton, London

*Rachel's Environment and Health Weekly* (1999), no 650, 13 May

Rawls, J (1971) *A Theory of Justice*, Oxford University Press, Cambridge, MA

Ray, A (1984) *Cost–Benefit Analysis: Issues and Methodologies*, Johns Hopkins University Press, Baltimore

Redclift, M (1988) 'Economic Models and Environmental Values' in Turner, R K (1988) *Sustainable Environmental Management*, Westview Press, Boulder

Reed, D (ed) (1997) *Structural Adjustment, the Environment and Sustainable Development*, Earthscan, London

Repetto, R, M Wells, C Beer and F Rossini (1987) *Natural Resource Accounting for Indonesia*, World Resources Institute, Washington, DC

Repetto, R, et al (1989) *Wasting Assets, Natural Resources in the National Income Accounts*, World Resources Institute, Washington, DC

Rich, B (1994) *Mortgaging the Earth*, Earthscan, London

Riddell, R (1981) *Ecodevelopment: Economics, Ecology and Development*, St Martin's Press, New York

Roan, S (1989) *Ozone Crisis*, Wiley, New York

Robinson, T J C (1989) *Economic Theories of Exhaustible Resources*, Routledge, London

Roe, D, B Dalal-Clayton and R Hughes (1995) *A Directory of Impact Assessment Guidelines*, International Institute for Environment and Development, IUCN/OECD, London

Romer, D (1996) *Advanced Macroeconomics*, McGraw-Hill, London

Ronnback, P (1999) 'The Ecological Basis for Economic Value of Seafood Production Supported by Mangrove Ecosystems', *Ecological Economics*, vol 29, no 2, pp235–252

Savage, D, M Burke and J Coupe (1974) *Economics of Environmental Improvement*, Houghton Mifflin, London

Schotter, A (1997) *Microeconomics: A Modern Approach*, Addison Wesley, New York

Schramm, G and J J Warford (1989) *Environmental Management and Economic Development*, Johns Hopkins University Press, Baltimore

Sen, A (1986) *On Economic Inequality*, Oxford University Press, Oxford

Serôa da Motta, R Huber and H J Ruitenbeek (1999) 'Market-based Instruments for Environmental Policymaking in Latin America and the Caribbean: Lessons from Eleven Countries', *Environment and Development Economics*, vol 4, part 2, May, pp177–202

Siebert, H (1987) *Economics of the Environment: Theory and Policy*, Springer-Verlag, New York

Simonis, U E (1990) *Beyond Growth: Elements of Sustainable Development*, Sigma, Berlin

Solow, R M (1974) 'Intergenerational Equity and Renewable Resources', *Review of Economic Studies, Symposium on the Economics of Exhaustible Resources*, pp29–45

Solow, R M (1986) 'On the Intergenerational Allocation of Natural Resources', *Scandinavian Journal of Economics*, vol 88, no 1, pp141–149

Speck, S (1999) 'Energy and Carbon Taxes and their Distributional Implications', *Energy Policy*, vol 27, pp659–667

Squire, L and H van der Tak (1975) *Economic Analysis of Projects*, Johns Hopkins University Press, Baltimore

Stanners, D and P Bourdeau (eds) (1995) *Europe's Environment: The Dobris Assessment*, Earthscan, London

Stead, R, P Curwin and K Lawler (1996) *Industrial Economics: Theory, Applications and Policy*, McGraw-Hill, London

Stevenson, G G (1991) *Common Property Economics: A General Theory and Land Use Applications*, Cambridge University Press, Cambridge

Stiglitz, J (1993) *Economics*, W W Norton, New York

Swanson, T (1994) *The International Regulation of Extinction*, MacMillan Press, Basingstoke

Therivel, R, E Wilson, S Thompson, D Heaney and D Pritchard (1992) *Strategic Environmental Assessment*, Earthscan, London

Tietenberg, T (1992a) *Environmental and Natural Resource Economics*, Harper Collins, New York

Tietenberg, T (1992b) *Innovation in Environmental Policy*, Edward Elgar, Cheltenham

Tietenberg, T (1994) *Economics and Environmental Policy*, Edward Elgar, Cheltenham

Tietenberg, T (1996) *Environmental and Natural Resource Economics*, Harper Collins, New York

Tol, R S J (1999) 'Spatial and Temporal Efficiency in Climate Change: Applications of FUND', *Environmental and Resource Economics*, vol 14, no 1, pp33–49

# References

Tolba, M and D El-Khaly (eds) (1992) *The World Environment 1972–1992: Two Decades of Challenge*, UNEP/Chapman and Hall, London

Toth, F (ed) (1998) *Cost–Benefit Analyses of Climate Change*, Birkhauser, Basel

Turner, R K (1988) *Sustainable Environmental Management*, Westview Press, Boulder

Turner, K, D Pearce and I Bateman (1994) *Environmental Economics: An Elementary Introduction*, The Johns Hopkins University Press, Baltimore

United Nations (1993a) *System of National Accounts 1993*, United Nations, New York

United Nations (1993b) *Agenda 21: Programme for Action for Sustainable Development and Rio Declaration*, United Nations, New York

UNDP (1999) *Human Development Report 1999*, Oxford University Press, Oxford

UN ECE/UNEP (1994) *Guidelines on Environmental Management in Countries in Transition*, Geneva

UN ECE (1994) *Environmental Action Plan for Central and Eastern Europe*, UN ECE, Geneva

UNEP (1993) *Economic Instruments for Environmental Protection*, UNEP, Paris

UNEP (2000) *Global Environment Outlook 2000*, UNEP, Paris. Available online at http://www.unep.org/geo2000/

USEPA (1998) 'Terms Of Environment', available at USEPA homepage at http://www.epa.gov/OCEPA terms

Vanclay, J (1999) 'On the Nature of Keystone Species', *Conservation Ecology* vol 3, no 1: r3. See http://www.consecol.org/vol3/iss1/resp3

Varian, H (1996) *Intermediate Microeconomics*, W W Norton, New York

Wallart, N (1994) 'La taxe environnementale est-elle un 'bon' impot?' Cahier no 94 12, Faculte des Sciences Economiques et Sociales, Universite de Genève (in French)

Water Quality Association (1997) *WQA Glossary of Terms* (online), Water Quality Association, http://www.wqa.org

Weinstein, M and W Stason (1977) 'Foundations of Cost-effectiveness Analysis for Health and Medical Practices', *New England Journal of Medicine*, vol 296, no 13, pp716–21

Weitzman, M (1998) 'Gamma Discounting for Global Warming', discussion paper, Harvard University, Cambridge, MA

Wigley, T M L (1999) *The Science of Climate Change Global and US Perspectives*, PEW Center on Global Climate Change, Arlington

World Bank (1993) *World Development Report 1993: Investing in Health*, Oxford University Press, Oxford

World Bank (1995), *Monitoring Environmental Progress: A Report on Work in Progress*, The World Bank, Washington, DC

World Commission on Environment and Development (1987) *Our Common Future*, Oxford University Press, Oxford

WWF, UNEP and IUCN (1991) *Caring for the Earth: A Strategy for Sustainable Living*, IUCN, UNEP and WWF, Gland

Young, M D (1992) *Sustainable Investment and Resource Use: Equity, Environmental Integrity and Economic Efficiency*, UNESCO MAB Series, vol 9

Zarrilli, S, V Jha and R Vossenaar (eds) (1997) *Eco-Labelling and International Trade*, Macmillan Press, Basingstoke

Zweifel, P and J-R Tyran (1994) 'Environmental Impairment Liability as an Instrument of Environmental Policy', *Ecological Economics*, vol 11, pp43–56